'An astonishing book: a collection of truly riveting stories of bravery, all brilliantly told. In terms of sheer drama and audacity, *SAS Great Escapes Two* goes where no fiction writer would dare venture'

Alex Gerlis, author of *Agent in the Shadows*

'Damien Lewis paints a uniquely vivid picture of the wartime SAS. Packed with detail, this fresh and dynamic book brings us as close to its remarkable members as we are ever likely to get'

Joshua Levine

Damien Lewis

SAS

GREAT
ESCAPES TWO

SIX UNTOLD EPIC ESCAPES MADE BY
WORLD WAR TWO HEROES

QUERCUS

First published in Great Britain in 2023 by Quercus Editions Ltd
This paperback published in 2024 by

QUERCUS

Quercus Editions Ltd
Carmelite House
50 Victoria Embankment
London EC4Y 0DZ

An Hachette UK company

A CIP catalogue record for this book is available
from the British Library

PB ISBN 978 1 52942 942 8
Ebook ISBN 978 1 52942 940 4

Picture credits (in order of appearance): 1, 2 – Fiona Ferguson;
3 – Stewart McDermott/Douglas Nash; 4 – National Army Museum; 5 – Bundesarchiv;
6, 11 – Imperial War Museum; 7 – Service Historique de la Défense; 8 – Sue Collinson;
9, 10 – The estate of Captain M. J. Pleydell MC; 12 – Commando/SRS; 14 – Author's collection;
13, 15, 16 – Jan Maingard; 17, 19, 20 – Avril Castelow; 18 – Christopher Muller

10 9 8 7 6 5 4 3 2 1

Typeset by CC Book Production
Printed and bound in Great Britain by Clays Ltd, Elcograf S.p.A.

For the great escapees whose stories are told in these pages, and for those of their comrades who did not make it home.

And for Christian Deehan,
the late grandson of Herbert Castelow MM
– gone but not forgotten.

Contents

Author's Note

There are sadly few survivors from the Second World War operations depicted in these pages. Throughout the writing of this book I have endeavoured to be in contact with as many as possible, plus surviving family members. If there are further witnesses to the stories told here who are inclined to come forward, please do get in touch, as I will endeavour to include further recollections in future editions.

The time spent by Allied servicemen and women as Special Forces was often traumatic and wreathed in layers of secrecy, and many chose to take their stories to their graves. Memories tend to differ and apparently none more so than those concerning operations behind enemy lines. The written accounts that do exist can tend to differ in their detail and timescale, and locations and chronologies are sometimes contradictory. That being said, I have endeavoured to provide an accurate sense of place, timescale and narrative to the stories depicted here. Where various accounts appear particularly confused, the methodology I have used is the 'most likely' scenario: if two or more testimonies or sources point to a particular time or place or sequence of events, I have treated that account as most likely.

The above notwithstanding, any mistakes herein are entirely of my own making and I would be happy to correct them in future editions.

*

A final note and an appeal for information. The real identities of some of the individuals portrayed in the following pages seems lost to time, but perhaps there may be readers who can help solve such mysteries. For example, the medic known as 'Johnson' in all contemporary accounts of the Operation Bigamy raid appears not to have used that name, and is formally recorded today as simply being of an 'unknown identity'. I have used the name 'Johnson' in this account, as no other is available. It appears as if he was known as 'Jakie' to the men of the SAS, and that he did not survive the war. If anyone has any further details which may help clarify his true identity, do please get in contact.

I am also keen to learn more about Operation Bulbasket, the escape from which forms the core story in Chapter Five of this book. It seems to me that there is a great deal more to be told about this incredible, yet ill-fated post-D-Day mission. I am particularly keen to hear from anyone with insight into Operation Bulbasket, including any family members of those who partook in the mission, or indeed those who may know more details about the extraordinarily successful RAF missions flown in support of the SAS men on the ground, or indeed anyone with insight into the war crimes investigations that followed.

My website – www.damienlewis.com – is the best means by which to make contact with me, and I extend my thanks to anyone who may be able to help.

Preface

Books have the potential to be extraordinary things. They can be immensely powerful. They can and do inspire people; they can turn an individual's fortunes around and change people's lives. I've always liked to think that perhaps my own had the potential to do something like that. At least, I'd always hoped so. In the summer of 2022 I was given some quite extraordinary insight into all of that . . . and in the most unexpected of ways.

The previous year I had published a book entitled *SAS Great Escapes*. It told the stories of seven amazing escapes executed by members of the wartime SAS. Almost a year after publication a message dropped into my email inbox, which had been sent to me via my author's website (damienlewis.com). The subject line was 'Your book saved my life'. As you can imagine, it caught my attention. I opened it, expecting to perhaps read about how one of my books had inspired a person to find new hope and meaning, via incredible tales of wartime courage, endurance and fortitude. What I read was utterly, utterly unexpected, unbelievably uplifting, and humbling beyond measure.

Earlier that summer, Tommy Soames, a primary school teacher and the author of the email, had taken a half-term holiday in Montenegro, in south-eastern Europe. He'd grabbed his backpack and set off. On the penultimate day of his trip, most of which he'd spent trekking in Montenegro's mountains and forests, he undertook a special journey. A fisherman had told him about a certain network of caverns deep in the hills – the Obod Caves. Located near the town of Rijeka Crnojevića, they sat amid an area of stunning emerald-green forest, interspersed with wild lakes and rivers. Checking out the fisherman's recommendation, Tommy had found just one review on Google, from an earlier visitor: 'Be sure to get to the end (it will not work without a flashlight), there is an underground river.'

Intrigued, and being something of an adventurer and an outdoor pursuits enthusiast, he set out early to hike the six kilometres to the cave. 'All I had on me was your book, a tin of sardines and a pack of dates in my backpack,' he wrote to me. He reached the cave, snapped a few photos of the entrance on his phone, and dived inside. Having explored many a cavern, he shrugged off any misgivings he might have felt about not having seen another soul during the trek, pressing on into the darkness. Ahead, the ground was a jumble of boulders and it began to drop off quite sharply. Behind, the light from the cave entrance faded to a small, distant speck of brightness. Above, there was the deafening shrieking of bats, a sound he knew well.

With his senses almost overburdened, Tommy heard the 'faint trickle of water far below'. He felt the adrenaline kick in at the thought that the underground river was within reach. The deeper he probed, the louder the sound of rushing water became, until it was almost deafening. At the same time there was a voice in Tommy's head screaming at him to turn back. But another, which proved far more powerful, urged him to continue and to see what he might find.

It took an hour to reach the river. Once there, he bent to the dark, surging water and made sure to fill his water bottle for the return climb. Then, he turned off his phone-torch, to 'momentarily allow the darkness to envelop' all, as he 'contemplated life a mile underground'. Curiosity sated, and with a few photos snapped of the extraordinary river, which surged over massive boulders, seeming to attain a golden glow in the light of Tommy's phone, he turned around and made for the exit. Forty-five minutes later his climb terminated in a dead end. Remaining calm, he executed an about-turn and retraced his steps, reasoning that there had to be two tunnels leading to the river.

He'd just picked the wrong one.

Reaching the water once more, he took a second exit and again began to climb. Some thirty minutes later, that tunnel began to narrow to such an extent that it was impossible to continue. It too was a dead end. Panic started to set in now, and moving at speed, Tommy retraced his route, treading faster and faster until he took a wrong step, slipping between two boulders. The next instant he was tumbling through the darkness, falling '10 . . . 12 feet', before smashing into the rock floor. As he lay there, 'crumpled in a heap', he thought to himself: 'Had I hit my head, this would have been my resting place for evermore.'

That thought was rapidly replaced by an even darker one: he might have survived the fall with only cuts and bruises, but he was never going to find his way out. 'I was hopelessly lost,' Tommy recounted. 'Water seemed to be gushing from every angle, from behind every boulder . . . At this point I convinced myself that I would die in that cave and my body would never be recovered.' Attempting to slow and steady his breathing, Tommy forced himself to imagine his mother and father and his brother and sister at home. He envisioned the police knocking on the door, to let them know that he was missing.

From there, his befuddled thoughts drifted to memories of a German woman that he had met the previous day, and somewhat fallen for. She had invited him to join her in the countryside near Berlin for her thirtieth birthday, in just a few weeks' time. He'd promised to make it. As he sat there, thinking of how he would never now see what his children might look like, he tried to paint a picture of them in his head, to give him something to cling onto, a cause for hope. Somewhat calmed and anchored by such thoughts, he decided to delve into his backpack, to see what solace or encouragement that might offer.

He munched on a few dates and sardines. Staring into the darkness, his mind drifted to thoughts of Theseus and the Minotaur and Ariadne's ball of thread. Theseus had managed to escape from the maze using the thread as his guide. He thought of Hansel and Gretel. They had tried to escape from the dark forest and the clutches of the witch by leaving a trail of breadcrumbs to follow. That got Tommy to thinking about maybe leaving a trail of dates on the floor of the tunnels, to mark off those that he had tried. But the dates were dark brown and the cave floor was dark brown, so they would never be visible.

Just then he caught sight of a gleam of white in the bottom of his rucksack. It was the book that he'd carried in with him; a book with seven chapters, of which only the last remained to read. He reached for the book and tore out a page. He scrunched it up and dropped it on the cave floor. One flash of his phone-torch and it showed up like a beacon. Feeling a 'glimmer of hope trickle into my bones', Tommy set off, leaving a line of balled-up pages to form a trail behind him, indicating that this tunnel had already been tried, and was a dead end.

In that fashion, he reached the river once more. Pausing for a few seconds, he played the light over the book's cover: *SAS Great Escapes*. What kind of a cruel irony was that, he wondered. He was tearing apart that book, in an effort to pull off his own great escape. Despite normally only going to church at around Christmas or Easter time, Tommy began to pray. Furiously. Begging God that he be allowed one more chance at life, and to emerge from this cavernous hell unscathed.

That done, he chose another route leading away from the river, and set off, 'tearing page after page into little pieces . . . placing each shred of writing with purpose, on a visible part of each boulder, pressing it gently into the mud to prevent it from being blown away by some faint underground breeze'.

Ascent three, his first using the torn pages of the book, failed.

Ascent four led him to another dead end.

Ascent five . . . same result.

Each climb had been met with a building sense of hope, only to lead to crushing disappointment when the tunnel ran into yet another dead end.

Each time, Tommy returned to the very same point where he had first filled up his water bottle, hours earlier. Before long he was surrounded by a crescent of paper trails, each of which led off into a dark tunnel. As he played his light across them, they seemed to form a clock face, with the only untried exits lying at the nine o'clock to eleven o'clock angle. By now, he was feeling less and less in touch with reality and his own sanity, as his sense of self-control seemed to slip further and further away. Exhausted, disorientated, battered and chilled to the bone, bit by bit he could feel his will to fight – his hunger to be free and to live – ebbing away. With the cave system being such a mind-bending labyrinth, he 'could scarcely tell which way was up or down' any more.

At this, his lowest ebb, when resigning himself to what seemed to be inevitable – to perishing here in the darkness – his mind drifted to thoughts of the torn and dirty book that he was still clutching in his hand. For the past week he'd been reading it, having bought it on a whim at Stansted Airport. The one thing those escape stories had drummed into him, page after page, was how the SAS men portrayed had managed to stay calm under the most intense pressures and life-threatening situations, and how they came up with the most ingenious solutions, time and time again, in order to escape. Above all, they never once gave up or gave in.

'I truly believe this is what made me think so clearly when I started to despair,' Tommy wrote to me. 'Without your book, I think I would have either gone insane with disorientation; lost the remaining 10% of battery life my phone had left; or simply smashed my head in a blind panic, before anyone even had the chance to come and look for me . . . not that anyone even knew for sure where I was. I hadn't seen anyone on the hike there, never mind in the cave.'

His resolve stiffened by such thoughts, Tommy chose one of the exits between nine and eleven o'clock and set out once more. He pressed on for twenty to thirty minutes, all the while mechanically ripping out pages, and leaving a scrunched trail behind. Finally, he caught what he imagined might be the distant sound of screeching bats. Or was that just his mind playing tricks? It had been doing more and more of that, as the disorientation worsened. Since reaching the river the first time around, he'd noticed one or two bats fluttering about, but no sign of any massive colonies, and few of their distinctive cries.

As the noise drifted to his desperate senses again and again, he started to move faster, urged on by a faint pulse of hope. Oddly, every boulder he passed somehow felt 'simultaneously familiar but strange'. He surged forward, the tunnel twisting one way and the other, as the squeaking grew in intensity and the roar of the water receded into a distant murmur far to his rear. Glancing up from the small pool of light cast by his torch, Tommy noticed something odd, far ahead. There was a 'faint jagged white outline on the cave wall'.

After seven hours underground, such was his state of 'desperation and disorientation' that hallucinations had begun to fog his vision. Instead of the 'white outline' representing the light from the cave entrance shining down the dark tunnel and hitting the far wall, Tommy somehow perceived it as a snowdrift. A snowdrift? How could there be a snowdrift here? Maybe it was a patch of snow secreted deep in the icy bowels of the cave? Maybe he'd been descending, not climbing, for all of this time? Maybe this was another dead end?

'Every sinew of my being gave up and I strained to turn back into the depths of the cave,' Tommy recounted. But something told him that he'd tried every other way, and compelled him to press on. He kept repeating that sentiment, over and over in his head: *press on, press on, press on. Like the guys in the book, never ever give up.*

Finally, he drew near to the shaft of light cast by the entrance. As he played his hand through it, he realised what it was and what it had to signify. Turning the corner, he spied the cave exit, lying fifty metres beyond. Overcome with emotion, he sank to his knees and wept uncontrollably, 'my body convulsing in disbelief at my survival'. When Tommy felt able to stand again, he stumbled to the exit, after which he began the long hike back to the village from which he had set out, many hours before.

It was well after dark by the time he got there. He was shaking from head to toe, covered in blood and caked in mud. When the local woman who had sorted Tommy's accommodation and the like first caught sight of him, she went white with shock. 'Oh God, what attacked you?' she asked. It turned out that the forests around there were populated by brown bears, and she'd just presumed that Tommy must have been set upon by one of those. In truth, the bears had been the least of his worries.

Back in his room, Tommy realised the one final overarching irony to what had just occurred. As he contemplated the book, with its torn pages stained by blood and grime, he realised he had ripped out all up to page 259, the opening of Chapter Seven, 'Across Enemy Lines'. That chapter was the last, and the only one that he had not yet read. It had taken him all the previous pages, torn out and balled up, to find his way out of the nightmare; out of the Obod Caves.

Tommy finished off his message to me with these sentiments. 'I haven't been able to finish the book yet, given the memories attached to the mud and blood stains on the rest of the shredded pages . . . As a side note, I don't think it's the fact that I had just any old book in my bag that enabled me to escape. I've thought about it a lot and just can't see any way I would have made it out without your book. For that, I am forever grateful. It's quite feasible I wouldn't even have had a book in my bag at all, as I hadn't read one for a while. I just wandered into WH Smith and was taken by the title and thought I'd give it a go, having always been a fan of prison escape stories and films.'

In short, *SAS Great Escapes* really was the book that had saved one young man's life. Simply incredible. It had done so both physically, by providing that life-saving paper-trail and that handrail to get Tommy out of the caves. But more importantly, it had done so psychologically and emotionally, as Tommy had used the inspiration behind those stories of superhuman endurance and spirit to stiffen his own resolve and to spur him on, when his body and his mind were telling him how much easier it would be to simply give up.

In light of Tommy's incredible story of survival and escape, and of the triumph of the human spirit, I decided that this book, *SAS Great Escapes Two*, the sequel, really did need to be written. By coincidence, several caves feature in the following tales – both in the sun-blasted North African desert and in the dust-dry hills of Crete. In both instances, those caverns play a key role in the escapees' incredible stories.

In celebration of Tommy's escape, here is *SAS Great Escapes Two*, in all its life-enhancing, life-affirming detail.

Damien Lewis,
Dorset,
November 2022

Chapter One

BACK FROM THE DEAD

December 1941, North Africa

It was New Year's Eve, and the five desert-worn Chevrolet trucks got on the move early, pushing north across the dawn terrain. At a distant rendezvous, a force of fellow raiders was awaiting collection by what the SAS had affectionately named 'the Desert Taxi Company'. The Chevys were operated by the men of the Long Range Desert Group (LRDG), the reconnaissance and intelligence-gathering specialists, and the SAS were here strictly as passengers, to be ferried to and from the targets that they sought to destroy.

The convoy had been on the move for a little under three hours, when they heard the noise they most dreaded – the drone of an aeroengine, as a warplane powered through the thin blue. Worried eyes scanned the skies. Shortly, a twin-engine Messerschmitt Bf 110 *Zerstörer* – Destroyer; a heavy fighter-bomber – melted out of the burning sun. Just as soon as they'd heard the distant engine beat the convoy had halted, for in the open desert movement drew the eye, and on these kinds of missions that could spell disaster.

The enemy warplane seemed to pass right over without the slightest pause or alteration of course, suggesting that the convoy had escaped notice, which was fortunate, for the open terrain offered barely a hint of any cover. But just as those riding in the vehicles were starting to relax a little, the aircraft was seen to tilt one wing, as it came around in a tight, screaming turn.

'He's coming back!' someone yelled. The warning came from Sergeant Jim 'Gentleman' Almonds, one of the more senior ranks among the SAS patrol riding in those vehicles.

With nothing left to lose, the convoy broke and scattered. Some made for a distant outcrop of rocks about two miles away, speeding across the bone-shaking ground. The enemy pilot executed another, lower pass, before sweeping around once more to attack from out of the sun. Dropping down until it was skimming the desert sands – 'in for the kill . . . attacking hard', Almonds would note in his diary – the Messerschmitt's four machine guns, plus its two nose-mounted 20mm cannons unleashed hell, large-calibre rounds tearing into the desert, throwing up spurts of blasted rock and sand.

Answering fire with fire, the weapons on the British vehicles spat defiance. Right along the scattered line the machine guns roared, belching out a hail of lead. The noise was deafening, as smoke drifted through the hot air, and blasted rock and spent bullet casings cascaded all around. But it was soon obvious what an unequal contest this was going to prove. Relying on their long experience – these elite warriors had soldiered here for months, and knew the desert, and how to fight in it, intimately – groups of men began to dive from their vehicles, abandoning the

Chevys, which were the proverbial bullet-magnets, and scurrying for cover. Here and there larger boulders and thin scrub dotted the landscape, and if they could make it into their shade, they might slip into a place of relative safety.

Almonds' Chevy had already been raked with a long burst of rounds, and as he dashed away he grabbed his Bren light machine gun, the weapon with which he'd been returning fire at the enemy warplane. Even as he ran, he noticed that one man remained resolutely at his station, seemingly searching for something in the front passenger compartment. It was Lieutenant John 'Jock' Steel Lewes, the SAS's tough-as-old-boots training officer – one of the founders of the unit, and the commander of their patrol.

Almonds yelled for Lewes to abandon the Chevy and to make for cover, even as he and his fellows dashed into the lee of a rocky knoll. From there they began to play a vicious game of 'ring a roses', putting the bulk of the boulder between them and the attacking warplane's bullets, before darting out with the Bren to unleash fire as it sped past. Finally, the enemy pilot called off the attack. It seemed to the hunted men that some of their Bren rounds must have hit the Messerschmitt's rear gunner's compartment, which housed one of the warplane's two- or three-man crew.

As the aircraft powered away, Almonds and the others broke cover and raced for their vehicle. There was not a moment to lose. They found their Chevy riddled with bullets and shrapnel, but still just about drivable. Miraculously, the fuel and water drums strapped into its pickup-style rear were still intact. Desperate to get under way – the enemy pilot would have radioed in his position, calling for further air-attacks – they could see no sign of Jock Lewes anywhere. The SAS commander's fate remained a mystery. Firing up the vehicle, they got going, aiming to put as much distance between themselves and the attack site as possible.

But all too quickly a flight of Junkers Ju 87 'Stuka' dive-bombers were on their tail. Pulling to a halt, SAS and LRDG alike dashed for a nearby patch of low scrub, burrowing deep into the undergrowth and throwing sand and grit over exposed skin and hair, half burying themselves in the process. The Stuka pilots knew the form: repeatedly they dived, raking the bush with long bursts of fire, spurts of blasted sand erupting all around those figures cowering beneath the thin cover. The urge to flinch – to run – was all-consuming, but these men knew that to do so would spell certain death, and so they forced themselves to remain motionless, frozen under the fearsome onslaught.

A little distance away, a first Chevy rocked with bullet strikes before exploding, hungry flames licking outward from the ruptured fuel tanks, chasing the petrol greedily, as it drained into the hot sand. First one, then two, and eventually four columns of thick black smoke barrelled into the sky, as four of the patrol's five vehicles were blasted into a blazing, fiery ruin.

The horrific duel was kept up all that day, as the Stukas were replaced in pairs, one flight peeling off while another took over, swooping in to join the hunt. It wasn't until four o'clock that afternoon that the last of the dive-bombers droned away, disappearing over the distant horizon, whereupon Almonds, plus those of his fellows who had survived, were finally able to break cover. They gathered their scattered forces and did a head count. Incredibly, only one man seemed to be missing – Lieutenant Jock Lewes.

Gradually, they pieced together what must have happened.

It seemed that Lewes had been hit in the leg while still in the Chevy. As he'd tried to make it to some cover the warplane had pounced again, finishing him off with a burst to the back. He must have died very quickly, which was about the only consolation that Almonds and the others could think of. Lewes was the sole fatality from that long day of hell, but of all the men then present he was the least they could afford to lose. The loss to the SAS – then barely six months old, and engaged in only its second series of such missions – was incalculable.

Captain David Stirling, the SAS's founder, saw Lewes as being indispensable to the fledgling unit – his deputy who not only trained recruits in the all-important crafts of water-discipline and desert marching, but was their explosives expert to boot. Indeed, Lewes had been nicknamed the 'Wizard', due to his magical way with conjuring up novel explosive concoctions. The most recent was the aptly named 'Lewes bomb', a small incendiary charge that was perfect for a raider to carry on his person, as he stole onto an enemy airbase to blow up the ranks of waiting warplanes. Typically, their Chevys had been stuffed with dozens of Lewes bombs, for they had become the stock-in-trade of the SAS.

Lewes was buried in a shallow grave in the open desert. Once that grim task was over, the men of the SAS and LRDG took stock. They had one barely serviceable vehicle. It was riddled with holes, and two of the tyres had burst, but it had suffered no damage that couldn't be fixed by scavenging parts from the wreckage of the other Chevys. The key thing was that the water and petrol it carried had somehow survived the hours of strafing, for without that they would be going nowhere, at least by wheeled transport. They were nine men all-told, and with Almonds being the most senior surviving rank it fell to him to muster the means and the wherewithal to get them back to friendly lines.

Almonds decided they should hide until it was fully dark – a Fieseler Storch spotter plane had buzzed them, and no one believed the hunt was over – after which they'd clamber onto the one surviving vehicle and head for the Jalo oasis, then the SAS's base of operations. It was little short of 500 kilometres south-east of their present position, by the convoluted route they would have to take, which would constitute some challenge in their one overloaded Chevy. But there was no other option. As they hid among the scattered cover and the light drained from the landscape, Almonds tried to come to terms with the fact that Jock Lewes was gone. Later, he would write in his diary, lamenting how 'one of the bravest men I have ever met, an officer and a gentleman', had been left 'lying out in the desert, barely covered with sand . . . Not even a stone marks the spot.'

But Almonds also found himself wrestling with another disturbing conundrum. Even as the enemy warplanes had struck, their convoy had been en route to collect that other party of SAS raiders. Yet right now, there seemed precious little they could do to help them. With only the one vehicle remaining and all stores in perilously short supply, they had to save their own skins. As had been drilled into them from the earliest days of SAS training, they had to be prepared to leave men behind, if the success of the mission depended upon it. Well, right now the very survival of Almonds and the men of this patrol depended on them making a beeline for home.

They would leave what little water they could spare in a hide, which was the best they could manage.

*

It was forty-eight hours later when the lone Chevy carrying that party of nine limped into Jalo, having traversed wild, desolate country in a non-stop run. 'A hot meal, roll up in a borrowed blanket and Goodnight Lockie,' Almonds noted of the moment, Lockie being his wife, Iris. The following morning, he delivered the news of their sad loss to David Stirling. At first the SAS commander looked visibly shaken, as he tried to take it all in. He and Lewes went way back and they had been close. Then, typically, the SAS founder tried to mask one emotion with another, stressing to Almonds how they needed to learn from the incident and to refine their training, to better cope in future with such air-attacks. But that in turn brought him right back to the core of the present dilemma – that Lewes had devised nearly all their training regimes, so who was now to take over?

Despite the shock and the sadness at their loss, at least Almonds and his eight fellows had made it back alive. Even as they had set a course for Jalo, so the raiding party that they had been tasked to collect was facing the challenge of a lifetime. If Almonds and company's escape had been extraordinary – Almonds would be awarded the Military Cross (MC) for leading his party to safety – the predicament faced by that missing SAS patrol seemed utterly nightmarish; impossible.

To all appearances, they were either facing a long and torturous death, or capture by the enemy.

If anything, the leader of that missing patrol was an even more iconic figure than Jock Lewes. Since the SAS's inception, in July 1941, there had been three sets of raids. The first, Operation Squatter, an airborne insertion by parachute-borne troops, had ended disastrously, as wild storms had swept the desert and injured and killed many. The second set of raids, mounted in November 1941, had been make or break, for after the debacle of Squatter the SAS had been facing disbandment. Never popular with high command – seen as piratical upstarts engaged in a decidedly ungentlemanly means of waging war – they had absolutely needed to strike home.

The first to do so in those November raids – they had been ferried to their targets by the LRDG, eschewing airborne means – was the superlative warrior-commander, Lieutenant Blair 'Paddy' Mayne. Mayne, a northern Irishman who would come to epitomise the very essence and spirit of the SAS, had struck at the airbase at Tamet, wrecking two dozen enemy warplanes. Days later, Lieutenant Bill 'Skin' Fraser had gone one better, reporting of his raid on Agedabia airfield: 'Spent one night in the middle of the Germans, who were digging in . . . Walked into drome and destroyed 37 planes without opposition . . . may have been more, as planes were closely packed.' That report was vintage Fraser: terse, sparse and replete with archetypal British phlegm.

On first glance, Fraser seemed far from being the stereotype of a Special Forces warrior. But appearances can be deceptive. Tall and gangly of frame – skinny almost, hence the nickname – with sticky-out ears and a doleful, shy expression, Fraser hailed from a long-lived Scottish military clan. His forebears had served in the Gordon Highlanders, but Fraser was the first to do so as an officer, and there was a part of him that doubted if he was truly officer calibre, or class, much that his combat record should belie any such fears. Wounded in action during the bitter June 1940 retreat to Dunkirk, Fraser had been evacuated from France to Britain. Once there, hungering to avenge his fallen comrades, he had volunteered for

Special Service, joining the ranks of the newly formed No. 11 (Scottish) Commando.

Even as the British and Allied troops had been whisked off the bullet-torn beaches of France, so Britain's wartime leader, Winston Churchill, had struck a tone of extraordinary boldness and defiance. Just days after Dunkirk, he'd called for the spirit of offence to prevail, ordering his commanders to prepare for 'offensive operations against the enemy's coastline'. Plans were to be drawn up for 'constant smash-and-grab raids by numbers of irregular troops'. Churchill urged these Special Service recruits to 'land secretly by night and kill or capture the invader', creating 'alarm and havoc' at every turn. With all the territory seized by the enemy, they had long and vulnerable supply-lines, and Churchill urged his raiders to 'make hay while the sun shines'.

The formation of the commandos was the chief response to Churchill's exhortations. Fraser – always quiet, a deep-thinker – had gone into action with No. 11 Commando in Syria, in a daring amphibious landing that had won singular acclaim, despite the terrible cost paid in lives and blood. But shortly, No. 11 Commando – along with Nos 7 & 8, which together had formed the Middle East Commando – had been disbanded. When Churchill learned of this, he was enraged. 'The Middle East Command have indeed maltreated and thrown away this invaluable force,' he thundered, in a 'MOST SECRET' missive of July 1942. Decrying how those three elite commando units 'have been frittered away', he ordered them be 'reconstituted as soon as possible'.

By then Bill Fraser had siezed the initiative, volunteering for the newly formed SAS. Churchill continued to push for more raiding operations, which were the key to boosting Allied morale, stressing how 'a few successful raids would be most valuable. They would encourage the Russians in their struggle and would be heartening evidence to the Chancelleries of Europe that we are capable of offensive action.' (War on the Eastern Front had recently been declared.) North Africa made for perfect terrain for such missions, Churchill averred, while stressing that laying waste to the enemy's airbases was of paramount importance.

In short order Fraser had become the 'smash-and-grab' raider par excellence, with thirty-seven warplanes to his name. But right now, at the SAS's Jalo headquarters, he and his men had been reported as missing in action.

Seventy-two hours earlier, Fraser and his men had been dropped in the desert just to the south of a garish monument erected by the Italian Fascist leader, Benito Mussolini, to celebrate his nation's colonial triumphs in Africa. Formally the Arco dei Fileni, it was known to all in Allied command as 'Marble Arch', due to its resemblance to the famous London landmark of the same name. Adjacent to the towering, angular edifice, which rose from the desert like some alien apparition, lay an enemy airbase, or so Fraser and his men had been briefed. Their mission, codenamed 'Operation Number Five (B)', was to get onto that airstrip unseen and undetected, and to lace its warplanes with Lewes bombs, before making their getaway.

They'd hidden out for twenty-four hours, then moved in on foot under cover of darkness, and laden with their explosive charges. Unfortunately, they'd found the target to be all-but deserted. In fact, it was little more than a 'landing strip with a shed', one of Fraser's men had commented, ruefully. With not a single aircraft to attack, the raiders had melted away into the night, to await collection by the LRDG. They were disappointed not to have hit the jackpot, of course, having had a totally 'wasted journey'.

As they lay up in hiding they vowed to put it all down to experience, and to seek better target intelligence the next time around. Yet slowly, inexorably, the grim reality had dawned upon them that right now, there might well never be a 'next time around'.

From their hideout – 'a small hollow in the desert, partially screened by soft sand and surrounded by sparse scrub' – they'd taken turns on look-out. For two days they'd waited for the column of Chevys to emerge from the desert wastes, which stretched for hundreds of miles in all directions, bar north, where the coastal strip and the Mediterranean lay just a few kilometres away. Of the five raiders, two were, like Fraser, seasoned irregular warriors. They weren't 'unduly worried', for the timing of the pickup would be dictated by the LRDG, and whenever Lewes, Almonds and their party had managed to execute their own attack.

But by sundown on the third day they'd started to sense that maybe they 'were in trouble'. They'd noticed a series of columns of smoke on the horizon and heard the sounds of distant battle. While they couldn't know it for certain, they'd feared that maybe that was the Desert Taxi Company taking a pounding from enemy warplanes. By then, each man had little more than half a bottle of water remaining, and with no sign of the LRDG, they placed themselves on the kind of water strictures that Jock Lewes had drilled into them during the long months of training, doing 'little more than moisten our lips'.

Minds turned to the inevitable – what to do if, as now seemed possible, they had been abandoned. Fraser's second-in-command was Sergeant Duncan Robert Tait, a man who'd already earned an almost mythical reputation in the war. Tait, a fellow No. 11 Commando veteran, had served on the same amphibious operation as Fraser, when, in June 1941, Allied forces had moved to seize Syria, to stop it being used as a base for enemy warplanes. Due to a complex set of factors, not aided by delays and the men being dropped on the wrong beaches, the commandos had found themselves fighting a series of running battles, while vastly outnumbered and outgunned by the enemy.

Attempting to escape and evade back to friendly lines, Tait's party had been caught on the enemy wire, all bar one being killed or forced to surrender. Tait alone had remained determined to make a getaway, and he had resorted to quite extraordinary means to do so. He'd stolen through the darkness towards the sea, slipped into its salty embrace and proceeded to swim for several kilometres, in the process crossing from enemy to friendly territory. Tait had come ashore to a hero's welcome, and despite the crippling losses suffered by No. 11 Commando. He would be awarded the Military Medal (MM) for his daring escape, coupled with his earlier standout heroics as the battle raged.

Since then, Tait had joined Fraser in signing up for the SAS, distinguishing himself once more by conjuring up the design for the unit's iconic badge, the so-called 'winged dagger' as it has become known, which more accurately depicts either the flaming sword of Damocles, or King Arthur's Excalibur. More to the point, he'd served as Fraser's second-in-command on the Agedabia raid, their 'bag' of thirty-seven warplanes earning him a bar to his MM – his second such decoration in the space of six months. Tait, known to all as 'Bob', was square-jawed and classically good-looking, being blessed with open, no-nonsense features. Like Fraser he was a fellow Gordon Highlander. His suggestion, now that their patrol very likely faced a desperate march across the desert on little or no water, was characteristically upbeat and bullish: they should head for the coastal highway, hijack a suitable enemy vehicle and drive right through the desert back to Jalo.

Tait's plan had a certain, delicious simplicity to it, plus the upside was that they could carry all of their weaponry, ammo and Lewes bombs with them, so arriving back at base 'ready for the next raid'. What was more, once they were on the move with their own wheels, they might come across other targets of opportunity and be able to strike. Lastly, and above all, everyone appreciated the idea of *not* having to walk. But there were also the all-too-obvious downsides. Firstly, they would need to cross several hundred kilometres of trackless desert without the one navigational aid that made the LRDG's forays so reliable: the sun-compass.

Basically, this resembled a knitting needle set vertically in a circular disc, the shadow from which enabled a navigator to plot direction of travel. Mounted on a Chevy's dashboard, and with an adjustable circular dial to account for the movement of the sun, it allowed a patrol to plot its course while on the move, and without having to worry about the interference a standard magnetic compass was prone to (metal tended to upset its true bearing). Few enemy vehicles would carry a sun-compass, especially since it was the singular invention of the LRDG's founder, Major Ralph Bagnold. The second downside to Tait's hijack-and-scarper plan was the possibility that the enemy vehicle might break down in the open desert, leaving them facing a dire predicament indeed.

Fraser reckoned that they'd be better off sticking as close to the coastline as possible, pushing east towards the nearest British lines, which they believed to be some 300 kilometres away. It would constitute a hellish journey, especially as they would be moving on foot through hostile territory, and they would need to scavenge and steal food and water to sustain themselves. Even if they did succeed in covering that kind of distance without being killed or captured, or dying of heat, thirst and exhaustion, there was still the very real challenge of crossing over the Axis – German and Italian – front lines. After which, they'd have to make it back into friendly territory without being shot by their own side.

Still, on balance Fraser's plan was seen as having the greater potential, though each man was aware that right now 'every desert soldier's nightmare was coming true'. Daunted by what lay before them, the five men decided to remain in their place of hiding until the very last moment, in case the LRDG patrol was simply delayed.

By day six, they were down to their last remaining drops of water. With the approach of evening, they faced the inevitable: the moment of departure. At dusk, they busied themselves burying all excess kit, including their precious Lewes bombs, and even their weaponry. It was each man's choice what armaments he carried, as long as there was a decent balance of firepower across the patrols. A similar rule pertained to dress, each man choosing to operate in whatever bits and bobs of uniform, or otherwise, he most felt comfortable wearing. Even so, when Fraser ordered one of his men to abandon his Thompson sub-machine gun, that was seen as being a step too far.

Corporal John 'Jack' Vincent Byrne was a resolutely tough

soldier and an SAS original, plus he was one of Bill Fraser's regulars. A fellow veteran of the 1st Battalion the Gordon Highlanders, Byrne had likewise only escaped from the June 1940 hell of the retreat from France due to his injuries. Like Fraser, he'd fought with maniacal ferocity in defence of the evacuation beaches, being injured twice, the second time during bloody hand-to-hand combat with German troops. Wounded by a bayonet thrust, he'd been left for dead, but rescued by some French villagers who had carried him to the beachhead. From there he was rushed onto a waiting ship, which steamed for British shores. Just as soon as he was on the mend, Byrne had volunteered for Special Service and had gone to join No. 11 Commando.

Byrne has been born into hardship, being brought up in the harsh school of knocks. Hailing from Preston, he'd grown up in 'a tough Lancashire orphanage' where there was little option but to take care of oneself or go under. He'd gone on to attend the Army Apprentices College, in Chepstow, Wales, which trained the next generation of soldiers. There, he'd learned key practical skills – carpentry, metalwork, electronics – plus the foundations of good military acumen, including 'leadership', 'adventure training' and 'character development'. In 1939 he'd lied about his age – he was barely seventeen – to join the Gordon Highlanders. After France, he'd gone on to fight alongside Fraser and Tait in the parched Syrian hills, after which he'd joined them in volunteering for the SAS.

Byrne was a single-minded, plain-spoken individual, and when he raised an objection people tended to listen. 'Bill told me to toss the Tommy gun into a hole,' he would write in his war memoirs, *The General Salutes A Soldier*. 'When I protested he said I could keep the weapon, provided it was clearly understood that I would not ask anyone to help carry it.' The Thompson sub-machine gun weighed well over five kilos, when loaded. Byrne wasn't particularly bothered. Known as the 'Chicago Piano', the 'Trench Sweeper' or the 'Trench Broom', it was a favourite weapon among the raiders, due to the punch it packed. 'I agreed at once,' was Byrne's singular response to Fraser's exhortation.

At first light the five men set forth. 'Started to walk back with very little food and no water,' Fraser would record, with typical understatement, in the SAS War Diary. This was a record of the unit's war service, compiled by the men themselves and told in a manner 'devoid of glamour or romance', as the 'simple cold, blunt facts of British soldiers who preferred to fight in a technique all of their own'. Well, right now five of these men were about to attempt to escape and evade following a 'technique all of their own', and the extraordinary trials that lay before them would challenge the imagination of even the most gifted thriller writer.

Each of the five hefted an Italian Army-issue backpack – far superior to the standard British equivalent – holding whatever provisions they had left. Mostly, this consisted of a few biscuits, a little cheese and some raisins, plus a tin of emergency chocolate. As Byrne pointed out, while these were the kind of rations that would normally last a man for barely two days, it was 'more than sufficient' for what lay ahead, as the human body could go without food for weeks on end. It was water that would be the key issue, as each man had just a few drops remaining in his bottle. Before leaving, they agreed between themselves the iron discipline they would adhere to – 'not to drink until dusk'. But it would quickly become clear that they had tarried too long in their desert hideout, eking out their meagre water supplies, and the five were in 'no condition to march'.

They set out in single file, a tiny string of figures in the vast emptiness, and assailed by the blazing sun. The marching discipline that Fraser decreed was to push on for fifty minutes, rest for ten, then repeat and repeat ad nauseum. Each of the five would take turns in the lead, trying to match the pace set by his predecessor. All morning no one so much as breathed a word, as parched lips gasped for air in the burning heat. At midday, as they halted for their break, the five gathered in a circle and gazed into each other's faces, each reading the others' expressions and their thoughts. What each man detected was a sense of 'indescribable misery'. Seeing their fellow's abject suffering drew the five closer together and they began to talk. But not the barest 'spark of hope' was expressed by anyone. What possible reasons could they find to be hopeful?

'Someone suggested this was how we would end, sitting together in a group,' Byrne remarked. In the midst of the empty, sun-blasted wilderness, who could take issue with that? In any case, no one had the energy to argue or disagree.

Resolution was overtaken by a leaden weariness. Still they kept moving, forcing one foot in front of the other, stamping into the hot, clinging sand, before lifting the rear leg up like 'automata' and taking another step. The one thing that seemed to keep them going was the promise of the ten-minute break at the top of the hour. As that moment approached, they would bunch together until just inches separated them, so they could sit down as one and take that blessed breather, gasping in the parched air. Once the ten minutes' rest was done, the man in the rear would take up the lead, leapfrogging the weary line, and bang on cue he would begin marching on, without a word to his fellows.

Only once during that first day's trials did anyone break the routine, the figure bringing up the rear failing to take up pole position in a timely manner. When he rejoined the party and went to take up the lead, someone asked him if he was all right.

'Of course I am,' he countered, pointedly. 'I stopped for a crap, that's all. What's wrong with that? Come on, it's time.'

And with that he set off, stomping into the hot sands.

The sky burned with a blinding ferocity, the light and heat of the sun being thrown back by the sand, so it was as if the marchers were being roasted from all sides. There was not the slightest scrap of proper cover or the chance to escape from the desert oven. They longed for sunglasses or the luxury of a wide hat, to cast a little shade. Around 3.6 million square miles in area, the Sahara – *as-sahra al-kubra*; the Great Desert, in Arabic – is almost as large as Europe. It is largely devoid of human life, especially as it lacks life-giving water. These men had crossed it by both land and by air, and they had fought in and among its vastness, so they knew its wild beauty and its deadly strictures most personally. Being marooned here, bereft of water, was no recipe for survival.

At dusk on that first day, five exhausted figures scraped shallow holes in the soft sand, and climbed into their makeshift shelters to try to sleep. Curled into the one blanket that each man carried, they tried to conserve body heat, as the temperature began to plummet. Paradoxically, as soon as the Saharan sun goes down the heat dissipates, and the nights can be bitingly cold. From highs of around 38 degrees Celsius during the day, the temperature plummets to minus 4 degrees during the hours of darkness. Often, there would be a crust of frost dusting the dunes, come daybreak. Restless in the biting, bone-numbing chill, Byrne found himself lying awake and unable to resist treating himself to a smoke, plus the delicious luxury of moistening his lips with a dash of water.

Long before daybreak all were awake, sitting bolt upright and shivering uncontrollably. They were keen to get moving, to work some warmth and life back into icy limbs. As soon as it was light enough, they set forth. All that day they somehow kept at it, sticking to their rigid marching regime, and despite the fact that they were now into day five without drinking more than the barest sips of water. By mid-afternoon someone made the suggestion that they rest through the remaining heat, and push on come nightfall, into the cool of darkness. Gratefully, the five did just that, crawling beneath their blankets in an effort to seek a little shade. The blankets also served a second purpose, something that Jock Lewes had drilled into them during their repeated training marches. A blanket thrown over the body broke up the human form, providing a form of DIY camouflage and making it far less easy to be spotted from the air.

That evening, before setting out into the velvety purple and charcoal hues of the dunes, the fugitives drank the last of their water. A few remaining drops, like delicious nectar, and the bottles were bone dry. They abandoned their marching routine, for in the freezing cold and the starlit expanse of the desert night it was better simply to keep moving. If they risked stealing a rest break, frozen limbs might seize up, hence keeping the long march going right through the witching hours, until dawn.

Resuming the daytime regime, they pushed on. By mid-morning they had detected a dancing, ephemeral shimmer on the eastern horizon – something they had been expecting, if the route they were steering was true. As they pushed ahead, the image seemed to stabilise and crystalise more fully, revealing the distant forms of Libya's salt lakes – Bir Al Akhariyah, with further east again, Ma'tan Al Jafr, each an expanse some sixty-odd kilometres from end to end. The blinding, glistening whiteness gave the lie to the hope of any life-giving water they might harbour, for the lakes were fiercely saline and poisonous to humans. The fugitives knew this, of course. It was part of the desert lore they'd had drilled into them. Their training camp at Kabrit lay deep in the Egyptian desert, situated on the shores of that nation's Great Bitter Lake, itself a sea of salinity that was undrinkable.

As the water of these Saharan lakes evaporated under the burning sun, so the concentration of the salt became greatly enhanced, ending up being many times that of any sea. Eventually, it was unable to sustain anything like the rich diversity of life that inhabits the oceans. Even the most basic organisms struggled to survive, and often the toxic waters harboured only single-cell creatures, like algae, which somehow could still thrive there. But none of that meant that the fugitive's feverish minds didn't dream and hope, and allow a collective delusion to grow among them and to increasingly take hold.

It took two hours to reach the nearest shoreline – salt-encrusted, devoid of nearly all greenery and with a harsh, retching tang to the air that alone should have furnished ample warning. But in the interim, every man among the five had conjured up some reason, and given voice to it, as to why the waters would have miraculously been rendered potable. Despite the very appearance of the lake – 'without vegetation or life of any description' – all were convinced that somehow, here lay their salvation, with the result that the last few kilometres had developed into a frenzied speed march.

Flinging themselves down at the shoreline, they drank greedily, but instantly spat out the nauseous, vile brew. But still the delusion – the desert madness – gripped them. A figure stumbled around the shoreline, intent on trying another patch of the lake's expanse, desperate to prove that there at least the water was life-giving and sweet. Taking his cue, the rest hurried after, hope springing eternal in the hearts of the tortured and suffering. Of course, that patch of water proved no better, but all were gripped by a form of insanity now, and for an hour or more they dashed to and fro, trying to find the sweet-spot and to drink their fill.

With beards and nostrils dusted in a thick layer of whiteness – crystalized salt – the five crazed figures were 'indeed a sorry sight'. But still the bitter lesson was yet to be learned. The utter hopelessness of their predicament – they were still a good 200 kilometres distant from friendly lines – combined with the crushing fatigue, and the effects of the salt they had already imbibed, caused these men to partially lose their minds, not to mention their powers of good judgement or discernment.

'The more we tasted the lake water, the more difficult it became to decide whether it was salty or not,' wrote Byrne.

They began to bicker. Someone accused someone else of making this patch of the lake saline, simply by dipping his salt encrusted features into it. Someone else argued most volubly that of course saltwater was good to drink. He tried to demonstrate this by filling his water bottle to the brim, then necking a good half of its contents. Figures began to vomit up whatever they had imbibed, as the classic symptoms of such poisoning began to take hold. Normal seawater is four times as saline as a human's bodily fluids. The salinity of the Saharan salt lakes is far more extreme. Very quickly, drinking such water results in muscle cramps, a dry mouth and extreme thirst. Nausea, weakness and delirium ensue, as the scrambled human brain reasons that the only way to slake the body's desperate thirst is to drink more of the same. Catastrophic organ failure, coma and death soon follow.

For the five desperate fugitives, salvation came in the form of some caves. Exhausted beyond measure, disorientated, plagued by stomach cramps and worse, one by one the five men stumbled into their shelter. That blessed escape from the pounding sun – utterly unexpected, and the first real shade in well over a week – proved a life-saver. Dotted along the northern shore of the Bir Al Akhariyah lake, the caves provided a moment's respite in which the worst of their desert madness could be mastered. But not a man among the five of them was under any illusion any more: they were all going to perish, unless they found some means to get life-giving water.

It was Bill Fraser, plus another of the five, Jeffrey 'Jeff' DuVivier, who suggested how they might do so. DuVivier, with rounded features, a shock of wild sandy hair and eyes that always seemed to be laughing, was another Gordon Highlander and No. 11 Commando veteran. A waiter in a Felixstowe hotel prior to the war, DuVivier had volunteered for the SAS, for it seemed to offer real promise that they 'were going to see some action'. Action they were certainly seeing on the shores of Bir Al Akhariyah, but not quite of the kind that DuVivier had craved. 'It was absolute hell,' he would remark of their ordeal, 'but the worst part of it was that our transports were destroyed.'

At any other time, Fraser's and DuVivier's suggestion would have been given short shrift, for they proposed transforming the toxic mix of the lake into something eminently drinkable. They would concoct a makeshift still, purify the lake's contents and transform it into that lifesaving elixir – pure, potable water. At its simplest, a still could be made from a British Army billy-can, with a bowl floating inside it, and an upturned lid on top. With a fire kindled beneath the billy, the lid would capture the evaporated water, and it would drip down into the bowl. That, at least, was the theory. In practice, the others thought Fraser and DuVivier stir-crazy, simply for suggesting that those vile waters could be rendered any way pure. But lacking any better suggestion they set to it with a vengeance, ferrying water from the lake, plus wet sand, to act as a makeshift coolant.

As the sun crept ever higher, in the guts of the cave the still bubbled and hissed. By sunset, a paltry pint of water had been captured. As it was steaming hot, tea was prepared, and the five men settled down to their heavenly brew. Only it wasn't. The first sip proved it to taste 'just like urine', and the five men were all too familiar with that, having already resorted to drinking their own pee during the long trek east across the desert. Fraser and DuVivier forced themselves to down the 'terrible concoction', but the others found it too noisome, and could not keep it down for long. Sadly, their cave distillery was not looking like the answer to their life-and-death predicament.

It was now that Bob Tait voiced an alternative proposition. While the contents of the salt lakes were known to be poisonous, there were sometimes wells sunk in the neighbouring terrain, for the water, when filtered through the earth's substrata, could be made drinkable. With the cool of evening settling over the landscape, it was worth taking a look, Tait reasoned. Fraser agreed, so long as those forming the search party left their water bottles behind, to aid with the ongoing process of distilling. Tate and Byrne decided to set out, taking a fifth member of the patrol, Trooper Arthur Philips, of the Royal Warwickshire Regiment.

While the desperate trio's supposed impetus was searching for a well, instinctively the search led them north towards the coastline. In that way they stumbled across the main highway, which, from the northern tip of the lake, was barely five kilometres distant. 'Within the hour the three of us were standing by the coast road, watching enemy vehicles pass in both directions,' Byrne wrote of the moment.

Now they were there, Tait's original suggestion – that they hijack an enemy truck and use that to make their getaway – seemed all too tangible, not to mention impossible to resist. This road formed German General Erwin Rommel's main supply route, along which his war materiel had to be ferried, from the coastal ports eastwards towards his frontline positions. It was rarely devoid of traffic. Keeping to the southern flank of the highway, Tait, Byrne and Philips flitted through the darkened terrain, until they came to a point of natural pause – a vehicle park. A row of empty drums marked off a space beside the road, being large enough to accommodate several trucks.

Right now, that pull-in was deserted. But none of the trio figured it would remain so for long, especially with the volume of traffic that tended to crowd Rommel's supply route. Byrne slipped his Tommy gun from his shoulder. All through their travails he had refused to discard it. Taking up position, he kept the others covered as they went about shifting around the drums, which fortunately proved to be empty. None of them would have had the strength to move them otherwise. In that way they closed down the parking space, until it could accommodate just the one vehicle. That done, they took cover beside the empty lot and waited.

The minutes ticked by, as the trio considered their predicament.

This was an absolute life-or-death situation, and in more ways than one. While they might be killed or wounded while attempting to snatch a vehicle, if they didn't take the risk they were as good as dead anyway. Their resolve hardened. Sixty minutes slipped by, before a lone set of headlamps slowed on approach to the pull-in. It was a large covered truck, and, just as they were hoping, it nosed carefully into the parking space, coming to rest with its tailboard towards the hidden watchers. The trio spread out, so they could keep an eye on three sides of the vehicle: front, near-side and rear. Positions set, they waited for those riding in the truck to alight, as they took a cigarette break, or a pee stop, or whatever they had pulled over for.

No one emerged, which begged the question – why had the truck stopped at all? Tait, Byrne and Philips crept forward, pausing at the vehicle's rear to check that it was unoccupied. After a brief listening watch, straining their ears for any sign of life, they were satisfied that no enemy soldiers were inside. Moving silently, they stole towards the cab. Tait took the right-hand side, while Byrne and Philips made for the other. As the latter braced himself to wrench the door open, Byrne readied his weapon. An instant later the door was yanked wide, the truck's startled occupants finding themselves staring down the barrel of a Tommy gun wielded by one of the most dishevelled and des-perate-looking individuals they had ever laid eyes on. None of the SAS trio had shaved or washed for weeks, let alone cut their hair. After days under the blistering sun, and sleeping out in the freezing desert, the description 'piratical' didn't even come close.

Pretty much at the same moment, Tait threw the opposite door wide, grabbed the nearest German soldier and dragged him bodily from his seat. Byrne had realised right away why the truck had halted. The driver and his mate had been examining a miniature pistol, via torchlight. Presumably, it was some kind of a war trophy that they had retrieved from the battlegrounds. Byrne reached in and grabbed it – just in case the one remaining German entertained any ideas about putting up any resistance – and slipped it into his pocket. That done, he pulled the driver from behind the wheel.

In short order the raiders secured the two captives 'in the approved manner' – face down on the roadside, hands clasped behind their necks. The shock with which they'd responded to the hijacking was hardly surprising. One moment they were there, hundreds of kilometres behind their own lines, trundling along in what they believed was the safety offered by friendly territory, and the next they had been set upon by a fearsome trio of bandits, with not the slightest idea of how their desperate-looking assailants had even come to be there. As for Tate, Byrne and Philips, they faced their own dilemma right now. A search of the truck revealed manna from heaven: a jerrycan full of fresh water. The question was how to get it back to their lakeside cave.

They could try to take the truck, but the terrain around Bir Al Akhariyah was boggy, treacherous and marsh-like. They resolved they'd have to carry the water to the cave. There, they could drink their fill, and thus replenished and revitalised they could return to the truck and get motoring on their way, heading east on the highway. After two dozen kilometres they would be able turn south into the open desert, skirting around the fringes of the lake. Plan sorted, there was just one matter to deal with: the prisoners. There seemed to be no option but to take the two hapless Germans with them, in which case they figured their captives might as well carry the water.

The five set off, pushing south on foot and making for the cave. They were half a mile short when Tait signalled a halt. He glanced at the prisoners, before announcing: 'Sod it, let's turn 'em loose. By the time we collect the others and walk back to the lorry – that's if Bill agrees – it'll be nearly daylight.'

Tait had a point. No one fancied motoring east on Rommel's main supply road in broad daylight, while trying to make like the enemy. With their present unorthodox appearances, they weren't about to fool anyone for very long.

Using hand gestures, they motioned for the captives to set down the jerrycan and to scarper, heading back the way they'd come. But the pair seemed rooted to the spot and they looked visibly petrified. Most likely, they feared they were about to be shot in the back, just as soon as they turned tail on their captors. Both men appeared strikingly young, and it took the trio's best efforts to reassure them that they weren't about to be mown down in cold blood. When finally the pair had got the message, one of them, who spoke a little halting English, confessed that they were actually Austrian, not German . . . as if that made the slightest difference. In fact, it only served to annoy Tait and Byrne, who much preferred facing their 'deadly enemies, to their running dogs'.

Tait eyed the pair. 'We always shoot Austrians,' he growled, with quiet menace.

Panic filled the prisoners' eyes. 'I was born in Hamburg,' one exclaimed, as if hailing from Germany's second largest city might save him from Tait's murderous intent.

'All right,' Tait feigned, as if that had convinced him to show a little mercy. 'Clear off then.'

With that the pair turned and hurried into the darkness.

The three fugitives paused, for the call of the water was too powerful to resist. They were just about to take a nip, when out of the night emerged two familiar figures. The pair of erstwhile prisoners were back, eyes saucer-wide with fear. They blurted out that they were afraid of getting lost in the dark, and would prefer to remain captives, if they possibly could. Tait was having none of it. He grabbed the pair, pointed to a star that lay low on the horizon and just to the right of where their lorry was located, and showed them how to use it to steer their way home.

'Follow that star to the road, then turn left and keep going until you reach your lorry. And don't come back.'

With those words ringing in their ears the pair were well and truly dispatched. Tate, Byrne and Philips paused to take a drink. The water was stone cold and beyond perfection. They followed up with a smoke, and feeling thus reinvigorated they pressed on. To say their reappearance at the cave – and bearing water! – was like a miraculous apparition was an understatement. The welcome they received from Fraser and DuVivier defied description. Someone suggested brewing tea. It was vetoed. The purloined water was too fine and delectable to do anything but imbibe it cool and 'raw'. As they quaffed their fill, the five felt their appetites returning. They broke out their cheese and biscuits, and feeling thus revitalised they considered next steps.

Having filled their water bottles, they hefted the jerrycan and resolved to push east on foot, aiming to put a good distance between themselves and their cave hideout. Shortly, the enemy were bound to learn of the trio's presence in the area and they needed to make tracks, using the last of the night hours in which to do so. They set out, marching hard until dawn. By the gathering light they spied another cave. This one was far shallower, with barely a roof to speak of, being formed from where the wind had scoured out a shallow cliff in the salt-encrusted terrain. It would suffice. Crawling into its hollow, they settled in for the wait. Hopefully, the enemy would conclude that for a force of raiders to be so far behind enemy lines, they would have to have their own transport, in which case they would be long gone.

Evidently, no one made any great effort to scour the terrain, for there was zero sign of any follow-up or search party. At midday the five set out again, with full bellies and full water bottles, and with a newfound confidence that belied all their earlier tribulations, plus the madness that had seized them on the shores of the salt lake. There was still not the slightest sign of any enemy in pursuit. That night they would sleep relatively deep and sound, and for the first time since they had commenced their marathon getaway.

Over the next thirty-six hours they continued pushing eastwards, resuming their fifty-minutes' marching, interspersed with ten minutes' break routine. Spirits were high, and with their reinvigorated bodies and clear heads their legs ate up the miles. By now, Fraser reckoned they had skirted the northern shore of the second salt lake, Mat'an Al Jafr, slipping between its glistening expanse and the coast road where it swept past the Gulf of Sidra, the most southerly point of the Mediterranean. That meant they'd covered well over 100 kilometres, so more than a third of their journey.

All went well until the afternoon of their third day out from Bir Al Akhariyah's caves. Even as the five fugitives nursed the remaining liquid in their two-pint water bottles, an ominous apparition crept across the desert horizon. By its hollow, eerie, spectral wail they could hear it before they saw it, and out here in the desert there was, of course, no escape. Piling up to several hundred feet in height, the churning mass appeared like a ghostly tsunami, as it bore down on the escapees with remorseless intent. The desert tempest blocked out the sun, turning the sky an unearthly orange, and long before the cloud of roiling dust had engulfed them. The point man resolved to march on, stubbornly advancing into the storm's wild embrace.

Minutes later they were sucked into its maw – five tiny figures silhouetted against the howling belly of the beast. For thirty minutes they tried to fight their way onwards, until it was clear that to continue was courting death or disaster. If nothing else they risked losing each other in the maelstrom, and to break the fellowship would be a terrible blow to their newfound morale and their spirits. There was no option but to huddle together in the heart of the storm, 'curling up in the sand until the worst was over', as the wind-whipped grit and dust tore into exposed skin and eyes.

Eventually the sky cleared. It revealed that their surroundings had been transformed, and not in any way that the fugitives had been expecting. Somehow, under the blanket of that desert tempest, an enemy supply column had moved into the area, camping up so as to avoid the very same storm from which Fraser and his men had taken shelter. As far as they could see, there were ranks of soft-skinned army trucks. The closest vehicle, which had a tent pitched beside it, was no more than a few dozen yards away. After all they had endured, it was an eerie and most disturbing apparition to behold.

As Fraser and his men shook off the layer of sand that had blown across them and tried to muster themselves, so did the enemy. Figures could be seen moving about, yelling to each other in Italian. Keeping his cool, Fraser reasoned that any curious enemy troops would very likely presume that he and his men were some of their own. It made no sense for them to be anything other than a part of their convoy. On his instructions, the five fugitives rose from the sand and turned away from the convoy, moving as one in the opposite direction. Covered in dust as they were, there was little to distinguish them from the enemy, and no one cried out so much as a word of challenge. A hundred yards from the Italian encampment they crested a rise. Beyond it lay a shallow scrape in the desert. They flung themselves down into its shelter, after which they set about studying their adversaries.

Via their binoculars they noted that one vehicle sat apart from the others. That was their obvious prey. Dusk wasn't so far away, and the Italian military encampment was clearly there to stay, at least until the following morning. Come nightfall they would move in and strike. Tait took a bearing on that lone truck, and the five settled down to wait. When it was fully dark, Tait took up the lead, and via a compass bearing led them directly to their target. It loomed out of the desert night, a blocky silhouette sharp against the starry skies, which had been scrubbed clear by the storm.

Chinks of light bled out from the enemy vehicle. A blanket had been hung to cover its canvas rear, but not very well, and the glimmer of an oil lantern could be seen burning inside. The attempt at a blackout wasn't very effective, and a group of very voluble Italians were visible, messing around and joking in the truck's rear. As three kept watch, Fraser and Philips stole across the night sands to check on the truck's cab. Finding it to be empty, they retraced their steps, after which Fraser, cool as a cucumber, swept aside the blanket and without a word clambered aboard. The hubbub of Italian voices was instantly stilled. Philips, who was a good deal shorter than Fraser, hung on to the tailboard for a few seconds, before he too managed to vault over and drop inside.

The Italian soldiers, figuring the distinctly unfriendly-seeming strangers had to be Germans, started explaining that they were Italians, which meant that they were all on the same side. But as Fraser started to rifle through the contents of the truck, with Philips keeping a close watch, and with Tate, Byrne and DuVivier covering them with their weapons, it gradually dawned on the Italians that their unexpected visitors had to be on the opposing side of this war. Realising these wild-looking men had to be British, or at least serving with British forces, they all fell silent once more.

Fraser began tossing out anything that caught his eye – provisions and kit for their ongoing journey. First a tin of jam, followed by one of sardines, after which came a portable petrol stove. Philips hefted a large water bottle and threw it to Tait, who by now was at the vehicle's rear, weapon at the ready. Tait unscrewed the top and took a swig, before gagging and spitting out the contents. It was actually full of petrol, and Tait was not best pleased. He moved around to the engine compartment and tried to tap the radiator, for that should contain water enough to replenish their bottles, but the cap was rusted solid.

Tempers began to fray. Surely, the entire truck could not be bereft of water, the key booty the fugitives sought? They gathered at the rear and ordered the Italians down, at gunpoint. Four managed to exit the truck, but a fifth was so terrified that he hung onto a strut and would not be dissuaded by any means. None of the Italians were armed, which seemed decidedly odd. DuVivier

41

spoke a little French, which the Italians seemed to understand, and he managed to get them to explain exactly who and what they were. They were Italian Army cooks, hence the truck containing little more than their bedding and the few tins of food that Fraser had discovered.

Seizing the moment, DuVivier warned the hapless Italians that British forces had broken through their lines, and that they had the entire Italian encampment surrounded. They were preparing to attack come first light. They left those Italian Army cooks convinced that they were doomed, especially as DuVivier had threatened that should they try to leave their vehicle or otherwise raise the alarm, they would be cut down in a hail of Tommy gun fire. Warning given and understood, Fraser and his men departed with their booty, determined to put a good distance between themselves and the enemy camp come dawn. Miraculously, the bluff must have worked, for none of the thousands of enemy troops came chasing after them either on foot or by vehicle.

It was the early morning of 7 January 1942 when they pushed onwards into the western slopes of Wadi El Faregh – a deep, water-worn chasm that cut through the desert. Moving across broken, rough ground strewn with giant boulders and uprooted trees – detritus from recent floodwaters – it proved challenging to keep track of their progress, especially in the pre-dawn darkness. Still, Fraser figured they had covered an incredible distance to date, completing some 200 kilometres of their journey by foot. By rights, if the Allied front was still in the place where they had last known it to be, they should be no more than 50 kilometres short of their own forward lines.

The wadi provided excellent cover, so Fraser decided they should lie up for all of that day, and get moving again come nightfall. Water remained a critical issue, having failed to secure any from the Italians. But all being well, they might make friendly lines that night, if they marched at a fierce pace all through the dark hours. In decidedly high spirits the five gathered in a circle for a makeshift feast – falling first upon the tin of jam. It was a big one, maybe two pounds in weight. Each man readied his spoon, as they decided upon a conveyor-belt dip-system as the fairest means to distribute the booty, each sinking in his spoon and sucking it dry, one after the other.

Tait, his breath still reeking of petrol fumes, was allowed to go first, for it was famously difficult to get that taste out of one's mouth. Maybe the jam would do the trick. But watching him drive in his spoon and 'stuff it into his filthy black beard with exaggerated relish' fairly turned the others' stomachs. Several suspected that Tait was simply acting up, in the hope of putting the others off the feast, which would mean more for him. But then they stole a glance at the other faces in the circle, realising that each was about as monstrous and repellent as the other, and that Tait's appearance was actually nothing particularly special. No wonder the Italian chefs had been petrified.

Jam polished off, the tinned sardines were next – one and a half of the small, silvery fish per man, with the residue of oil left for anyone who fancied it. The tinned pears were saved for last. So utterly delicious, they were divvied up with 'great exactness, including the juice'. Thus refreshed, the five fugitives lay up in good cover and shade all that day, husbanding their strength for the last big push. They set out come nightfall on what they hoped was the final march to safety.

Moving north out of the wadi and then turning eastwards, they stumbled upon a well-used track, one they had not been expecting. Before they could assess what it might signify, a vehicle bore down on them, a pair of hooded headlamps spearing the gloom. Ducking into cover, Fraser and his men let it rumble past. Having done so, they put their heads together, deciding it was time to seize the moment. The next vehicle to come along that track would be theirs. Philips, the smallest among them, volunteered to step into the open at the appropriate moment. With a blanket draped over his head, hopefully the occupants would conclude that he was a local Arab, and slow down, at which point Fraser and his men would emerge, guns at the ready, to 'knock off the vehicle'.

An hour crept by, before a second set of shaded headlamps emerged from the darkness, bouncing along the rough ground. Philips stepped into the light, blanket appropriately draped across his shoulders, and turned to face the oncoming vehicle. It didn't seem to slow its pace, but when it was around a dozen yards away the lone SAS man stepped right into its path. The driver had no option but to run Philips over, or to swerve aside. He chose to do the latter, coming to a halt at the trackside. Within seconds, Fraser and his men had the two occupants dragged out of the vehicle and flat on their faces in the dirt. Having hurled their captives' weapons into the darkness, the hijackers demanded water, only to be told by their captives that there was none. A thorough search of the vehicle proved them to be telling the truth. Even the radiator water, when tried, proved to be rank with salt.

Still, at least they had a prize of sorts – the vehicle. It was a small, open-topped Mercedes car fitted with a wireless set. While it would be a tight fit, they could just about all cram inside. Fraser ordered the German driver back behind the wheel, reasoning that he was sure to be able to find his way through, especially as he would keep a pistol jammed into the man's neck. He was particularly keen for the German to navigate with due care, for the enemy frontline was defended by minefields. That agreed, he and Tait crammed themselves into the front passenger seat, beside their hapless German, while the remaining three – plus the other captive – squeezed into the rear.

The driver-captive turned out to speak a little English. 'I am Austrian,' he declared, seemingly in an effort to curry favour with his captors.

Tait barked out a laugh. 'Dammit,' he growled. 'I didn't want to shoot anyone today.'

Fraser ordered the man to head north, making for the main coast road. They reached it without incident, pulling off the rough ground onto the smooth surface, whereupon Fraser signalled a right-hand turn, so taking the route running east towards the frontline. The highway was crammed with traffic, as Rommel's convoys took full advantage of the hours of darkness in which to move, for there was little risk of the Royal Air Force targeting them from out of the desert skies. They reached the coastal settlement of Mersa Brega, but beyond that the route ahead looked devoid of traffic. Not a set of headlamps seemed to piece the darkness.

With the road having 'suddenly emptied' the driver slowed his pace. Fraser demanded to know what was happening. The way ahead was mined, the German explained. If they pushed onwards, they were dicing with death. Fraser ordered him to take the next turning right, into the desert, no matter what kind of route it might be. The driver did just that, and shortly the fugitives found themselves crawling along a deeply rutted track. The man behind the wheel kept complaining that the entire area was mined, as he reduced their progress to a dead slow. Up ahead a fork in the track appeared. There were no warning signs, nor anything to indicate where either route might lead. The driver seemed confused as to which track to take, and amid the chaos and uncertainty he failed to opt for either, instead driving the Mercedes right into a salt marsh.

The vehicle slewed to a glugging, slumping halt, as the wheels cut through the salt crust and it sank to its haunches. Fraser and his men clambered out, as did their German captives. Together the seven – friend and foe alike – tried to prise the Mercedes free and to manhandle it back onto firm ground. But the terrain was boggy and treacherous, and the attempt to rescue their mired wheels proved hopeless. Fraser turned to the two Germans and told them to make themselves scarce. Their usefulness was over. He indicated they should trek back the way they had come, heading for the road and their own side.

The five fugitives waited until their former captives were well out of sight. The madcap ride had taken its toll in terms of frayed nerves and fatigue. The on-again off-again race towards friendly lines had ended in failure, leaving them 'weary and disappointed'. But they faced no option, now the car was bogged down. It was east they had to head, and on foot once more.

Getting through the marshy ground proved a noisy and tiring procedure, as their boots constantly broke through the crusty, friable surface and sank deep. In the back of their minds were the German driver's dark warnings – that the entire area was mined. Finally, they broke out of the salt marshes and pressed on, moving cautiously through the still night air, for anywhere hereabouts there were likely to be hostile forces manning front-line positions. As they crept ahead, senses alert and straining, at any moment they expected to stumble upon their foes.

At last, a faint blush of dawn illuminated the skies to the east, as the first rays of the sun peeped above the chill horizon. The light revealed a forsaken landscape that seemed to offer not the slightest scrap of cover. It was the worst kind of terrain to be marooned in, especially at a moment such as this. Fraser ordered his men to lie face-down in the sand, unmoving, making best use of their blankets and whatever other coverings they might possess, in an effort to break up the human form. It stood to reason that the enemy would have constructed observation posts, overlooking their defensive positions. If Fraser and his men were spied at this – what they hoped was the final stage of their epic escape and evasion – that would be the bitterest blow of all.

The sun rose higher. It seared into the surrounding desert, the predicament of the five worsened by the heat thrown off by the sand. As they tried to burrow deeper, to better hide, the intense temperatures burned into their exposed bodies. The torture was 'aggravated by having to hug the ground so closely and by the absence of water', as Byrne described it, 'but we stuck to it all day long without uttering a single word'. It was well after last light when Fraser broke the quiet, giving the order that they could at last risk movement, as they prepared to get going again.

They set off stumbling into the darkness, pushing slowly and silently east. Sometime a little short of midnight a revolting, sickly-sweet scent drifted to them on the desert air. It was a smell they knew only too well by this stage of the war. It was the stench of decay and of death. It grew in strength and potency with each step, signalling the approach of some kind of killing ground. Finally, 'with the vile stench in our nostrils the whole time', the five stumbled into the ghostly setting of a mass grave. On two sides stretched a long, dark trench, broken open by what could only have been grave-robbers. Corpses had been dragged out, and the bodies of the dead lay in grisly, haphazard abandon, piled on top of each other in grotesque heaps.

In places, the horrific forms of arms, legs, feet and even heads protruded from the ground, as if the dead were rising up. All the corpses seemed to be British, or at least to be dressed in British uniform. There was no easy way around the hell-scape. Instead, the desperadoes were forced to set a course right through it, 'stumbling on through the bodies'. The horrific stench seemed to seep right into their beings. Even when they were through the worst, still 'the cloying, sickening smell stayed with us'. No matter that they were battle-hardened warriors, they'd been haunted by the experience, which left them 'much chastened by the fate of our comrades'.

Inching ahead with utmost care, their progress came to a sudden halt when a single, stark challenge cut the night. Throwing themselves down, they lay stock still, pulses racing, 'hearts pounding the desert'. Had they been spotted? If not, why then that solitary cry of alarm? Or perhaps there had been no shout at all? Perhaps it was simply tortured minds playing tricks? In hushed tones they tried to work out just what they might have heard. Convinced it had indeed been a challenge, they concluded there had to be some kind of a watch-post up ahead. Accordingly, they set a course a little to the north of where the enemy position had to lie, and got moving again. As there were no further cries of alarm, they figured they must have steered past that first point of danger.

But just as they were starting to relax a little and increase their rate of march, a series of shots tore apart the night. First one, then two, and eventually as many as a dozen cracks of rifle fire echoed across the desert, as the whine of bullets cut the air. Once more, the hunted dropped to their bellies. The outburst of gunfire was followed by a great deal of yelling, but eventually both the gunfire, and the shouts, died down to nothing. Silence enveloped all. Finally, Fraser gave the signal to get going once more, only this time they were to inch backwards, moving on all fours, retracing their steps.

For fifty yards they wormed on their bellies, retreating the way they had come. Only then did they risk clambering to their feet, whereupon Fraser decided to set a course slightly to the south of their previous one. They began to advance once more, moving with utmost care. If a figure so much as knocked a pebble free, all froze, straining their ears for a full minute or more. This stop-start progress seemed to continue for a lifetime, as they inched their way through the dark terrain, all the while growing increasingly convinced that right now they were transiting the enemy's front lines.

Finally, a faint glimmer of light emerged from out of the darkness somewhere up ahead. As the figures crept forwards, it didn't particularly seem to grow any closer, as if it were some form of spectral apparition dancing before their eyes, taunting and mocking their progress. Finally, it appeared to jump out of the night, becoming instantly recognisable for what it indeed was. Up ahead was a lone tent, inside of which burned a paraffin lantern. What on earth this solo camper might be doing here, amid this war-blasted, benighted landscape, was anyone's guess. Eventually, the five watchers reached the only conclusion that seemed even vaguely feasible: it had to be some kind of an Arab camp, for only the locals would risk showing a light.

The tent was large, with a long, flat profile, and maybe four feet in height. As they studied it, they fancied they again caught the horrible 'whiff of death'. Why the tent would be showing a light if all inside were dead, was beyond reckoning. But the longer they observed the mystery encampment, the stronger the sense of death became. Convinced at first that it was the stench of the mass grave clinging to their clothing, the certainty overtook them that the tent itself was the source of the smell.

Fraser decided to toss a small pebble onto the roof of the tent, to see if it harboured any living soul. It landed with a soft plop, and elicited an immediate response. A figure sat bolt upright, searching all about, his head almost touching the canvas roof. Finally, whoever it was lay down to rest once more. It was confounding. With no other option, the five men crawled forward, flicked aside the canvas covering and slid inside. As they did so, they were met with a 'putrid smell of death that was almost overpowering'. The figure they'd spied earlier crawled towards them. It was an Arab male and beside him was a small child.

The five fugitives greeted him in the traditional manner, then gestured that they were desperate for water. By way of response the Arab pointed towards a British Army fuel tin, which had had the top cut off, to form a crude kind of a water butt. It was half full and a small tin bowl floated on its surface. It was foul, and 'tainted by the smell of death', but even so the five drank deeply, they were so desperate. In mixed broken English and Arabic the two sides – Arab, and British soldiers – managed to make themselves understood. There were two dead bodies in the tent, a woman and a child, the Arab explained. They were his wife and his other child. Presumably, more victims of this war. The Arab told them that both the German and British forces would visit him at night, sometimes within an hour of each other, though the Italians never came. His tent was pitched in some kind of no-man's-land, the hiatus between two mighty armies at war.

Fraser asked in what direction lay the nearest British positions. The Arab gestured to where they were – east of there again. Thanking him for his hospitality they bade their farewells.

They were so close now. The night was still. What could stop them? At the approach of dawn Fraser and his men found themselves creeping through a mighty boulder field. Cautious as ever, he decided they would take cover here and see what first light might bring. It revealed a graveyard of military vehicles, scores of burned-out armoured cars and tanks littering the terrain. A quick rifle through some of the debris, and some tins of food were discovered. Though they had been roasted as the vehicles burned, in the very centre the escapees found there was still a core of edible food.

The boulder-strewn landscape stretched eastwards, dropping into a narrow ravine. It made sense to push on, for in such terrain their careful progress should remain unobserved. Slowly but surely the five escapees made their way down into the shadowed depths of the dry gully. Glancing up and eastwards, they spied the first of a rank of armoured cars, perched atop a vantage point on the far side. They were almost instantly recognisable as being the forces of the King's Dragoon Guards, especially as their unmistakeable red, blue and yellow pennants – displaying a distinctive double-headed imperial eagle – were lying limp and still in the torpid air.

Fraser and his men had spent some time with the forces of the

King's Dragoon Guards after their remarkable raid on Agedabia airfield, when they'd blown to pieces those thirty-seven enemy warplanes. It had been their armoured cars that had helped speed them back to the safety of Allied lines. Arguably, there was no better unit to welcome the five fugitives home this time around. Once they'd managed to attract their attention, the commander of the armoured car patrol sent a force of men scrambling down into the ravine to investigate.

'They must have thought we were a band of savages,' remarked one of the fugitives, 'with our long matted hair and beards. Faces and hands caked in dirt, and torn ragged clothes.' Once the men of the King's Dragoon Guards had managed to identify just who this band of desperadoes might be, they led the miracle escapees on their last steps to safety.

Shortly, Fraser and his fellows were loaded aboard a British Army truck to be whisked eastwards again, with an armoured car providing escort. Fraser took the front passenger's seat, while Tait, Byrne, DuVivier and Philips were ensconced in the rear. There they discovered some mouth-watering booty – two jars of Army-issue rum, plus a crate of Libby's evaporated milk. It proved too much to resist, but they reckoned they couldn't scoff the lot without offering some to Fraser, the man who deserved the lion's share of the credit for getting them out of that hell alive.

Tait banged on the driver's cab, trying to attract his attention. 'Stop! We need to take a leak!'

The truck didn't so much as slow its progress. Instead, Fraser yelled back a typical riposte: 'Do it over the tailboard. What the hell's the matter with you?'

The four figures in the rear were about to get stuck in to the booty, when the driver slowed his pace enough for Fraser to leap down and dash around to the back, whereupon he clambered aboard.

'What's wrong?' he demanded, as soon as he was inside.

By way of reply, Tait gestured at the heap of loot. Fraser eyed it for a second, before pulling out his mug and holding it out. 'How much have you drunk already?' he asked.

By the time the truck had reached its destination, the entire lot had been polished off – rum, milk and all. Somewhat unsteadily, the five escapees clambered down and tried to muster themselves into some kind of order. Attempting to stand to attention in a 'dead straight line . . . our bodies jutted out at odd angles,' Byrne recalled. Fraser tried to whip up a salute, as a smart young British Army major came out to greet them.

'I'm afraid we owe you for two jars of rum and twenty-four tins of milk,' Fraser blurted out, by way of introduction.

For a moment there was a stunned silence, as the major tried to assimilate what he'd just heard. He couldn't help but burst out laughing.

'I don't believe it,' he stammered. 'It's not possible.'

He strolled around to the rear of the truck to investigate, and of course, the evidence – twenty-four empty tins, two empty jars – spoke for itself. The major turned away from the vehicle, trying his best to hide his consternation and his mirth.

He gestured at the pile of empties. 'Forget it,' he declared. After all that the five men had endured and survived, they'd more than earned it.

Before speeding on from that location, Fraser approached Byrne and asked for the miniature pistol – the one that Byrne had taken from the two German truckers. He wanted it as a gift for the major, to say thank you. Fraser returned bearing a small silver hip flask, which was a gift in return from the major.

He handed it to Byrne. 'Here. I'm sure you're more than able to carry that, as well as your Tommy gun.'

'Can I keep it?' Byrne queried.

Of course, Fraser told him.

What the SAS lieutenant didn't reveal was just how useful their incredible escape was going to prove to the British forces then mustering at the battlefront. Having executed 'one of the greatest survival epics of the North Africa war', the return of Fraser and his men to the SAS's Kabrit base was further delayed by the need to impart some choice intelligence to British headquarters. As Fraser would report, they had made it through the front lines 'just as [the] big push was going in . . . [and] we were able to give very valuable information . . .' In other words, in the process of executing a nerve-shredding escape from deep inside enemy territory, Fraser and his party had gathered some crucial intelligence, which they had passed on to Eighth Army high command. Fraser's eyewitness account was viewed as being so valuable that he was flown directly to Cairo, where he had made his report in person to General Neil Ritchie, Eighth Army's commander, and to its Intelligence Branch.

By the time Fraser, Tait, Byrne, DuVivier and Philips had made it back to Kabrit, they had been missing for the best part of a month. Unsurprisingly, all had presumed that the five men were gone for good – either captured, or dead and buried. By the time the ghosts of 'Operation Number Five (B)' melted out of the desert heat-haze, it was as if Fraser and his party had returned from the grave. When Fraser went to retire to his tent, one that he had last slept in fully six weeks earlier, he found it occupied by a fresh recruit. 'We were told that we had been given up for dead,' DuVivier commented, of their return to Kabrit.

In truth, the traumatic experiences of their tortuous trek would haunt the five escapees for many months to come. During that long desert escape, 'I learnt what it meant to be thirsty, what it meant to be desperately hungry and whacked to the wide world,' DuVivier would write. 'It would fill a book to tell all our adventures on that journey.' At times they'd resorted to 'eating lizards, berries and snails', so desperately famished and dehydrated had they become. Long after their death-defying getaway, neither Fraser nor any of his patrol could bear the smell of cooking. If they caught the scent of food, they simply had to eat right away, gorging themselves.

For leading his men to safety against seemingly impossible odds, Fraser would be awarded the MC, the citation for which would praise his peerless leadership and his undaunted spirit, which had continuously bolstered the morale of his men when all had seemed hopeless. Typically, he would conclude in his report on their incredible escape that the 'men under my command behaved admirably ... and made the task much easier by their cheerfulness and readiness to obey orders. Particularly noticeable was their determination not to be captured under any circumstances.'

Our next great escapees would demonstrate similar steely determination to avoid capture at all costs. Their extraordinary tale takes us from the sun-blasted desert to deep beneath the ocean, as a submarine steams stealthily towards the enemy coastline.

Chapter Two

LAST STAND AT HERAKLION

June 1942, Alexandria, Egypt

The submarine commanders had got into a somewhat unorthodox habit, one intended to signal that a successful Special Service mission had just been executed by their craft. They would steam back into their base at Alexandria harbour, Egypt, with the distinctive skull and crossbones – the Jolly Roger – flying from their vessel's conning tower. While it wasn't exactly standard Royal Naval practice, it was peculiarly fitting when bearing in mind the kind of patrols they were ferrying to and from their targets, which were under orders to 'make hay while the sun shines' by executing 'constant smash-and-grab raids'.

It was June 1942, and the commander of the *Triton* – a ship named after the mythical son of Poseidon and Amphitrite, the ancient Greek god and goddess of the sea – was keen to get his present mission under way, and to run the skull and crossbones up his submarine's stubby 'mast'. The *Triton* was actually a Greek vessel, the rump of that nation's war-fleet having escaped Greece upon the April 1941 invasion by the forces of Nazi Germany. The Greek flotilla that had steamed for Alexandria had included a First World War armoured cruiser, the *Georgios Averof*, the flagship of the fleet, together with half a dozen destroyers and various smaller surface ships, plus five submarines, one of which was the *Triton*.

The *Triton*'s captain, Lieutenant Commander E. Condoyannis, knew the shores of the target area intimately. A Greek national, his vessel executed regular patrols off the island of Crete, which the German military had seized in a series of airborne attacks and monumental battles, in May 1941. It was his personal knowledge of the Cretan seas that had landed Condoyannis the present mission – to drop a party of SAS raiders on a remote stretch of the island's coastline. Once ashore, they were to lay waste to one of the main aerodromes, which served as a key base for Luftwaffe operations across the Eastern Mediterranean.

The present mission was in part at the behest of Churchill. Across the North African desert and the Mediterranean, a series of daring raids were in the offing, all of which had the sole aim of helping to ensure that the relief convoys sailing from Alexandria would make it through. For months now Britain's island fortress of Malta, which lies off the toe of Italy, had been under a brutal siege, and supplies were running desperately low. If Malta fell, Churchill feared the Mediterranean would be lost, with catastrophic consequences. It would be a 'disaster of the first magnitude', he warned, stressing the 'vital importance of the safe arrival of our convoys at Malta'. Conversely, if Malta did manage to weather the siege, General Rommel feared a similar calamity on the Axis side – that they would end up losing the war in North Africa.

For months, German and Italian warplanes had hounded both the island itself, and those vessels that attempted to run the gauntlet, laden with supplies. So it was that the decision had been taken to try to destroy as many of those aircraft *on the ground*, in a series of daring raids. If they could be blown to pieces at their airstrips, the Malta convoys might forge a passage through. Hence the SAS being charged to head west across the vast wastes of the Sahara, in order to attack a string of Axis aerodromes. But they were also to slip anchor and journey north across some 600 kilometres of the Mediterranean, to strike at Crete.

In support of the coming Malta convoys, codenamed Operation Vigorous, the SAS were to target seven enemy airbases strung along the coastal region of the desert, but also one situated at the Cretan coastal town of Heraklion. After a string of successful SAS operations, this series of closely coordinated raids was arguably their most ambitious undertaking to date. A high-level propaganda war concerning such raiding activities had broken out between the British and German governments. Berlin was issuing false communiqués about individual missions, packed with misleading information, and unfortunately these were being picked up by the British press, with damaging consequences for the war effort.

Eventually, Britain's Ministry of Information intervened, countering with a pithy riposte: 'The enemy is betraying anxiety about our intentions with regard to the coast of the occupied territory and hopes by making exaggerated claims to elicit information . . .' In other words, the enemy were on a fishing expedition, as they tried to flush out intelligence regarding just how the raiders functioned and how to tackle the threat. On one level, their 'anxiety' proved that Churchill's 'butcher and bolt' policy was hitting home, striking at the heart of the enemy's comfort and their certitude. If nowhere was safe along the length and breadth of enemy-occupied territories, then *no one* was safe, regardless of their rank or status, and that offered a serious blow to the enemy's morale.

With that in mind, two SAS officers gathered in an Alexandria warship's operations room, hell-bent on striking another signal blow to the enemy's spirits. The pair were there to discuss 'Operation Number Ten (D)', as their mission had been code-named, their raid by 'Submarine and motorboat' on Crete. Maps and reports were pinned to the walls and spread across a nearby table, as the two commanders were briefed on the specifics of their mission – 'to attack, by night . . . to destroy as many aircraft as possible . . . and to cause maximum damage to the vital installations of the airfield, to the ammunition and fuel dumps'.

Both men were long-experienced special duty volunteers, but this was to be their first ever mission with the SAS. One was a Frenchman, Major Georges Roger Pierre Bergé, a short, powerful, wild boar of a man, who was known to be quick witted and sharp tongued, and who did not suffer fools. Just five foot six inches in height, and with his deep-set brilliant-green eyes and shock of unruly dark hair, Bergé was excitable and irascible. Recently, he'd arrived at the SAS's Kabrit training camp, along with sixty-five battle-hardened French parachutists of the *1ère Compagnie d'Infanterie de l'Air* – 1st Air Infantry Company. They were on loan to the SAS, hungry for action, and especially keen to match the kind of stunning successes that the desert raiders had scored.

With their country occupied by the forces of Nazi Germany, Bergé and his fellow countrymen had 'quite literally everything to fight for', as they sought to drive the invaders from their lands.

As he made clear, he would accept nothing but the best from his men. 'We have a terrible challenge to live up to,' Bergé warned them, regarding their joining the ranks of the SAS. 'They have already a hundred planes to their name. We will have to work double time to catch up.' Indeed, Bergé urged his recruits to aim for the stars: 'We must not only catch up with, but overtake Stirling's men.'

In truth, by now – early June 1942 – the SAS's tally of wrecked enemy warplanes was well in excess of one hundred. The lion's share had fallen to Mayne and Fraser. Bergé and his men could hardly fail to be impressed. Wounded in the 1940 battle for France, the French commander had already earned a Croix de Guerre, plus a British Military Cross. Making his way to Britain in early 1941, he'd had the honour of being one of the first Frenchmen to be parachuted back into his homeland, on Operation Savanna, a mission masterminded by the Special Operations Executive (SOE). Otherwise known as Churchill's 'Ministry for Ungentlemanly Warfare', the SOE had been founded to execute the kind of black, deniable operations that governments are not supposed to engage in: industrial sabotage, subversion, bribery and fraud, blackmail, smuggling, raising guerrilla armies, money laundering and assassinations.

Operation Savanna had the last of those dark arts in mind.

Bergé and his small team were charged to attack *Kampfgeschwader* 100 (KG 100), the Luftwaffe's specialist Pathfinder squadron, whose job it was to steer the night-time bombing formations onto targets across Britain. They were to ambush the bus that carried the pilots to their airbase and to kill them all. Due to outdated intelligence the mission had failed, but Bergé had remained in France, engaged upon resistance business.

He'd returned to Britain by submarine, and gone on to play a key role in setting up a Special Training Station for the SOE, at which prospective French agents were readied for deployment back into France. Keen to see action, Bergé had answered SAS founder David Stirling's call for volunteers for the SAS. In securing Bergé and his sixty-five Free French paratroopers, Stirling had struck lucky, for all had been through RAF Ringway, near Manchester, the British military's parachutist's school.

They had arrived at the SAS's Kabrit base battle-experienced and jump-ready.

The second figure in that Alexandria warship's ops room was Captain George Patrick John Rushworth Jellicoe, the 2nd Earl Jellicoe, scion of one of the foremost martial families in Britain. His father, Admiral Sir John Jellicoe, had commanded the British fleet during the 1916 Battle of Jutland, the largest naval clash of the First World War. Admiral Jellicoe had died in 1935, being buried in St Paul's Cathedral, with a commemorative bust in Trafalgar Square and a long list of distinguished titles to his name. His son, George, had inherited the mantle, but with his thirst for danger and the 'thick coat of self-deprecation' that he tended to wear, he was also ideal material for the SAS.

By family tradition and expectation, Jellicoe had been destined to join the Royal Navy. However, by his own admission he'd had a habit of wetting the bed at boarding school, and he didn't fancy 'peeing in a hammock with somebody underneath', that being the standard kind of accommodation aboard ship. Studying at Trinity College, Cambridge, he'd made three of his closest friends, but all would be killed in the coming conflict; one, in the 1940 defence of France. With war declared, Jellicoe had gone to Sandhurst for officer training, but hated it, and particularly the 'mindless' square-bashing and drill. Instead, he'd signed up as a junior rank with the Scots Guards, in an effort to get to the war, and thereafter as a volunteer for Special Service.

Deployed to North Africa, Jellicoe had found himself at the port fortress of Tobruk, which was then under siege by the enemy. Executing a night recce on German positions, Jellicoe and his six-man patrol had been overrun during a surprise enemy advance. What had followed was a desperate, eighty-mile escape and evasion across the desert, during which Jellicoe had been shot in the back, but had still made it through to friendly lines. Typically, he'd refused to get his injuries properly treated, returning directly to the fight instead, until the wound had become infected. Sent to see Captain Malcolm Pleydell, a medic attached to his unit, he was promptly dispatched to an Alexandria hospital. (Pleydell would shortly volunteer for the SAS himself, as the unit's first doctor.)

Recuperating after his hospitalisation, Jellicoe had run into David Stirling in a Cairo bar. Shortly thereafter, on 30 April 1942, he was signed up to the SAS. Jellicoe had arrived at their Kabrit base, '23 years old, brown as a nut, with a nose like the Iron Duke's [the Duke of Wellington]' plus an 'extensive capacity for irony'. He'd been allocated a tent as his quarters, being informed that the 'chap' who normally slept there was 'away'. Jellicoe had promptly slung his kit and dropped off to sleep, only to be awakened by the unexpected return of the tent's rightful owner. It was none other than Captain Blair 'Paddy' Mayne, the Irishman whose peerless soldiering and inspired leadership would win him the Distinguished Service Order (DSO) no fewer than four times during the war.

Mayne's welcome was to expel Jellicoe from the tent, no

messing. Jellicoe wasn't about to argue. Mayne had 'already made a great name for himself', as Jellicoe fully appreciated, whereas he was just the newbie. Barely a month after being summarily ejected from the SAS commander's tent, Jellicoe had landed his first mission – the Heraklion raid. Serving as Bergé's deputy, he was chosen in large part due to his fluent French, having spent time living in both France and Germany before the war. With Lieutenant Kostas 'Costis' Petrakis, a Greek soldier and Cretan native serving as their guide, plus three further French SAS making up their number, the only language all would be able to understand was French, which was to be the lingua franca of the mission.

Bergé and Jellicoe studied the charts and maps, along with Lieutenant Commander Condoyannis. Together, they selected a small beach at Karteros, on the northern Cretan coast, as the point at which they would put ashore. From there the coast road snaked west for three or four kilometres, leading directly to the target airfield. The plan of attack was as follows. Condoyannis would navigate the *Triton* to within a few kilometres of the shore, before surfacing so the SAS could launch their inflatable dinghies. Those three boats, heavily laden with explosives, weaponry and supplies, would be towed towards the beach, getting 'as close as possible', after which the raiders would be cut loose and paddle to shore. From there, they would trek into the hills and lie up in a vantage point overlooking the target, awaiting the date to strike, the night of 12/13 June 1942. Meanwhile, Lieutenant Petrakis would dress himself in local Cretan clothes and execute a reconnaissance of the airfield on foot, checking that the location of the guard posts, sentries and other key defences were as Bergé and Jellicoe had been told.

With the plan of attack sorted, there remained two other matters to attend to. While Jellicoe was to pay a fleeting visit to RAF headquarters, in Cairo, Bergé hurried back to Kabrit to select his team. He had exactly the men in mind for a mission such as this. In Cairo, Jellicoe's aim was to secure an agreement from the RAF not to carry out any bombing raids on Heraklion during the night of the attack. The last thing any of them wanted was to get blown up by their own side. That was the deal that was struck, but their window of attack would be more no more than twenty-four hours, Jellicoe was warned. Once their time was up, the RAF would resume bombing operations with a vengeance.

At Kabrit, Bergé paraded his men. Word had done the rounds that their inaugural mission, and the first ever seaborne raid by the SAS, was in the offing. Figures had been lobbying their commander to be selected. One, Corporal Jack Sibard, had gone to see Bergé privately, to voice his disquiet. A long-standing member of Bergé's unit, Sibard was '*inquiet et déçu*' – anxious and upset – for he felt certain he wouldn't be picked. Bergé immediately silenced any such protestations. Sibard would be going, and theirs would be '*la plus dangereuse*' – *the most dangerous* – mission imaginable. '*Elle sera pénible*' – it will be tough – Bergé had warned him.

Sibard had yet to see any military action, although he had survived being torpedoed by the enemy, in May 1940, when serving in the French merchant navy. Regardless, he thrilled to the prospect of the coming raid. For his part, Bergé confessed that he had just won promotion to acting major, but did not feel that he especially deserved it. 'When we have succeeded in blowing up the planes, then you can address me as "major",' he cautioned.

*

In front of the large tent at Kabrit that doubled as the officer's mess and operations room, Bergé addressed his men. Following weeks of relentless training, all had taken part in a trial raid against RAF Heliopolis, an airbase that lay 100 kilometres due east of Kabrit. They'd spent days crossing the desert on foot, after which they'd slipped onto the landing strip and laced the ranks of British warplanes with sticky labels declaring 'BOMB'. That alone had proved they were ready. Bergé had a choice selection of recruits from which to choose, but he could afford to take only three. Sibard was already in, of course, and he had little doubt who else to pick.

'Mouhot, Sibard, Léostic, stay with me,' he barked. The rest were dismissed.

Corporal Jacques Mouhot was about as archetypal an elite paratrooper as one could imagine. Big-boned, square-jawed, dashing-looking, he was the son of a career army officer who had been schooled at Saint-Cyr, the French equivalent to Sandhurst. A lover of sports, he had been working as a ski instructor prior to the war. He had gone on to fight in the defence of France, and when his unit was overrun he was one of the few to escape. In circumstances that 'defied imagination', he had slipped out of France into North Africa, and via Tangier had made it to the British territory of Gibraltar, and from there to London, whereupon he had promptly volunteered for parachute training.

Something of a Casanova – 'a darling of the girls' – Mouhot was a lover of life in all its forms. He adored partying. 'When we're out, we're out!' he would declare. But he was also a fine soldier, one who could be incredibly calm and perceptive at moments of greatest danger. Blessed with a ready wit and a good dose of sangfroid, he also had the stamina and prowess of a natural sportsman. Held in the highest regard by his younger comrades – Mouhot was thirty years of age, making him the 'old man' of the unit – Bergé viewed him as one of his very best. Events on Crete were to prove him a fine judge of character.

At the opposite end of the spectrum there was Léostic, the final member of their raiding party. Pierre Léostic had lied about his age on making it to Britain and volunteering for the Free French parachutists. He was barely sixteen, but had feigned a greater maturity, and had been accepted for jump-training. By the time he'd reached Kabrit, Léostic had just turned eighteen, and 'Pierrot', as everyone called him, promptly became the baby of the unit. Prior to that, Johnny Cooper, one of Stirling's originals, had been known to all as 'The Kid', for he had likewise lied about his age in order to join the British military. But Léostic was decidedly more fresh-faced and youthful, and Bergé had very much taken him under his wing.

Team selected, they made haste to Alexandria, where the Royal Hellenic Navy (RHN) submarine *Triton* awaited. Built in the late 1920s, the ageing vessel was getting decidedly 'long in the tooth' by June 1942. Despite the fact that she was 'pretty ancient', as Jellicoe commented, he had every confidence in her captain, for Commander Condoyannis was 'absolutely first rate'. In utmost secrecy – the enemy had spies everywhere – the raiders were ferried out to the submarine, along with their heaps of gear. Cramped, and never designed to carry such a body of passengers, the *Triton* was going to be crowded. Three-way hot-bunking was the order of the day, as each man tried to snatch an eight-hour rest period, one after the other.

Jellicoe and Bergé gathered with the submarine's commander, as he opened his final instructions. They were stamped 'TOP

SECRET. This order must be burned after its execution. It must not be allowed to fall into the hands of the enemy.' Commander Condoyannis was further warned: 'As it is likely you will encounter several enemy patrols in the landing area, both from the air and from the surface, as well as surveillance off the coast by searchlights at night, it will be necessary to exercise great care during the entire operation.' His orders concluded that RHN *Triton*'s part in the coming mission would be viewed as 'accomplished as soon as the patrol leave the submarine'.

Interestingly, the orders were copied to the 'Chief of The Intelligence Service' – more formally, the British Secret Intelligence Service (SIS), or MI6 – for the collection of the raiders at mission's end was to be partly their responsibility. The SIS already had their people positioned on Crete, agents who were feeding back priceless intelligence on the enemy. It would be up to one of those individuals to ensure that Bergé, Jellicoe and their team were plucked off the coast to safety, once Heraklion's airbase had been consigned to the flames. A passphrase had been set to use with the SIS agents: Bergé, Jellicoe et al. were to introduce themselves with the phrase, 'I am Captain Madolis.'

After nightfall on 7 June the *Triton* set sail. Bergé, Jellicoe and their team were ecstatic. Finally, they were embarked upon a mission to strike hard and deep against the hated enemy.

'Can you believe it?' one exclaimed. 'In a submarine!'

Catching the spirt, another joked: 'Why bother parachuting into battle, when you can just join the Navy!'

Shortly after lunch on the tenth, the *Triton* nosed cautiously towards what Commander Condoyannis reckoned was the intended point to prepare the dinghies. The *Triton*'s captain upped periscope to study the shoreline. It showed as a long, low, dark mass obscured every now and again by the waves that lapped over the periscope's upper end. Condoyannis ordered the vessel to dive to about a dozen metres, where it would hold its position until H-hour – nightfall. Only under the cover of darkness could they risk launching the boats.

But suddenly the calm of the *Triton*'s bridge was cut by a frisson of alarm. One of the sonar operators glanced up from his set. He'd detected the noise of a squadron of ships bearing down on their position. Moments later the klaxon blared and the watertight hatches slammed shut, as the *Triton* began to dive. Bergé and his party were ensconced in the middle of the vessel, and of course they had little idea what was happening. They strained their ears for the slightest tell-tale sound, as the submarine dipped her bows and sank like a stone.

Down, down they went, as the depth gauges showed twenty metres, then thirty, then broke through the forty-metre mark. At forty-two metres the descent slowed and the submarine levelled off, but the pressure on the SAS party's eardrums was horrendous, as was the strain on their nerves. All around them not a soul breathed a word, or so much as moved a muscle, as they tried to remain perfectly still. Then, through the eerie silence that permeated the hull, the faint throb of a ship's screws could be heard.

The *Triton* was almost motionless, as the vessel's giant batteries powered her instruments and her engines, and she drifted in a current that swept along the seabed. Bergé, Jellicoe and their men knew now the horrible feeling of being submerged and hunted. One by one a flotilla of ships thundered overhead, but other than the beat of their screws, silence reigned. For Mouhot, the keen sportsman and ski-instructor, being confined in this tin coffin was torture; 'unbreathable' was how he described it. But thankfully, there was no crump of explosions as depth charges were released, nor the shattering impact as they detonated in the water to either side of the decades-old submarine.

Eventually, the order was given to ascend and to 'up-periscope' once more. A quick scan proved the waters to be clear of enemy shipping. The sea was calm, the night black as pitch. Perfect conditions for making the drop. The coastline was clearly visible, standing out like a thick dark band against the sky. As the *Triton* surfaced, all got busy preparing the dinghies for release. Then, a faint light was spotted on the shoreline. It glowed intermittently: light, dark, light, dark and so on. As those on the submarine studied it, the pinprick moved back and forth along the shore, quartering a section of beach some 200 metres from end to end. Over and over again the same movement was executed, until all were certain – the light was a cigarette being enjoyed by a sentry.

Mindful of his orders, Commander Condoyannis decided to cast the dinghies off at this point, and to abandon any effort at towing them closer to shore, for under the eyes of the enemy sentry that would be sure to invite disaster. Hurriedly, Bergé, Jellicoe and their crew threw their gear aboard. Into one dinghy they loaded the heaviest kit: weapons, ammo, grenades, Lewes bombs, rucksacks. That vessel would be towed behind the others, into which the raiders now divided themselves – Jellicoe, Mouhot and Petrakis in the one, Bergé, Sibard and Léostic in the other. Positions set, they cast off from the trusty *Triton* and began to paddle, blunt prows turning towards land.

It was close to midnight, and Condoyannis cried out a faint farewell across the water: 'Goodbye! *Bonne chance!* Good luck. *Kali Tychi!*' That last – good luck in Greek.

69

Unbeknown to Bergé and his men, they were going to need it.

Something didn't look quite right. As the six men dug deep with their paddles, they realised the shore appeared far too distant. More like half a dozen kilometres or more, as opposed to the one or two they had been expecting. In truth, while submerged and hiding from the enemy the *Triton* had drifted east a good thirty kilometres. Rather than having a relatively easy paddle to land, something of an epic lay before the raiders, and there was no way in the world that they were going to reach Karteros, their intended point of landfall. In fact, no one had a clue where exactly they might come ashore.

Someone spied a long, low humpy silhouette rising from the waves, due west of where they were positioned. It could only be the island of Dia, which they knew lay ten kilometres due north of Heraklion. There also appeared to be a strong current running, pushing them further east all the while. The only point to aim for on the shoreline was the sentry's cigarette. Nothing else provided a clearly visible marker. With that as their target, they paddled with all the strength and gusto they could muster, and slowly but surely the pinprick of light seemed to grow a little most distinct.

Then a dinghy sprang a leak. Jellicoe, always impeccably attired when on missions, swept off his peaked officer's cap and began to bale, gold trim flashing in the faint light. For an hour the epic battle continued – sea-current against muscle-power, frustrated by a leaky dinghy. Finally, a sheer cliff reared out of the darkness. They had been swept east of the sentry's stretch of watch, coming in to land at a narrow creek, with a rocky path terminating at the base of the cliffs. Leaping ashore, the six men went about unloading the dinghies as quickly and silently as possible.

Without realising it, they had arrived at the mouth of the San

Barbara river, which lay some 35 kilometres east of their target. Mouhot and Jellicoe stripped naked now. Loading the empty dinghies with rocks, they waded into the sea and swam back out the way they had come. Once they'd reached a good depth, they used their commando knives to slash the boats and sank them beneath the waves. That way, all traces of their presence should be obliterated, come dawn.

With Jellicoe and Mouhot back ashore and dressed once more, the six took stock. The only hint of life was the 'light splash of the surf'. That was the upside – there was no sign that their landing had been discovered. The downside was they had little idea exactly where they were or the route they should take. There was nothing that they could do about it now. Instead, they shouldered their loads, turned towards the cliffs and began to climb. It was just before three o'clock in the morning of 11 June as they set forth into the hills, scrambling up a slope of rocky scree.

They had just forty-eight hours to make it to Heraklion, and the window to attack.

The party were painfully overloaded for a trek by foot over the distance that now lay before them. Each carried a 30-kilogram pack, stuffed full of rations (dates, raisins, chocolate, bully beef, biscuits), water, detonators (packed into a separate oilskin bag, to keep them dry), plus sixteen Lewes bombs per man. There were also grenades, compass, maps and dagger, plus the weight of their personal weapon that each man carried – a Colt 1911 '45' pistol, plus a Beretta Model 38 sub-machine gun (Italian military issue). Sibard had packed a knuckle-duster-knife combo, a particularly fearsome-looking weapon, while Bergé had sawn off the wooden stock of his Beretta, in an effort to lighten his load.

They also had medical kits, courtesy of Malcolm Pleydell,

the doctor who had first treated Jellicoe for his gunshot wound, prior to their both joining the SAS. Jellicoe it was who'd asked for those emergency kits, which were designed to be 'as small as possible', each wrapped in a waterproof covering. They included salt, morphia tablets (in case of injuries), dressings, Vaseline, plus a small saw. But as both Bergé and Jellicoe were starting to appreciate, theirs was far too burdensome a load for this kind of a journey, and especially over such punishing terrain.

Lieutenant Petrakis, their local man, had a sense where they might be. As per the plan, he'd donned civilian clothes just as soon as they had reached the shore. Figuring they'd landed somewhere to the east of the coastal town Malia, he led the way. The path before them would be 'extremely difficult', he warned, as it wound through high rocky bluffs, and over mountains thick with dry, thorny scrub. They pushed on through the night hours, the weight of their packs seeming to grow heavier and heavier still. Finally, they paused by a deep ravine, deciding to dump all but the most essential kit, though Jellicoe, stubbornly, refused to jettison much of his own.

Marching on in silence, the 'exhaustion of everyone' became ever more evident. At dawn, Bergé called a halt. There was a ruined sheep-shelter near by – a decent-enough place to lie up in shade. That day, some locals found the SAS party. The Cretans never seemed to miss a thing, and as the German forces were starting to realise, they were determined to resist the occupation and drive out the invaders. Bergé and Jellicoe had been briefed that the locals were likely to be friendly, and to rely upon the help of the Cretan resistance. That day, the party that would become known to all on Crete as the famous 'sabotage organisation of Captain Jellicoe', were offered water and a little food.

With nightfall, they set out again heading west, 'stumbling, cursing under their breaths', but still making steady progress. At one point, the darkness and the silence were torn asunder, as flashes rent the horizon, followed by the rolling, rumbling thunder of distant explosions. Unwittingly, the RAF had just revealed to the raiders the location of their target. 'Their' aerodrome was taking a pasting from British warplanes. As the exhausted watchers soaked up the spectacle, their spirits were buoyed. Heraklion airbase didn't look so impossibly distant any more, the Frenchmen declared happily.

'Bravo the British!'

At first light on 12 June the six men found shelter in a deep cave. Bergé and Jellicoe reckoned they were within striking distance of their target. They would rest here for the day, and make their final approach come nightfall. That way, they'd hit their window of opportunity – the twenty-four hours during which the RAF had agreed to pause their attacks. First watch was set, while the others slept the sleep of the dead. Jellicoe and Bergé had decided to take it. They had more reasons than simple vigilance to do so. Jellicoe had been popping 'bennies' – Benzedrine, a powerful amphetamine-like stimulant – to sustain him on the long march. He'd likewise convinced Bergé of the benefits of using the pills, which were part of the standard raiding kit now carried by the SAS.

The two commanders sat at the cave entrance, shivering in the cold light of dawn, their minds buzzing. They killed time by cleaning their weapons and going over the plan of attack. They figured they were some ten to fifteen kilometres short of the airbase. They should be able to dump most of their kit in the cave, so as to travel light and fast. They decided to leave Petrakis as a

73

guard and lookout, and to discard all excess weight. Other than their pistols and daggers, they'd carry Lewes bombs, water, and little else.

Bergé decided to go one step further. They'd deployed wearing mechanic's-style overalls, covering their military uniforms. That was standard SAS attire, adopted during parachute training, for the coverall served the purpose of reducing the risk of any kit snagging during a jump. Bergé reasoned that now was the time to dump their distinctive headgear, as well. They would go in bareheaded, for in their mechanic-style overalls he reckoned they could very possibly pass as a German maintenance crew. To the Frenchman's amusement, Jellicoe baulked. Ditching his cap – that was something that no officer of His Majesty's Armed Forces would ever do lightly. In any case, it had already proved invaluable bailing out the leaking dinghy.

At dusk the five raiders set out, moving light and fast. Just prior to midnight they crested a ridge cloaked with olive trees and vineyards, the airbase itself emerging from the darkened plain that stretched before them. They stopped dead, staring at 'their' airfield. Not a man among them spoke. This moment had been so longed-for, so hotly anticipated, and despite all the odds finally they had made it. Heraklion airbase hugged the coast, stretching for three kilometres in an east–west direction. From their studies of aerial reconnaissance photos, Bergé and Jellicoe planned to strike from the south, for north lay only the sea, and the approach route from the east was bisected by a busy road. With little time to waste they needed to press on.

They set off at once, moving through the darkness. There was barely a sliver of moon, it being a waning crescent. Perfect conditions to attack. But the terrain underfoot proved far from ideal.

As they dropped from the high ground, the way was thick with loose scree. No matter how carefully they tried to move, every now and again a rock broke free, 'tumbling noisily' downslope, and skittering towards the airbase perimeter. They pressed on, the target growing closer with every step, the muted sound of engines and distant voices reaching them on the still air. But suddenly a slice of darker ground yawned before them. The five raiders stopped abruptly, as a ravine opened 'vertical, at their feet'. Some twenty yards across, the chasm plummeted to hidden depths, while on the far side the wire fence of the airbase could be seen rising before them.

They were astonished to have blundered into this hidden abyss. There hadn't been the slightest suggestion that such a feature might exist on any of their maps, or the aerial photos. In truth, it ran all along the southern perimeter of the airbase, effectively barring any route of entry. Burning with frustration, they quartered its southern edge, but inevitably first one rock and then another tumbled off and ricocheted into the depths below. On the far side of the ravine, a distinctive noise cut the night: the sharp sound of a bullet being ratcheted into the breech of a rifle. There was a sentry positioned beside the wire, unseen, but no more than a few dozen yards away.

The raiders froze. Long moments passed during which no one dared risk the slightest move. As the seconds ticked by, the feared shots did not ring out, and finally Bergé was able to signal that his men should pull back. As one, they melted silently into the darkness. Once he felt they'd put enough distance between themselves and the ravine, Bergé called a halt. Reluctantly, he made the only decision he felt he could sensibly reach under the present circumstances.

'We do not attack tonight,' he declared. 'To do so would be foolish. This ravine, which we were not warned about, blocks our way . . .'

If they tried to press on, even if they could scale the chasm, the noise of doing so would alert the enemy. They would risk 'raising the alarm, before we have even begun to carry out our mission. Besides,' Bergé added, 'it's too late. It's soon going to be daybreak.' It was well past 3.00 a.m. by now, and first light was not so far away.

They'd pull back into the high ground, Bergé announced, and wait until the following evening to strike. He'd need Sibard and Mouhot to trek back to the cave to warn Petrakis, but they would have to make it back again by sunset, to join the attack, he cautioned. Plan sorted, they proceeded to search out a decent hiding place, finding a narrow cleft in the hills. It offered good cover and should provide a point from which to spy out the air-base. Sibard and Mouhot departed, while the remainder settled down to rest and wait.

With dawn came the realisation of just what a fine vantage point they had chosen. The entire length of Heraklion aerodrome stretched before them. With their binoculars, they carried out a careful study of the target. A road snaked through the centre of the airbase, bisecting it from the south-west corner to the north-east. That was the main route running from Heraklion to Malia town. Bergé and Jellicoe were amazed to see how busy that highway was, and also just what kind of traffic made use of it. It was far from being military transport only. Instead, there were local farmers heading off to their vineyards on foot, horse-drawn carts loaded with fruit and vegetables, and even the odd priest sat astride his donkey, legs flapping to the 'slow rhythm of the steed'.

The hidden watchers couldn't help but find it amusing. What kind of commander allowed such a mishmash of locals to pass through his base apparently unheeded? They counted as many as sixty-six German warplanes parked to either side of the twin runways, mostly the twin-engine Junkers Ju 88s, a multi-purpose airframe known as the *Mädchen für alles* – the maid of all work. The Ju 88 could function as a bomber, a night-fighter and a reconnaissance aircraft, and serving as a torpedo-bomber it was a menace to Allied shipping. They were the prize. But there were also the larger forms of triple-engine Ju 52 transport aircraft, plus the slim, sleek silhouettes of Messerschmitt Bf 109s, then one of the most advanced fighter planes in the war.

On spying the rich selection of targets – these 'objects of the SAS's lust' – Bergé and Jellicoe felt their paces quicken. They swallowed more Benzedrine to stave off fatigue, as flights took off and landed before their eyes. They also studied the defences. 'Hard-walled' blast barriers lined much of the road. Ranks of long, narrow buildings lay behind those – they could only be barrack blocks. Here and there, tented camps and wooden huts – more accommodation for the enemy troops – dotted the base. To the far north lay a massive structure – 'a veritable prison' – more barracks and military quarters, they reckoned.

As the day wore on, the watchers logged how the airbase scheduled the ongoing sorties. At the eastern end of the runways, those warplanes returning from missions were mustered, arranged in tightly packed ranks and shielded by 'low-walled blast shelters'. There they were bombed-up and refuelled for forthcoming missions. They counted twenty or more aircraft crammed together chiefly relying upon those blast walls to shield them from attacks from the air. Well, indeed they might – but not from a Lewes bomb slipped onto a wing right beside the fuel tank and primed to blow. There were more warplanes scattered around the opposite side of the runways, but they were widely spaced out. It was clear to both Bergé and Jellicoe where they would find the richest selection of targets.

To the northern end of the twin asphalt runways lay a group of structures that had to house the airbase's truck depots, and the bomb and fuel dumps. They were duly noted. That the greatest concentration of warplanes lay slap-bang in the middle of a tented-encampment – troop quarters – didn't escape remark. The raiders would be forced to operate right under the enemy's noses. More to the point, the only feasible route into their target lay in the south-western corner and on the far side of the airbase. They'd have to cross the entire length of the base to be able to strike at the greatest number of warplanes, but there was no other way.

As Bergé observed to Jellicoe, excitedly, 'Qui ose gagne' – who dares wins.

Just prior to sundown Sibard and Mouhot returned. Typically, they'd had a series of wild adventures during their journey to and from the cave, including being treated to a feast of lamb stew courtesy of a Cretan shepherd, and being buzzed by a low-flying Fieseler Storch spotter aircraft. Caught in the open, they'd opted to hide in plain sight, making as if they were farmers working the vineyards, even pausing to wave and offer 'friendly gestures that the pilot could clearly see'. They returned to the hideout full of their stories and local knowledge, including where to find the nearest source of water.

The rest of the raiders were parched. Sibard offered to lead them to the nearest well. They reached it, only to discover that the water lay some ten yards below ground, in the depths of the shadows. As they peered in, wondering just how to reach it, an apparition appeared, 'as beautiful as any fairy tale princess'. A young Cretan woman had come to draw water, and she promptly offered them the use of the bucket and rope that she carried. By nightfall, all five of the raiders were comparatively well rested, and had managed to drink and eat their fill. After that day's spying on the airbase, all felt sure of their route in and the means of the coming attack. Confidence and morale were at an all-time high.

At dusk, a flight of Ju 88s touched down. Once the aircraft had taxied to a standstill, the watchers could see the pilots gathering together, talking and gesticulating excitedly – they were clearly swopping tales of what appeared to be a successful mission. If anything, seeing that only quickened the raiders' hunger to hit home.

As darkness descended, so the gathering night was torn apart by the scream of an alarm. The rhythmic wail of an air-raid siren echoed across the airbase. A dull rumble in the distance soon became a roar, as a flight of RAF bombers came speeding in to attack. From their vantage point the SAS had a ringside seat. Soon, the muffled crumps of explosions and the staccato blasts of anti-aircraft fire beat out their tattoo. Bergé, Jellicoe and the others could see each and every bomb-strike, and amazingly not one seemed to fall on its supposed target. Neither of the runways, let alone any of the bomb dumps or the warplanes, had been hit. It was a sobering sight. For all of its dramatic sound and pyrotechnics, that air-attack had failed to score any serious hits.

At 10.00 p.m. Bergé gave the order to set out. Less than an hour later they'd reached their planned entry point onto the airbase.

They took cover in a ditch and watched. A troop of German soldiers were returning from Heraklion, most probably after a night out on the town. Moving on foot, their ranks kept stomping past, their boots hammering into the dusty road no more than a few metres away from the hidden watchers. Finally, the last of the long column of soldiers thumped by.

Swiftly and silently, moving on the soft rubber soles of their specialist boots, the shadowy figures slipped across the road and made a dash for the wire. There, Léostic – the eighteen-year-old raider – knelt with wire cutters and began to fashion an opening. One by one the five slipped through. Creeping ahead, they came to a second fence, for the airbase boasted a double wire perimeter. Again Léostic bent to his task, as he went about snipping the first strands. But moments later he froze, as did the rest of the patrol. Voices – German voices – rang out in the darkness, accompanied by the scrunch of boots on gravel. An enemy patrol was approaching, moving along the wire.

Caught in the open, the raiders had nowhere to run or to hide. The first of the enemy soldiers seemed to pass without noticing them, but then one of the figures paused. A hand reached forwards, groping through the strands of barbed wire, before a torch beam lanced the gloom. It played over the forms of five figures clad in overalls lying prone on the ground. As chance would have it, Bergé and Mouhot were the nearest to the German sentry, and that would be the salvation of the entire patrol.

'*Was machst du da?*' – 'What are you doing there?' – the German soldier demanded, suspiciously.

Acting with his signature coolness when facing danger, Mouhot grabbed his haversack more tightly, clutched it to him as if it were a duvet and he were deep in his dreams, and issued a loud, inebriated-sounding belch. He followed it with a burst of incomprehensible, 'drunken' gibberish, topping the entire performance off with a stream of deafening hiccups.

The German barked out a laugh. *'Du bist gut besoffen, mein Lieber!'* – 'You are well drunk, my friend!' He gave Mouhot a 'friendly tap with his boot', before turning to leave.

Still laughing to himself, the sentry hurried after his comrades, calling to them about what he'd just seen – a bunch of maintenance guys blind drunk and collapsed beside the wire. 'What are they like!' he rounded off his tale, his fellow soldiers joining in the merriment.

With that, the sound of the enemy's chat and their footfalls faded away. No doubt about it, Mouhot's nerve and his coolness had saved the day. That, combined with Bergé's decision to dispense with their distinctive head gear. Jellicoe and Mouhot had hit it off from the very start, and from his place at the rear of the party – Jellicoe had volunteered to be the tail-end-Charlie, guarding their backs – he whispered a few words of congratulations. Mouhot's drunken act had been utterly 'inspired', Jellicoe declared, and had demonstrated extraordinary powers of 'quick-thinking'. Mouhot had nicknamed Jellicoe 'Curly' or 'The Belted Earl', the former for his wild and unruly dark hair, the latter due to his high-born roots. Jellicoe's praise was a boon to the Frenchman, spurring him on.

But the raiders had barely had time to congratulate themselves, or to recover from the scare, before the next crisis was upon them. For the second time that evening, the familiar wail of air-raid sirens cut through the night. A second flight of RAF warplanes was in-bound. Urging Léostic to hurry, the five men wormed their way through the narrow entryway that he had sliced through the wire, and they dashed ahead. Seeking cover, they crawled in beside a neat stack of 'long metal cylinders', before realising what they actually were: it was a stockpile of 500-pound bombs.

With the flight of twin-engine RAF Blenheims swooping low to 'hammer the base again', the raiders just had to hope that this time around, the 'airmen won't hit the bullseye'. Even as they hugged the ground and prayed for the pilots to miss the bomb dump, Sibard let out a strangled cry of alarm.

'My commander, I have lost my belt!' Somehow, Sibard's webbing, holding his pistol and grenades, must have been snagged on the wire.

'Go get it and be quick!' Bergé ordered.

Dashing through the darkness, Sibard was blessed with extraordinary luck, unerringly finding his way to the very spot where they'd crawled through the wire. Grabbing his belt and its weapons, he raced back to join his fellows, being struck by how perfectly their forms blended in with the shadows of the bomb dump. No sooner had he thrown himself into that uncertain cover, than a group of half a dozen enemy soldiers came hurrying out of the night. Bent low, they made a beeline straight to the wire, to the very spot where Mouhot had executed his inebriated mechanic's act.

Having discovered the group of 'drunkards', once they had returned to their quarters the patrolmen had telephoned the airbase's engineering department to offer a friendly warning. It wouldn't look good if a squad of their technicians was discovered flat out beside the wire come daybreak, comatose with drink. But the response they'd received was confounding. According to Heraklion's Chief Aircraft Engineer, they didn't have a technical team out and about anywhere within that sector of the airfield.

The German troops had set out to investigate, hence their reappearance right now. As they executed a hurried search of the wire, the first of the Blenheim's 500-pound bombs screamed through the night, the flash of the explosions pulsing over the airbase. Realising that the party of 'drunks' had disappeared, the German soldiers did the only sensible thing – they made a dash for the air-raid shelters. For a second or so, the SAS raiders offered their thanks to those RAF pilots braving the darkened skies above them: 'This bombing – what luck!'

Taking advantage of the confusion and chaos caused by the air-raid, the five figures broke cover and flitted ahead. It made sense to risk the RAF's bombs, for the base was largely deserted as the enemy took cover. They reached the eastern side of the airbase without being spotted, or blown up by their own side, at which point the raiders slipped into their prearranged routines. As Mouhot and Sibard stole towards the nearest Ju 88s, Bergé and Léostic gave cover, while Jellicoe slipped away on a raiding mission all of his own. Their Lewes bombs had been fitted with ninety-minute delay fuses, to give the raiders time to set their charges and make good their getaway. But right away, Mouhot and Sibard realised they had a problem. The twin-engine Ju 88s sat a dozen feet off the ground at the point where the wings met the fuselage, which was precisely where they needed to plant their charges.

The Lewes bomb was an ingenious mixture, a pound of plastic explosive (PE) mixed with a quarter pound of thermite – a highly inflammable metal powder – topped off with a good dash of diesel oil. The single greatest advantage of the fiendish concoction was its light weight, combined with its destructive power when placed close to an aircraft's fuel supply. The blast caused by the PE punched through the fuel tank, at which point the burning thermite-diesel mixture would ignite its contents, transforming the warplane into a raging inferno. But only if the charge could be placed on the wing right beside the fuel supply.

Mouhot and Sibard's solution right now was based upon brute strength and improvisation. With Sibard acting as the anchor-man, Mouhot clambered onto his shoulders, whereupon Sibard hoisted him up until he was high enough to haul himself onto that first Ju 88's wing. Under the sleek metal skin beneath Mouhot's feet sat a tank containing some 415 litres of aviation fuel (with a little short of 1,700 litres being spread across the warplane's four, inner and outer wing-tanks). Having crushed the timer pencil's glass vial – the fuse was triggered by a process of acid eating through a copper wire – Mouhot placed the charge, wrapped in its hessian bag, snug beside the junction between the wing and the fuselage.

That done, he slipped down again, and he and Sibard darted across to the next target. That too was served with its charge in similar fashion. One after another the two Frenchmen did the lifting act, lacing fifteen warplanes with Lewes bombs, and without so much as a cry of challenge from any of the airbase's defenders. But as they approached target number sixteen, they hit an unwelcome obstruction, practically stumbling over a pair of forms lying beside the warplane. As Mouhot and Sibard warily eyed the recumbent Germans, they realised that they were sound asleep, somehow having napped through the entire air-raid, 'like children, their heads cradled by white sheets'.

For a long moment the two raiders fingered their blades – their sleek, commando fighting knives. But eventually discretion – not to mention, common mercy – got the better of them. They were here to blow to pieces enemy warplanes and to avoid combat wherever possible. Indeed, that was the credo of the SAS. They didn't seek to fight. Instead, they sought to sow destruction, chaos, fear and uncertainty, before melting away into the night . . . '*Sleep in peace . . . dream of your Liebchen*' – sweethearts – the raiders told the pair of German soldiers, before stealing across to the waiting warplane. That, too, was given its gift of a Lewes bomb, after which Mouhot and Sibard placed more of their charges on four further Ju 88s that they'd noticed, lined up beside a hangar.

Jellicoe, meanwhile, had crept north a good five hundred yards, alone and unaided, remarking to Bergé as he had left: 'Commandant, I'm just heading off to see if there is anything else to be done.'

Beyond the twin runways lay what he and Bergé had earlier identified as the airbase's main warehouses, its bomb and fuel dumps, plus the vehicle depot. With his signature '*flegme britannique*' – British phlegm – Jellicoe not only set his charges on a bomb dump and a dozen trucks, but he also decided that a close inspection of the largest hangar was in order. Slipping inside, he found the place to be crammed with aircraft spare parts, plus crates of aero-engines. Moving with 'a calm and dignified step', according to his French comrades, Jellicoe proceeded to lace the hangar with bombs.

But even as the raiders went about their deadly work, so the first of the charges on the planes detonated. As the initial blast rent the night, ripping into that warplane, so the raiders feared the enemy would be alerted to their presence. But not a bit of it. It looked as if the RAF air-raid – now long-gone – was still providing 'cover'. Delayed-action bombs were used by both the RAF and the Luftwaffe, with the intention of frustrating any clearance and reconstruction work across airfields. They spread terror and chaos, for repair crews and bomb-disposal teams were often caught in the blasts. Bergé, Jellicoe and co. could only imagine the enemy had failed to react to that first detonation mistaking it for '*bombes à retardement*' – delayed-action bombs.

As they gathered at a central point, the five SAS men were torn. On the one hand, to tarry any longer would surely be 'unseemly, surely unwise'. On the other, the alert had yet to be sounded. Another Lewes bomb detonated, the crump of the explosion echoing across the still-deserted airbase. Seizing the moment, the raiders dashed about, placing the last of their charges. More trucks, an Me 109, plus one Dornier Do 17 – a *Schnellbomber*; fast-bomber – were all targeted. Last but not least, a Lewes bomb was set aboard a Fieseler Storch spotter plane – maybe the one that had buzzed Sibard and Mouhot earlier – making twenty-three enemy aircraft in total that had been sown with charges.

But as more of the explosives began to detonate, the alarm was finally sounded. It was 2.00 a.m. by now, and to all sides figures began to dash about, as yet more explosions rent the night. Bergé led the charge, taking the main road that bisected the airbase and steering his party due west, towards the exit. They jogged past the main barracks. Scores of enemy troops were hurrying about in confusion, as they tried to work out what on earth could be causing such a devastating string of explosions.

Pressing on, the raiders blundered into an unseen obstruction – a garbage dump, which was piled high with empty tin cans. Someone made a wrong move in the darkness and a heap collapsed, cascading about noisily. The sound was deafening.

Holding his nerve, Bergé called his team together and they pressed on, moving at 'patrol pace', and acting as if they had every right to be there. An enemy soldier dashed out, rifle 'pointed and cocked'. He had been drawn to the racket caused by the tumbling cans.

'*Halt! Halt!*' the German sentry cried.

Barely pausing, Bergé strode towards him, his hand held out in a placatory gesture. He, plus Jellicoe and some of the others, spoke enough German to figure they could bluff it. With Austrians, Czechs, Hungarians and numerous other nationals serving in the German armed forces, they would rely upon their sheer confidence and front to ensure that their accents passed muster. Crying out greetings, and 'calmly, almost paternally' explaining that they were a maintenance crew going about their work, the enemy soldier seemed reassured. Finally, he lowered his weapon and hurried away.

As vehicles zipped to and fro, Bergé and his men pressed onwards, the exit to the airbase growing ever closer. With audacity to the fore, they fell in behind a squad of German troops moving at the double. Marching smartly, as if they were likewise being dispatched to execute their duties during this unprecedented assault on Heraklion airbase, the five SAS men slipped through the gates. Moving in the wake of the enemy soldiers, they finally managed to disappear, peeling off into the darkness. As far as they could tell, not a soul had noticed anything amiss and they were home and dry.

Pushing south into the high ground, the raiders were gripped by an all-consuming sense of exhilaration, as further explosions rang out from behind them. At one point Jellicoe was heard to exclaim, with a wild laugh, how it was all 'a perfectly normal outing', before moving forward to congratulate Mouhot.

'Without your extraordinary instincts, the mission was ruined,' The Belted Earl confided in the Frenchman. 'Bravo, Mouhot! It is thanks to you that it was such a success!'

A ripple of laughter ran down the line of raiders. All were in agreement. Mouhot, the drunken snorer, was the hero of the hour.

They kept climbing, before Bergé called a short halt. Settling into the cover of some vine groves, the raiders surveyed their handiwork, as below them further explosions pulsed across the airbase, and scores of fires raged. At last there came the grand finale, as Jellicoe's charges, planted among the bomb dump, detonated, the entire sky seeming to be set ablaze. A massive series of blasts followed, the sound echoing off the bowl of hills that cradled the airbase.

As he studied the spectacular scene of fiery devastation, Bergé declared: 'You are all deserving of the Croix de Guerre. You too, Lord Jellicoe, will get the French Croix de Guerre!'

Everyone laughed.

But beneath the euphoria there was also a frisson of concern. Eying their handiwork – the carnage that five determined and resourceful raiders had wrought – it was clear what a hornet's nest they had stirred up. They didn't doubt for one moment that they would be hunted remorselessly and pursued with a vengeance. Ahead of them lay a 60-kilometre escape and evasion – as the crow flies – which would involve traversing the island from coast to coast, moving due south towards a rendezvous on that distant shore. There, Lieutenant Commander John Campbell, a British naval captain commanding a converted trawler, was primed to whisk them away from a remote Cretan beach. At Krotos village, a tiny settlement lying a little inland from the sea-cliffs, an SIS agent would be waiting to shepherd them into Campbell's embrace.

Yet the route to get to Krotos was anything but easy. It lay across extraordinarily rugged and punishing terrain. They would have to navigate the jagged spine of mountains that form the backbone of Crete, steering just to the east of Mount Ida, the island's highpoint, which rises to over 8,000 feet. There was also another, wholly unexpected problem that raised its ugly head. Léostic confessed that he was in great pain. Despite his youth, he'd always been seen as being one of the best marchers in the entire French SAS contingent – this 'force of nature', as Bergé described him. Léostic removed his boots to reveal that his feet were horribly blistered and bloody. He could only think it was down to ill-fitting footwear. As he and Mouhot had the same size feet, the latter suggested that they swop boots. It was worth a try.

Footwear exchanged, the five set off, hurrying into the darkness, determined to put as much distance between themselves and the burning airbase come dawn. Léostic was still hobbling, but he reassured all that he was good to continue. Tired legs pushed on, but after a while Jellicoe was gripped by an unsettling feeling. Each time he glanced at the sky, he grew increasingly convinced that Polaris, the North Star, was absolutely not where it should be. By rights, they were pressing south-east, to link up with Petrakis at their cave hideout, which would put Polaris low on the horizon to their left. But Jellicoe reckoned it lay bang in their path, which meant that Bergé was steering them due north.

Eventually, the route was corrected and five exhausted figures stumbled into the cave, to be met by a euphoric Petrakis. While the Greek lieutenant couldn't see the airbase itself, he'd heard the cacophony of explosions and had known that they had hit home.

Petrakis had befriended a local miller, and as all were ravenous they headed to his place to see if he might rustle up a meal. Shortly, they were sitting down to a feast of bacon and potato stew, washed down by a strong local wine. Nearby there was a stream. Bergé ordered all to wash and shave, before trying to get some rest. For what lay ahead it was essential to try to remain as presentable as any self-respecting Cretan villager would, so as not to stand out.

That night, they set off on foot, moving due south towards the mountains that reared before them – black, jagged silhouettes against a dark sky. In the distance a light cut high across the horizon, before hanging in the heavens and drifting slowly to earth, like a bright candle flame. It was a flare round. No doubt the enemy search parties were out in force. They switched direction and pressed on. They hit a long, punishing scree slope, stumbling and falling over the boulders in the darkness. All that night they marched, but the way proved energy-sapping and 'demoralising'. The one major positive was that Léostic was keeping up. But not a man among them doubted that all around, hunters were seeking their prey.

At first light on 15 June 1942 – some twenty-four hours after the raid on the airbase – Bergé called a break. As the sky lightened, an ominous feeling settled upon the party. By the looks of their surroundings, they'd only managed to put a bare few kilometres between themselves and Heraklion. Moving through 'this mountainous maze . . . these rocky labyrinths' in the darkness, and with the repeated changes of course, it looked as if they had lost their way. It was hugely disheartening, but at least their present location – a steep-sided dead end of a valley, thick with thorny scrub – looked far off the beaten track. They'd lie up there during the hours of daylight, Bergé decided, for there was little risk of discovery.

Petrakis volunteered to execute a walkabout in search of sustenance or guides. Dressed as a Cretan villager, he should pass muster. A few hours later he returned, together with a local couple. Both spoke good French, and the man explained that he was a reserve officer in the Greek Army. They brought food – courgettes, snails, sheep's cheese – plus fresh water. But despite their generosity and the risks they seemed willing to run, they looked deeply troubled.

Petrakis explained why. The Germans, enraged by the daring attack on Heraklion aerodrome, had seized dozens of locals as 'hostages'. Already, twenty had been executed. Their crime – not 'handing over' the saboteurs. The Greek reserve officer confirmed all of this with a sombre nod. German troops were everywhere, he added, combing every inch of terrain. Large financial rewards were being offered for any local who could lead them to the saboteurs. Dark punishments and further mass executions were being threatened, if those who had attacked the airbase weren't caught.

A pair of young guides were fetched from the nearby village. For the remainder of the daylight hours the party lay low and tried to husband their strength. At dusk, the raiders and their guides ate a meal, before preparing to set out. But at the last minute the two young men seemed to baulk. They knew the best route to reach the rendezvous with the waiting trawler. What had spooked them was the fear of being caught by the enemy. The Germans wouldn't just wreak vengeance on the two of them. Their entire families – maybe even their entire village – would be made to suffer.

Bergé was furious. Those two young men knew the planned

line of march of the raiders, not to mention their intended means of escape. He could not in all conscience set them free. Instead, he pulled out his pistol and the two young men fell to their knees. It 'was a terrible moment', even to consider killing 'in cold blood two men with whom they had just shared a meal'. Petrakis brokered a kind of a compromise. While one of the men was held, the other would be allowed to return to their village, to warn their families. That way, they could at least take precautions.

Some twenty minutes later the young man was back. Reminding each other that the Cretans were 'a people of honour, who could be trusted', the party of eight set off into the mountains. But no one was pretending that the mood was anything other than grim and dark. The very knowledge that their actions had resulted in twenty innocent deaths, and would very likely cause more, was a terrible burden to have to shoulder.

Shortly, they came across more evidence of these savage reprisals. Posters had been pasted across the length and breadth of the island, announcing that if any Cretans didn't betray the presence of the raiders, or offered them succour, all the males of that village would be 'put to the sword'. A group of 'hostages' were seized from the historic town of Chania, which lay 140 kilometres due west of Heraklion. There was little sense in targeting such a location, but the list of those executed was long. It included prominent local figures, including a seventy-year-old priest, several Jewish residents and a former Governor General of the island.

The news was shattering. Jellicoe was particularly shaken, pointing out that: 'The Germans must have known this [the raid] had not been done by Cretans.'

For three long days the fugitives pushed south, moving through a dry, rocky, precipitous moonscape, and resting up as much as possible during the hours of daylight. In this way they crossed the island's high ground, descending into the Messara Plain, at the southern tip of which lay Krotos village, and the drop beyond it 1,500 feet to the sea. A little short of there the party called a halt. Petrakis reported that his own village, Appessokari, lay only a short distance away. What better opportunity was there to beg food and water, he argued, for they were plagued by hunger and by thirst.

It was Friday 19 June, and Bergé took a long, searching look at the location where he had called a halt. Formed of an elongated basin-like depression, the depths of which were thick with dense brush, he figured this was a perfect place to set camp. While Petrakis went about scavenging food and drink, the raiders could rest in good cover and shade, well hidden from prying eyes. They were around half a dozen kilometres short of Krotos village, so well within reach. Rescue, and their route to safety across the seas, was well within their grasp.

Shortly, Petrakis returned bearing manna from heaven, or so it seemed: some chickens, bread, olives and cheese. Finding a perfect hideout – a low wall, surrounded by stout trees, and with a shallow ditch running off to one side, as a possible exit route in case of emergencies – they settled down to their feast. A watch was set. While one party prepared the chickens to roast over an open fire on a makeshift spit, another gathered firewood, and Jellicoe and Sibard went about crushing the olives. Using a pair of flat stones, they squeezed out the olive oil, to sprinkle over the birds as they cooked.

A young villager had accompanied Petrakis, and he offered to head back to Appessokari to fetch some wine. He returned bearing two flagons full of a rich, heady brew. It threw off a delicious fragrance of sun, of good times and the promise of escape and freedom. As they settled down to eat and drink, their spirits rose. But it was then that another fresh arrival pitched up. Once again it was an Appessokari resident, only this man was unusually portly for a Cretan villager. He introduced himself as the local innkeeper and a friend of Petrakis, and he offered to fetch them some more wine.

Bergé was instantly suspicious. There was something about the look of this newcomer – his 'faux-brotherly countenance' – that struck the French commander as being off, and especially his nervous, excitable manner. Turning to Petrakis, he remarked: 'There's something about that man I don't like.'

Petrakis confessed that he found it hard to vouch for the newcomer, for he'd left the village a good while ago and the innkeeper was a relatively new resident. Unable to properly fathom his disquiet, Bergé decided to let the man leave . . . to his eternal, undying regret.

Well fed and well watered, the party relaxed in the shade. With the mid-afternoon change of watch, Bergé made a snap decision. He felt the need to clarify the arrangements and the timings for the coming rendezvous with Commander Campbell and his trawler. Only their SIS contact would be able to provide those details. Bergé decided to send Jellicoe, a tough and fearless officer whom he'd come to hold in the very highest regard, along with Petrakis, their local man. While Petrakis should know the way to Krotos village, Jellicoe had the stature to make the link-up with the British SIS agent go like clockwork.

Shortly after 3.00 p.m. the pair set out. Krotos village lay some six kilometres further south, but a series of rocky ridges and hidden valleys lay ahead, and they would need to hurry to make it before nightfall. At the makeshift campsite, Bergé and his men settled down to wait. Once Jellicoe and Petrakis had made contact, they were charged to return with the party's final marching orders right away. As all appreciated, they were so near to getting out of there, having pulled off a truly historic raid.

At the approach of dusk, Bergé's intuition started to kick in. Somehow, he could sense a gathering danger. He ordered his men to pack their rucksacks, in case they needed to move out at short notice. He'd asked Jellicoe to return just as soon as he had news, and it was quite conceivable that he might make it back that evening. They'd long practised night marching and navigation, back at Kabrit, and with Petrakis as guide they should find the way.

Just then, Bergé spied some figures moving stealthily through the distant brush. Instantly, he knew they were the enemy. He yelled out a warning: 'Quick! Quick! Grab your weapons! Enemy troops!'

As he scanned their surroundings, he became aware of two columns of German troops – one moving in from the west, the other from the east. Already, they were caught in some kind of pincer movement, and it looked as if their location had been betrayed. With some twenty troops per column, they were outnumbered ten to one. Bergé ordered his three remaining men to follow him, as they tried to escape and evade to the south. For a short while they crawled through the scrub, only to spy a third enemy column closing in from the direction. If they'd had any doubts before, there were few remaining now. They were practically surrounded.

Bergé ordered his men to prepare to fight. Each would take

one of the four cardinals – defending their position to all sides. In that way he hoped to hold off this vastly superior force at least until nightfall, when they might manage to slip away under cover of darkness. Orders set, Bergé and Mouhot took cover behind the low wall, covering the north-west and south-west tangents. Sibard and Léostic took to the nearby ditch, covering the north-east and south-east sectors. Like that they hunkered down to wait.

'Don't move!' Bergé hissed. 'Don't shoot!'

The priority was to conserve ammunition and to avoid betraying their position until the very last moment. While they were still many yards distant, the enemy opened fire. Machine guns let off probing bursts, and volleys of grenades unleashed via a *Schiessbecher* – shooting cup; a special device attached to a rifle – detonated amid the thick scrub. But while the air might be thick with the howl of shrapnel and the whine of passing bullets, none of it was accurately targeting Bergé or his men. At least, not yet.

The four SAS had only their Beretta sub-machine guns, which were accurate up to around a hundred yards. They held their fire. A lone German trooper pressed forwards, perhaps doubting that those they hunted were here at all. When he was within range, Bergé fired a single, aimed burst and cut him down. For twenty minutes the stand-off continued, the enemy seeming reluctant to press home their attack. Bergé and his men loosed off the odd burst, whenever one dared to show himself. But the German troops had the advantage of the high-ground and they were clearly no amateurs. This had all the makings of a siege, and it was crystal clear who would be the first to run out of ammo.

Eventually, Léostic seemed to be overtaken with impatience at the standoff. 'Follow me! To the south!' he yelled at Sibard and the others. 'There's no one there!'

Seeing Léostic clamber to his feet, Sibard cried out a warning. 'No, Pierrot! No!'

At the same moment, Bergé ordered Léostic to hold his position.

'I can no longer obey you, my commander!' Léostic yelled back. Hungry for the fight, he seemed blind to the dangers.

Léostic broke cover, making some twenty yards, before the machine gun sited to their south barked out a savage burst. It cut the young Frenchman down. Even as he hit the ground, Léostic was heard to cry out for his mother. 'Mamma! Mamma!'

A second burst of fire stabbed out, this one raking the young Frenchman across the guts. There was a cry of agony, followed by the death rattle of punctured lungs, before a last burst silenced Léostic for good.

For an hour or more, the German troops hammered in concentrated bursts of fire, as Bergé and his two remaining men tried to fight them off. But with the cloak of darkness still a good sixty minutes away, time was running out. Their ammo was desperately short, and either they broke out and slipped away or they were done for. Finally, the three SAS fired their last rounds, and it was a case of every man for himself.

Sibard moved first, crawling in the opposite direction to that Léostic had taken. His escape attempt ended with a figure dressed in *Feldgrau* – the distinctive grey-green uniform of the German military – putting a gun to his head. He'd made thirty yards, no more. To his rear, Bergé made a break for it, but shortly he too was captured. Only Mouhot remained at large, the 'drunkard' from the airbase attack seeming to have utterly disappeared. Shouting, cursing, probing with their bayonets, the German troops crashed about searching every inch of terrain. Finally, Mouhot emerged from a bramble thicket, his face and arms running with blood from where the thorns had cut into him.

For an age the probing and the yelling continued, before the German commander gathered the survivors in one spot. 'One, two, three,' he yelled, his face twisted with fury, as he numbered off the captives. 'Four!' he stabbed a finger at the bloodied form of Léostic. 'Where are the other two?'

Faced only with silence, he repeated the question, his voice spiralling into a rage. 'Where are the other two?'

No one breathed a word, but if they had any doubt that they had been betrayed, it was long gone now. The enemy had known not only their position but the exact number making up their party. As if to confirm their worst suspicions, the captives spotted a familiar figure among the ranks of *Feldgrau*. It was the '*gros bonhomme*' – the fat fellow – the village innkeeper from earlier in the day.

With little fanfare, Bergé, Sibard and Mouhot were marched towards the nearest village. The entire population seemed to have turned out to watch – men, women and children gathering on their doorsteps, 'petrified, sombre, depressed', and some on the verge of tears. Seeing the distress of the locals, Bergé shook himself into some kind of semblance of order.

He turned to the others. 'Smarten your bearing,' he barked.

Mouhot and Sibard, overwhelmed with sadness at the loss of young Léostic, nevertheless heard him. In an instant they'd straightened their backs, lifted their heads, tried to brush down their uniforms, and quickened their steps, adopting a far more soldierly bearing.

'*Gallos! Gallos!*' – Gauls! Gauls! – the villagers cried, spying the distinctive insignia on the captives' battle dress. 'Frenchmen! They are French!'

The German commander brought the column to a halt. He ordered the three prisoners put against one wall. Each was fully expecting this to end in a hail of gunfire. But the cries of the villagers had filled them with an immense sense of pride, giving them the strength to face whatever was coming.

To one side, the innkeeper – the Judas – fussed to and fro, offering the German troops drinks. Wine was served, as some among the enemy ranks went about coddling a young boy, who looked to be no more than ten years of age. In short order the captives learned why. This was the innkeeper's son. He had dispatched this boy to run the 25 kilometres to the nearest large town, the location of the German garrison. It was he who had fetched the enemy troops, at his father's behest.

Maybe it was the effect of the wine, but for whatever reason the three captives weren't executed. Instead, the column moved out, heading west towards their headquarters. Sibard's boots had been falling apart, and it was now that they more or less disintegrated. Stumbling along on bloodied feet, blows and insults rained down upon him as his captors berated him to keep up. But the rocky path tore into his feet, and finally the enemy troops relented. From somewhere a donkey was produced, and Sibard was slung astride it. In an effort to prevent him from trotting away, Sibard was lashed tightly by his escorts, and Mouhot and Bergé were ordered to march at his sides.

In this manner they finally reached the enemy's base. They were led before a lieutenant in the Germany military. Young, impeccably dressed and faultlessly polite, their inquisitor began the first round of questioning.

'I apologise, I don't speak English,' he announced, in French. 'Do any of you speak French?'

'But we are French!' one of the captives retorted.

'Oh. Well, that changes everything,' the lieutenant replied.

Reaching for a phone, he called what had to be his superiors, reporting what he had learned, before returning to the task at hand. Scrupulously correct and proper, Bergé couldn't help but be charmed by the German's manner. Eventually, he handed the young lieutenant his binoculars – the same pair as had accompanied him during the battle for France, and at all points thereafter, and which he held so dear.

'I offer you these,' Bergé announced. 'They will be taken from me. I would prefer you to have them. At least that way, I know who inherits them.'

The young lieutenant seemed touched, but the entire situation was about to take a marked turn for the worse. A new figure arrived. Small, red-faced, senior in rank, as soon as he walked in the entire atmosphere turned.

'You are French?' he barked, incredulously. 'You are traitors and terrorists! You will be shot! At dawn on the 20th of June precisely.'

That meant at sunrise on the following morning.

A new and bruising round of questioning followed. The puce-faced commander seemed most enraged that two of the raiders had managed to escape the dragnet. Again and again he attempted to make the captives betray where the two missing men – Jellicoe and Petrakis – might be. The certainty of being executed the following morning made the captives even less inclined to talk. They would never have breathed a word anyway, but the fact that they were dead men walking only served to stiffen their resolve.

The German commander seemed driven to distraction, repeatedly threatening that they would be shot dead if they didn't speak up. In truth, he had every reason to be worried. The news of the Heraklion raid had reached the very highest echelons of the German military and the Nazi party leadership. Very quickly, a team of investigators had got to work on the wreckage of the warplanes, concluding that the raiders had been 'connoisseurs' who had placed their charges with great precision. Though twenty-three aircraft had been hit, the German authorities attempted to cover up the attack, to conceal the extent of the damage.

But still, heads were going to roll.

The SAS raid had been branded as 'extremely reckless' and 'rare in the history of this war'. Heraklion's commanders found themselves under attack for the 'surprising ease' with which the saboteurs had reached their targets, getting to the aircraft 'with impunity', supposedly betraying the lack of proper security and the guards. Incredibly, General Albert Kesselring, since 1941 the Commander-in-Chief South of all German armed forces, had intervened personally. From his headquarters in Italy, he had telephoned Heraklion, demanding answers, and that those responsible face the consequences.

From Berlin, Hermann Göring – as Reichsmarschall, the most senior rank in the entire German military – dispatched a senior military judge, to assist in the search for the culprits. At Heraklion, Captain J. Helbig, the commander of the flight of warplanes that had been hardest hit – Group I/LG1 – was dragged from his bed and ordered to report to his superiors in full dress uniform. Ironically, Helbig had repeatedly requested that the airbase's security be stiffened, as he feared it was wide open to attack. Despite this, General Kesselring made it clear that he held Helbig somehow personally responsible, and that the Luftwaffe captain was going to be the focus of his ire.

In time, two German generals were to be recalled to Berlin and dismissed of their command, as a result of the Heraklion raid. But for now, Bergé, Sibard and Mouhot were facing the worst of the blowback, as senior commanders feared for their careers, if not their very lives. The captives were whisked north by vehicle, as they were taken back to the scene of the attack – Heraklion airbase. They reached the eye of the storm, to face renewed verbal and physical assaults. Taken to the Luftwaffe barracks, there was just the one positive that they could foresee: at least they remained in the hands of the German military, as opposed to the dreaded Gestapo.

Bergé was dragged before the base commander, who once again began to threaten him and his men with death by firing squad. Fortunately, they had prepared for just such an eventuality back at their Kabrit base, during training. 'If you are captured, and threatened with execution because you are French,' they'd been told to point out that 'German officers who are being held in Cairo will answer for your execution.' Before leaving Alexandria, Bergé had been briefed about how several thousand German troops had been captured around Tobruk, in November 1941. He would use that to his advantage now.

Having first pointed out that he and his men were members of a regular army, deployed in uniform, and that they should be treated as bona fide prisoners of war, Bergé delivered the counter-punch. 'If you shoot us,' he declared, 'those German officers we captured . . . and whom we are holding in Egypt, will answer for our execution with their lives.' Moreover, a dozen or more German officers would be killed, Bergé explained, for the laws of retribution dictated that the British response should be punitive.

For now at least the threat seemed to have hit home. The three captives were slammed into solitary confinement, each to his own cell. Sibard had suffered a flesh wound during the firefight. Though he dismissed it as being of no consequence, his captors demand that they inspect it, for which he was ordered to strip. Sibard had been circumcised, and upon spying this the German officer's mood darkened. *'Jude?'* they demanded – are you Jewish?

Sibard denied it, but it was seemingly one more nail in the coffin. Locked up alone, each of the three was 'chafing at the bit'. Maybe, for now, they had avoided the firing squad. But what all hungered for was an opening – the hope that the barest chance of escape might present itself.

Back at the site where Bergé and his men had been captured, Jellicoe was contemplating the self-same thing himself: *escape*. The Belted Earl had made it to the rendezvous with their SIS liaison, and the pickup by trawler had been set. As Petrakis's boots had given out on him, Jellicoe had proceeded to return to the patrol's hideout, to fetch the others. He'd reached what he was certain was the correct location – that long bowl-shaped valley – but not a sign of his comrades could he find anywhere. Having searched the feature from end to end, he did the same with the adjacent valleys, but with no greater luck. It was night, so perhaps he had missed them in the darkness, he reasoned. He settled down to grab some rest, resolving to search again come morning.

Well before dawn, he was back at it. Shortly, he discovered some of the patrol's kit. But something struck him as being distinctly odd. 'I found some of their belongings, all very tidily arranged,' Jellicoe would remark. 'I knew immediately that something was wrong.' The discarded equipment was placed far too neatly. If Bergé and his men had needed to abandon this place, they would have left things in disarray. Sensing the hand of the enemy at work, it was at this moment that a group of boys from the nearby village appeared. Though Jellicoe could not understand all that they were saying, their gestures were all too clear. He was in danger, and he needed to make himself scarce.

Before getting the hell out of there, Jellicoe got the gist of what the boys were trying to tell him – that Bergé and his men had faced 'betrayal and disaster', and that the village innkeeper was the traitor. As he hurried away from that valley, Jellicoe felt a mixture of conflicting emotions. While he had once jokingly described Bergé and his Free French forces as being 'very French and very free', in truth he had developed a huge camaraderie with his brothers in arms. Intense behind-the-lines missions tended to forge extremely close bonds very rapidly, and this mission had been no exception.

Now, he could only imagine that they were facing the very darkest of fates. He was also haunted by the cost paid in blood for the Heraklion raid, and chiefly by the innocents – the Cretan villagers. Dozens had been executed and the reprisals were far from over, of that he felt certain. Jellicoe would be plagued by a deep sense of guilt, and he would never speak about those deaths for the rest of his days. Yet at the same time it was a Cretan villager – 'a very rare thing: a Greek quisling' – who had betrayed them, resulting in his SAS comrades being captured, and very possibly killed.

Such were the dark horrors of war.

Jellicoe made his way south, heading towards the shelter of a cave down on the shore, where Petrakis had agreed to rendezvous with him. On his approach, he was spotted by one David Sutherland, a lieutenant serving with the Special Boat Section (SBS), the sister – waterborne – raiding unit to the SAS. Together with a small party of men, Sutherland had been dropped on Crete to raid another airfield, but had found it devoid of warplanes. Frustrated and fatigued, Sutherland was amazed to spy Jellicoe, 'in khaki shorts and shirt', strolling along the beach, with an apparently jaunty spring to his step. As Sutherland knew full well, Jellicoe must have 'climbed two ranges of mountains and walked 120 miles' to get there, but somehow he seemed unfazed by his ordeal.

Together, they retired to the 'welcoming cool of the dark cave'. Sutherland had been nicknamed 'Dinky' by his men, due to his always seeming to be impeccably turned out, no matter where he might find himself. The cave was not to his liking. Jellicoe wasn't particularly to his liking, either, and especially since he 'had begun scratching his back like an ape'. The cave turned out to be flea-infested, hence The Belted Earl's itching. Even so, they were forced to spend a good forty-eight hours holed up there, as the hue and cry across Crete continued.

Finally, the night of their scheduled pickup was upon them. If all went to plan, Lieutenant John Campbell would steer HMS *Porcupine*, his motor-trawler, close in to shore, whereupon a rowing boat would ferry the escapees across to her decks. On a dark stretch of remote shoreline Jellicoe, Petrakis and Sutherland waited, as the clock ticked closer to midnight. There was a flash of foamy whiteness, and a rowing boat glided out of the night.

A 'shadowy figure' called out a cheery greeting. 'I'm Paddy Leigh Fermor. Who are you?'

'I'm George Jellicoe. Good luck.'

Fermor was the SOE's newest agent being delivered to these shores, and, together with his wireless operator, he was to start work with the island's partisans. Though they had managed only the briefest of 'shadowy greetings' across the water, Jellicoe and Fermor would become firm friends. Fermor would be struck by Jellicoe's 'initiative, and his inflexible determination and his knack of command', not to mention his 'gift for getting on with his soldiers'. Right then, in the early hours of 24 June 1942, Jellicoe's 'inflexible determination' had got him across Crete and out of the clutches of a vengeful enemy. Shortly, they would be motoring back towards friendly shores.

There was a slight delay, as a crowd of Cretans thronged the shoreline, demanding passage aboard the *Porcupine* so they could join Allied forces and fight. There were scores of them, but only a handful could be taken. Four days later, the *Porcupine* docked at Mersa Matruh, the Allied port on the Egyptian coast. Of the Heraklion SAS raiders, only one, The Belted Earl, had made it home. Determined not to be disheartened – to put on a brave face – Jellicoe headed directly for a Cairo wedding, for one of the SAS's most colourful characters was about to get hitched. He arrived, seeming to those present 'little the worse for his savage experiences on Crete'.

In truth, he was in bad shape. From the wedding, Jellicoe went more or less directly to Alexandria's 8th General Hospital, to get treatment and to recuperate. It wasn't such a bad experience, he reasoned. One of the nurses turned out to be Ivy Vassilopoulos, a beautiful Greek girl with whom Jellicoe was already closely acquainted. 'He was well looked after.' Even so, the Heraklion losses cast a long shadow. As the sole escapee, Jellicoe could only imagine that the rest of the patrol were either dead or facing long and unpleasant incarcerations as prisoners of war.

The upside was the damage caused to the enemy. Confirmed losses included twenty-three warplanes, and huge quantities of aviation fuel, ammunition and bombs. And, in the bigger picture scenario, a handful of the merchant ships sent to relieve Malta *had* made it through. For his part on the raid, Jellicoe – still just twenty-four years old – would be awarded the DSO. His citation read: 'His cool and resolute leadership, skill and courage throughout this very hazardous operation were mainly responsible for the high measure of success achieved.'

Jellicoe's brief report to Stirling on the Heraklion raid declared simply: 'Mission accomplished, sir.' Of course, that short, entirely upbeat phrase did much to conceal the losses they had suffered. Yet in fact, Jellicoe's would be but the first of the Heraklion great escapes . . .

From solitary confinement in the Luftwaffe's Heraklion barracks, Bergé, Mouhot and Sibard were flown north to Germany, just a few days after HMS *Porcupine* had pulled into her Egyptian berth. Driven west to Crete's Malème Airbase, for the flight by Ju 52 transport aircraft, they were under a close escort commanded by an Austrian officer. In a private moment that officer confessed to Bergé, in fluent French, that he was married to a Frenchwoman, and that he secretly held Bergé and his men in the very highest regard for the daring mission they had executed.

Flown to Frankfurt, escape attempt number one was about to be launched. Typically, it was Mouhot who broke out, 'managing to squeeze through the bars' of his cell, but he was swiftly recaptured. As Bergé was considered such a 'big fish' – the commander of the Free French SAS, no less – he was transferred to Oflag IV-C, at Colditz Castle, the high-security prison for those Allied officers who were viewed as being the 'real bad boys' – the serial escapees. Mouhot was sent to Oflag X-C, in Lübeck, in northern Germany. That camp was also for officers, Bergé having lied about Mouhot's rank in an effort to provide a little more protection to his comrade.

Three further escapes were attempted by Mouhot, one of which ended with his recapture just as he was poised to cross the border into Holland. Eventually, in the spring of 1943, he was successful. Talking his way onto a work party, Mouhot managed to break free while labouring in a rail yard, and he made it into Holland and Belgium by train and on foot. After transiting through France and Spain, he was hidden in the British Consulate in Barcelona for several weeks, before being spirited onwards to Gibraltar. From Gibraltar, Mouhot caught a flight to Bristol, arriving there on 10 September 1943.

In due course Mouhot was able to rejoin his comrades in the French SAS, when they returned to Britain to prepare for operations in support of the forthcoming D-Day landings. On the night of 5/6 June 1944, Mouhot would parachute back into France, landing in Brittany to harry, ambush and sabotage enemy forces. In the interim, he'd married an Englishwoman, Freda Edwards, and was shortly to become the father to their infant son.

In contrast to Mouhot, Bergé had failed to convince their captors that Sibard held an officer's rank. From Frankfurt, Sibard was transferred to an *Arbeitskommando*, a labour camp holding various nationalities, including Russians, Poles and a few exceptionally 'headstrong' British POWs. On 13 February 1943, Sibard managed to slip away from those guarding his work detail. Like Mouhot, he made his way to Spain and from there onwards to Britain, arriving there on 5 May. Of the Heraklion raid survivors, only Bergé, their commander, would fail to escape. In April 1945 he was freed from Colditz by the advancing Allied forces, along with David Stirling, the founder of the SAS.

Unfortunately, there was to be a sting in the tale of the Heraklion great escapes. Sadly, when Sibard related the story of his epic getaway, it was seen as being simply too extraordinary to be credible. On reaching London, all such escapees were subjected to a rigorous debriefing by Britain's intelligence service. Sibard's interrogator suspected him of being 'turned' – in other words, that he was now working for the enemy. Held in solitary confinement, Sibard was repeatedly interrogated, but through it all he held firm to his story.

In France, Sibard's mother was arrested by the Gestapo, as a result of his escape. When Sibard protested his innocence and objected to his treatment, those holding him in London retorted: 'We would rather keep ten innocents in prison than risk releasing a guilty one.' Sibard wasn't finally freed until 1 April 1945 – coincidentally, April Fool's Day. He returned to France and was fully exonerated. In 1946, Mouhot would be awarded the Croix de Guerre, among many other decorations. Sibard would go on to receive a high French order of merit, being appointed as a Knight of the Legion d'Honneur.

Several months after dropping the SAS party on Crete, RHN *Triton* was engaged in a six-hour battle with enemy warships. It ended with the venerable submarine being sunk by the German U-Jäger – submarine chaser – UJ 2210, and more than half of her crew were lost. In 1962, Lieutenant Petrakis hosted a reunion of the Heraklion raiders in Crete. At it, he christened his new-born son Pierre Léostic, in memory of the young French SAS member who had died on that extraordinarily successful raid, which had spawned an incredible series of escapes.

The Heraklion operation had brought this small band of warriors to the attention of the very highest echelons of German high command. That alone was testament to its outstanding achievements. But it would also have a flip-side. More and more often the raiders would find themselves in the enemy commander's spotlight, and in time they would attract the rage and the ire of the Führer, Adolf Hitler, himself. Increasingly, Hitler would take the actions of these elite warriors, and their successes, striking deep behind German lines, as a personal affront.

As the next great escapees would show, the SAS were poised to reap the whirlwind.

Chapter Three

FLIGHT FROM BIGAMY

September 1942, Libya

For those in the know, it was almost impossible to shake off the dark sense of foreboding. As he pulled his Willys jeep into a side wadi – a dry, narrow ravine that snaked down from the high ground towards the coastal plain – Captain Malcolm James Pleydell was gripped by a deep sense of worry for the fortunes of his fellow raiders. Strictly speaking he wasn't there as a combatant. Pleydell was the first medical doctor to be attached to the SAS, and a damn good one if the attitude of the men was anything to go by. Even so, he felt their predicament most personally; almost as if he were about to head into combat at their sides.

Pleydell's jeep epitomised his role. It had large Red Cross symbols painted on bonnet and doors, 'optimistically', as Pleydell readily confessed, for the chances of those fending off an enemy attack were slim in his experience. It bristled with medical equipment – stretchers slung along either side, a blood-transfusion box sandwiched between the front seats, and the entire rear of the vehicle jam-packed with panniers bulging with life-saving supplies. Each contained a wide selection of medical kit, so that if one were destroyed, Pleydell and his small team would not be lost for a particular drug or a dressing. Even so, to Pleydell the overloaded jeep still looked 'like a mobile Christmas tree'.

By now, he knew full well that his services – his medical aid post – would be far better off concentrated here in this wadi, where all knew how to find him, should they suffer casualties, as many feared they would. The previous evening the scales had truly fallen from the eyes of Pleydell and the other SAS officers. Their present mission, codenamed Operation Bigamy, had been foisted upon them by Middle East Headquarters (MEHQ). It was reviled from the very outset, for it sinned against every founding precept of the SAS. To make matters worse, they'd discovered that somehow, the details of their mission were known to the enemy, and long before they had even got close to their target.

Some twenty-four hours earlier, the massive column of vehicles – scores of jeeps and army trucks, carrying some two hundred SAS plus other assorted raiding forces – had pulled into the Jebel, this ridge of high ground running along the coast of North Africa, which left a slim neck of fertile land that rolled towards the sea, and upon which the main human settlements were located. Inland of the Jebel lay only the sun-baked wastes of the Sahara, which this massive column of vehicles had just spent several gruelling weeks traversing. Getting here had been a truly epic undertaking, for the SAS's Egypt base lay a good 1,500 kilometres east, and far longer by the route the raiders had been obliged to navigate, in order to cross the desert while avoiding the attentions of the enemy.

That evening Pleydell had joined the SAS's two most senior

commanders, as they'd warmed themselves around an open fire, for the desert nights were bitingly cold. They'd just had supper, the cooks in the mess-trucks doling out whatever they could muster, though after the long weeks in the desert fresh provisions were in desperately short supply. Pleydell had settled beside David Stirling, the SAS's founder, and Blair 'Paddy' Mayne, the man who had done so much to ratchet up the unit's score of enemy warplanes. He noticed there was a stranger in their midst. A stranger to Pleydell, at least ... Noticeably older looking – Mayne was twenty-seven, Stirling twenty-six, and Pleydell was still in his early twenties – the newcomer appeared quite at home in their company.

Captain Robert Marie Emanuel Mélot – 'Bob' to all who knew him here – was actually well into his late forties, and a decorated veteran of the First World War. Belgian by birth, he'd earned a Croix de Guerre while serving as a pilot in that nation's Air Force, getting wounded in 1917. Migrating to Egypt, he'd settled in Alexandria, married, raised a family, founded a thriving business and learned fluent Arabic, while spending his spare time exploring the desert, which held an enduring fascination for him. Volunteering for the Belgian Army at the outbreak of the Second World War, he was rejected on account of his age. Undaunted, Mélot had approached the British. Commissioned into the Druze Legion – one of the last cavalry units ever to be raised in war – Mélot took command of the unit's 4th Squadron, despite the fact that he was by no means a natural horseman. It proved a short-lived posting. Cavalry had sadly had its day in a time of modern, mechanised – *blitzkrieg*; lightning – warfare.

In the summer of 1941, Mélot had volunteered for Special Service, being dispatched into the desert on intelligence-gathering cloak-and-dagger business. By November, he'd helped lead an LRDG patrol to rescue the handful of survivors from Operation Flipper, the daring but failed attempt to assassinate General Rommel at his desert headquarters, which had been carried out by the men of No. 11 Commando. For a string of such missions, Mélot was awarded a Military Cross, the citation for which praised his numerous 'sorties behind enemy lines', during which he had demonstrated 'great energy and initiative, and a complete disregard for his personal safety'. It rounded off with a warning: 'In view of the secret nature of this officer's task details should not be published.'

In the late summer of 1942 Bob Mélot MC had quietly joined the ranks of the SAS, and expressly for 'the purpose of undertaking an operation'. Mélot – somewhat avuncular in appearance, but with a steeliness behind his gaze that belied the wear and tear of the passing years – had joined Stirling's raiders expressly for the present mission. He was tasked to journey into the Jebel long before the arrival of the main force, so as to spy out the lie of the land. He had been doing exactly that, with spectacular – some would argue shocking – results.

Mélot was introduced to Pleydell as 'an old friend of the unit', the Belgian breaking off from what he had been doing, which was questioning a 'timid looking Arab', in order to exchange greetings. Returning to the task in hand, he subjected that local man to something close to an interrogation. After a good few minutes of animated conversation, the Belgian eyed his comrades, as he proffered up an explanation of all that had been said. The Arab was a long-standing source of his, Mélot explained. He'd just executed a reconnaissance of Benghazi, their target, on foot. The news he'd brought back was alarming, to put it mildly.

There was every sign that the enemy knew full well that the SAS were coming. Mélot's agent was adamant that the Benghazi garrisons had long known of the coming attack and were 'ready to meet it'. Not only that, but they'd also learned the date of the planned raid – the night of 13 September 1942 – and had been busy laying minefields and preparing dug-in defences, plus emptying the city's port of shipping, and most of its airfields. Only one aerodrome remained active, and that had had a cordon of steel thrown around it, as thousands of reinforcements were rushed in to bolster the city's defences.

Once Mélot had finished speaking, there was an awkward, heavy silence. No one was particularly surprised at the news, but this was still deeply concerning. From the very start, Stirling and Mayne had known that the present undertaking had all the makings of a disaster. Some had even spoken of it as a suicide mission. Such a massive force, moving in such a huge convoy of vehicles, over such incredible distances, and all to a rigid timescale – it was almost inconceivable that they would escape notice. Operation Bigamy was antithetical to the SAS's founding principles – to strike by speed and surprise, at a time and place of their own choosing, so as to maximise the enemy's weakness and vulnerabilities.

But still, this level of potential calamity – that the enemy were forewarned and forearmed – was staggering.

'This Arab is quite reliable?' Stirling ventured, finally breaking the silence.

'I think so,' Mélot confirmed. 'I've often worked with him. Besides, why would he say these things if they aren't true? What can he gain from it? If he had *not* told us, then it *would* be possible that the Germans were bribing him. But I feel pretty certain that he is all right.'

If a man of Mélot's calibre and experience had every confidence in his source, who were Stirling and Mayne – or Pleydell – to doubt him? Stirling decided it was time to alert Cairo. He radioed through a warning concerning all they had learned. The response from MEHQ was utterly confounding. They were ordered to ignore all such 'bazaar gossip' and to proceed with their mission as planned. That mission supposedly involved punching through Benghazi's defences, seizing the port and blowing up as much enemy shipping as possible, plus destroying the harbour infra-structure, and having a pop at any airfields while they were at it. There was even a plan for one party to cut the undersea cable that linked Benghazi headquarters with Italy, so severing communi-cations, while another was to sink a ship in the harbour entrance, so blocking it completely.

Only now, the raiders were supposed to do all of that facing a massively strengthened enemy garrison who knew they were coming. The mood among the SAS commanders was dark. Mayne 'scarcely said a word', other than remarking that 'some hard scrapping' doubtless lay ahead. Even Pleydell – a doctor serving with the Royal Army Medical Corps; he'd only been attached to the SAS for a matter of months – could sense how dire things looked. They had lost their 'most powerful card: that of surprise.' But as they were under strict orders, what more could they do than face whatever the future might hold . . . with fatalism.

For Pleydell, it took a phrase from the Bible to best sum up this most gargantuan of screw-ups: 'Sufficient unto the day is the evil thereof.' In other words, each day brings its allotted burden of suffering, and this one appeared to be no different.

Those gathered around the fire decided not to warn the men about what Mélot had discovered. It would do little to help, for they had been ordered to attack come what may. A new approach route was mapped out, one designed to try to avoid the worst of the city's beefed-up defences. That might buy them a sliver of advantage. In light of what they had just learned, Pleydell reckoned it was wiser to site his medical aid post outside of the minefields and the city's fortified perimeter. Eventually, it was decided that he should remain on the Jebel, providing a focal point to which all might return once the raid was over, including any wounded.

So it was that Pleydell and his small medical team had nosed their vehicles into that narrow wadi, in readiness to set up shop. Easing off the main track that twisted 'snake-like round the easy slopes of the hills', they'd halted to wave farewell to the rest of the party. Shortly, the raiders would be splitting into two groups. One, led by Stirling and Mayne, would spearhead the – ill-fated? – thrust into Benghazi. The other, a far smaller party commanded by Mélot, would speed on ahead, tasked to destroy the city's radio outpost, which perched atop the Jebel, so no early warning of the attack could be beamed out by the city's defenders.

As the long column of heavily armed jeeps rumbled past Pleydell and his small team, one slowed to a halt. 'Oy! Quack!' a voice cried out. It was the unmistakeable tones of Bill Cumper, the SAS's explosives and demolitions expert, a die-hard practical joker whose irascible manner and black humour never failed to raise a smile. 'Oy! Mind you've got yer knives nice and sharp before we're back!' After a few more jibes about 'butcher's shops' and limbs being chopped off, Cumper turned his attention to a contingent of the French SAS, who also formed a part of the Benghazi raiding force.

'Onwards, mez amiz!' he cried, striking a faux-dramatic pose, with one hand clutching his heart and the other lancing sky-wards. 'Onwards! À la glory!' Needless to say, Cumper's French left a lot to be desired. With that, he 'revved up and dashed off after the others', with those riding in his jeep 'hanging on for dear life'.

Shortly, the last of the jeeps wound up and away over the crest of the nearest hill and were lost to view. The sun was fast setting, as Pleydell led his own small convoy – the one jeep, plus a medical truck – further down the wadi, nosing into some decent cover. Two low trees growing close together formed a natural arch, beneath which the truck fitted snugly, with the jeep secreted a little further on. Camouflage nets were slung over both, after which Pleydell and his team ripped up tufts of the long dry grass that clung to the wadi, and pulled down some thorny branches, all of which was scattered over the nets. That way, the vehicles should be rendered largely invisible from the air.

All that remained now was to wait. Over a quick supper and cigarettes, Pleydell chatted to his drivers, both of whom had turned out to be excellent companions. One, Trooper Austin, a salt-of-the-earth type, had proved to be 'as tender-hearted as any woman' when dealing with the wounded. The other, Trooper Shaw, had seemed surly and withdrawn at first. But over time Pleydell had realised that, like many quiet, reticent types, Shaw was as reliable and dependable as anyone when the going got tough. They talked well into the night, until a pack of jackals moved into the wadi, their wild, cackling cries and howls sounding 'horrible and frightening'.

Instinctively, Pleydell reached for his pistol, as he felt the hairs on the back of his neck bristle. In truth, those jackals weren't the real danger here. They would never try to tackle a live human prey. The enemy were the real threat, and especially if Mélot's dire warnings were to be proven correct. Shortly before midnight, a low, sonorous drone reverberated through the wadi. Bang on cue, a flight of warplanes roared across the dark skies. The RAF had agreed to hit Benghazi, to cause a diversion as cover for the SAS attack. Shortly, the flash of anti-aircraft fire and the distant crump of explosions signalled that the bombardment had begun.

Pleydell and his four-man team cast lots, to see who should sit the first watch. Pleydell won, but he opted to take the initial spell on sentry. Grabbing a blanket, a torch and a paperback – one of the *The Forsyte Saga* trilogy, which chronicles the adventures of a country solicitor, Soames Forsyte, and his fierce possessiveness over his beautiful wife, Irene – he chose a vantage point and settled down to read. In a peculiar sign of the kind of men who formed this maverick band of warriors, it was via Pleydell's love of literature that he had forged his closest bond with the foremost raider of all – Blair 'Paddy' Mayne. When he wasn't blasting apart enemy airbases, or dashing down the makeshift rugby field at their Kabrit training base – Mayne had played rugby both for Ireland and the British Lions – he was more often than not to be found with his head stuck in a book. Ironically these two men – SAS commander and SAS doctor – had got to know each other best when discussing literature and swopping the odd novel.

At 2.00 a.m. Pleydell shut his book and went to wake Shaw. Watch relieved, he wrapped himself closer in his blanket and settled down to doze. Below them on the coastal plane, Stirling, Mayne et al. should be poised to go into action, bludgeoning their way through the enemy's outer defences. Pleydell was just drifting off to sleep when he sensed something was amiss. As he strained his ears, he heard the faint whine of a vehicle engine in the distance. The noise kept coming and going, and it sounded as if the driver was unsure of his way; as if he were investigating each of the valleys that he passed.

Unable to sleep, Pleydell woke Austin. Together, he and the driver wandered over to see Shaw, who was standing sentry right then.

'Sounds like a jeep,' Shaw remarked. It did indeed.

A few minutes later the shadowy form of the vehicle hove into view, showing no lights so as not to attract the attention of the enemy. Flashing with a torch, they signalled the driver closer.

A voice cried out. 'Mr Mélot's been wounded, sir.'

'Badly?' Pleydell yelled a reply.

'In the stomach and legs. He's lost a good bit of blood and we can't bring him back . . .' There was also a second badly injured man, Pleydell was warned.

Pleydell, Shaw and Austin hurried to their vehicles, where they dragged aside the camouflage netting. Waking the rest of their team, they set off along the track in the wake of the jeep. Twenty minutes later they were flagged down by some of Mélot's party. They pulled over, to discover a figure lying on the ground and covered by a greatcoat. It was Mélot, surrounded by a silent group of his men. Pleydell greeted the Belgian, noticing how ashen-faced he looked, and that it seemed as if the past few hours had aged him greatly.

'Hallo, Doc,' Mélot replied, putting a brave face on things. 'There's nothing much the matter with me. Hand-grenade wounds, you know.'

Pleydell knelt beside him, cutting away his clothes where necessary to inspect his injuries. Mélot and his party had taken out that wireless station all right, but in his keenness to get at the enemy the Belgian had been caught in one of their own grenade blasts. The result, as Pleydell was quickly starting to realise, was that he was peppered with shrapnel from the abdomen down.

Pleydell told Mélot that he needed morphia and a blood plasma transfusion. Mélot tried to object. He'd walked most of the way here. He wasn't in any great pain. He was perfectly all right. They argued back and forth a bit, but Pleydell remained firm. Mélot was getting what he prescribed, no ifs or buts. One man, Johnson – one of Pleydell's medical orderlies – held up a plasma bag, getting the fluids into Mélot, while Pleydell went to fetch some extra blankets from their jeep, for it was bitterly cold.

Johnson, a bespectacled Londoner, had earned the nickname 'Razor Blade' due to his skill with the knife, and Pleydell knew Mélot was in good hands. During a previous mission – one of his first with the SAS – Pleydell had realised that his then medical orderly was astonishingly squeamish about anything remotely smacking of being at war. He'd refused to carry out the most basic combat-related duties – sentry rotations, or standing lookout – which were essential for all to share when operating in such small units. Worse, his conscience would not permit him 'to clean rifles, revolvers, or handle ammunition'. That man had had to go. With Razor Blade Johnson, Pleydell had few such concerns.

Even as he was rummaging through the jeep for those blankets, a stranger's voice rang out, catching the SAS doctor by complete surprise. 'I say . . . er, excuse me, do you happen to have seen David Stirling or Bob Mélot around here recently?' The accent was cut-glass Oxford, the figure seeming to have materialised from out of absolutely nowhere. Pleydell studied him for a long beat: plus-fours, tweedy checked jacket and knobbly walking stick. He looked as if he should have been on some Scottish estate, shooting grouse. What on earth was such a figure doing here? As politely as he could, Pleydell posed that very question, before the bizarre apparition hurried over to have words with Mélot.

In truth, this was one Alan Samuel Lyle-Smythe, sometime actor, writer and policeman, but right now serving as an agent of the Inter-Service Liaison Department (ISLD), the cover name for Britain's Secret Intelligence Service here in North Africa. Lyle-Smythe was of the firm opinion that the more quintessentially 'English' he looked, the more juicy snippets of intelligence he would be offered, hence his wandering around the Jebel dressed as he was. On one level he was right, for a local informant had passed him a warning that the present SAS mission was 'fatally compromised', the enemy 'lying in wait'. He'd come here to alert Stirling and Mélot, but he was of course too late.

Lyle-Smythe remained with them, trying to speak to the Belgian, but by now Mélot was addled with morphine. Finally, Pleydell got the wounded man loaded aboard their truck, for the journey back to the medical station, at which point the ISLD agent drifted into the darkness, just as 'mysteriously as he had emerged from it'. Later, Mélot would confess that he and Lyle-Smythe had worked together on several cloak-and-dagger missions, and that Pleydell's peculiar encounter with him was nothing out of the ordinary. The man was as singularly eccentric as they came.

Back in their wadi, they laid Mélot on a stretcher in the shelter of a bush, after which they set about camouflaging their vehicles again. By now the first blush of dawn was creeping across the landscape, and the last thing they needed was to be spotted by an enemy warplane. The second wounded man from the battle of the wireless station, Captain Chris Bailey, was brought in. With great care they carried him into some shade. Pleydell inspected his wounds. There was a tiny hole just above his heart. It had hardly bled at all, but Pleydell could tell at once how serious it was. Bailey's left lung had collapsed and he had a sucking pneumothorax – a chest wound that prevented oxygen from reaching his system.

Normally, with hospital treatment, his injuries would be pretty straightforward to deal with, Pleydell reflected. But here, with 1,300 kilometres of punishing terrain lying between them and the nearest friendly lines – the deep desert oasis of Kufra – 'the future did not look good'. Even now, at rest, the injured man was struggling for breath. How on earth was he to survive the interminable journey on the back of a burning-hot, jolting army truck, Pleydell wondered? For that matter, what chance was there that Bob Mélot might do the same?

Having made both men as comfortable as he could, Pleydell got the story of the wireless station battle out of some of the others. Typically, Mélot had led the charge. By yelling out in Italian that they were Germans troops, he had bluffed the guard force, resulting in a short but fierce firefight at close quarters. Despite being injured in the grenade blast, Mélot had continued fighting as if nothing much had happened. It was only after they had blown up the wireless equipment and the barracks, and seized two prisoners, that Mélot was forced to accept that he could stay on his feet no longer. In view of his injuries, Pleydell was amazed that he'd made it that far.

Dawn was almost upon them by now, and Pleydell's mind drifted to thoughts of how the main body of raiders might have fared. His musings were interrupted by the distinctive, high-pitched snarl of a liquid-cooled V12 aero-engine – an enemy warplane was in-bound. The sleek Me 109 fighter tore down the track above them, at about a hundred feet of altitude. In a tense silence Pleydell and his men waited, and then it came: the 'fast crackle of machine-gun fire, sounding hideous and frightening on the chill morning air'.

Soon, the skies were thick with enemy aircraft. Whatever fate might have befallen Stirling, Mayne and their forces at Benghazi, they had stirred up a veritable hornet's nest, that much was clear. The pilots were flying so low that a warplane would appear as if from nowhere, powering over the lip of the wadi with almost zero warning. Pleydell and his men knew that one wrong move could spell death. In an apparent lull between sorties, they decided to try to clean Mélot's wounds, cutting away the dead skin and dressing them properly. Twice, they were forced to freeze mid-task, as an enemy aircraft thundered over, and they tried to shield the white of the bandages from the skies.

On the second occasion, the pilot did not seem inclined to pass on by. Instead, he circled around their wadi at two hundred feet of altitude, scanning the terrain below. Painfully slowly, inch by careful inch, Pleydell and Johnson edged Mélot's stretcher further beneath the bush. He lay there, completely oblivious, 'snoring away blissfully' with his false teeth lying beside him. The pilot continued to search, and momentarily the engine note changed, as the aircraft dived, passing right over their position and hammering some bushes on the far side with long bursts of machine gunfire.

Thankfully, that patch of brush was devoid of any human presence. Pleydell and his men felt a frisson of pride that their positions were camouflaged so effectively as to be rendered all-but invisible. Yet elsewhere along the Jebel, the fortunes of their fellow raiders appeared to be far starker. From the north – the direction of the coastal plane and Benghazi – the crump of exploding bombs and the death-rattle of machine guns were clearly audible. Fearing the worst, Pleydell and his men could only pray for their comrades' safety.

As the hours ticked by and the sun rose higher, Pleydell was struck by an apparition, as incongruous as it was bewitching. An ancient-looking chameleon – the shape-shifting, hue-changing lizard – crawled onto a branch where Pleydell had taken cover. Seeming utterly oblivious to the danger, it sat there with that typical 'you can't teach me anything' look on its face, appearing both 'wise and pompous'. The SAS doctor was personally acquainted with the species, for he'd adopted an entire brood of chameleons during his previous medical posting. He'd named them after Churchill and his family, for the stately lizards seemed to typify Britain's wartime leader, each with a 'lower jaw thrust forward' as they went after their prey, while 'nothing, it seemed, could alter their purpose'.

Strictly speaking, Pleydell was a non-combatant, but he had more than earned his spurs in battle, and long before volunteering for the SAS. Serving as a medic at Dunkirk, he had overseen the evacuation of hundreds of injured, who had been loaded aboard a pleasure steamer – one of the fleet of 'little ships'. Attacked by a flight of Stukas, the vessel had been bracketed with bombs, and half blown out of the water. As she had raced to make a getaway she had collided with a British destroyer amid all the confusion and the darkness. She had survived, managing to limp her way across to British shores, but the carnage aboard that makeshift hospital ship had been horrifying.

'The force of the collision was terrific and threw us in a jumbled heap,' Pleydell recalled, of the moment of the impact, with 'wounded men and stretchers' scattered everywhere. 'The ship was listing heavily . . . and there was panic on the deck above. We could hear heavy army boots over our heads, thudding backwards and forwards, drumming a mad tattoo. At any moment it seemed that the sea would come flowing down . . . and we would be drowned like rats. It was not easy trying to sort out the wounded and the stretchers . . . Eventually, we extricated the bodies into some semblance of order, and decided to take the stretchers up on deck for a chance to escape.'

Despite his best efforts, Pleydell failed to get all the wounded back alive. He'd lost any number on that blighted ship. He was haunted by those memories, the experience leaving him suffering terrible flashbacks. 'So when did Dunkirk end? In June 1940?' Pleydell mused. It certainly hadn't for him. 'For months after the evacuation . . . I would find my pulse racing and my hands slippery with sweat.' Even so, he had deployed to North Africa, and in the spring of 1942 had volunteered for a frontline medical posting with the Coldstream Guards. He'd kept a diary, tiny writing scribbled in pencil, the words often seeming staccato and rushed. It was hardly surprising. Pleydell's duties had taken him well beyond the German frontline, as British forces had punched through Rommel's positions, only to become the hunted themselves.

'Shells flying around then tracer,' Pleydell noted in his diary. 'Small arms fire from the east. We slowly zigzagged away from the fire turning back . . . Thought my last hour of freedom had come and position seemed hopeless. German vehicles following on flanks of us and shelling. Dusk came to our rescue . . . Moved through German lines once again for 70 miles . . . No sleep. Very frightening day . . . Seemed certain we were to be put in the bag . . . Worst moment was after reaching German concentration group and it was almost a relief when they opened fire on us. Quiet. Re-joined by our forces. Fear this is the lull before the storm. Very tired.'

Courageous, self-effacing, empathetic, and possessed of his own eccentricities – epitomised by the Churchillian chameleon family – there was no better medic for a unit such as the SAS. Even so, today's trials would push even Pleydell to the limit, as would the days of hell to come. At midday, the sky cleared of enemy warplanes. It was uncanny. It was almost as if the German and Italian pilots had departed for a decent lunch, before returning to the kill. Pleydell and his team emerged from their places of hiding. No damage had been done, so they had seemingly got off very lightly.

Then a first vehicle appeared. It was a jeep, and cradled in the vehicle's camouflage net, as if in a DIY stretcher, was the first of the injured from the Benghazi raid. Pleydell used the net as a 'hammock' in which to lower the wounded man to the ground. The driver explained that the patient was in a serious way. His arm had been so smashed up that he kept asking for it to be amputated, to kill the pain. Pleydell administered a shot of morphine, and as it started to take effect the wounded man's cries – 'Chop off this bloody arm, for God's sake!' – gradually died away. Pleydell did his best to reassure him: 'Just you rest now. That's the main thing.'

More injured arrived. Flesh wounds mostly. Nothing that was life-threatening. As Pleydell and his team went about cleaning and dressing the injuries, they asked after the fortunes of the mission, though it was quite clear that all had not gone well. Gradually the story emerged. The long column of jeeps had driven towards Benghazi, crawling along a road in the thick darkness, the route being sown with mines on either side. They'd reached an odd kind of a roadblock, formed by a single barrier that could be tilted up to enable passage through. Bill Cumper, riding in Stirling's jeep, had leapt out to raise the barrier. As he'd done so, he'd gestured theatrically and cried out, 'Let battle commence!'

As if on Cumper's cue, all hell had let loose. From their dug-in positions the enemy had let rip, opening up on the SAS column with mortars, machine guns and Breda 20mm cannons. As the lead jeep, driven by Gentleman Jim Almonds, had roared through the roadblock, it was caught in a hail of fire and it blew itself to pieces. It had been packed full of explosives, which were intended for sabotaging any ships moored in Benghazi harbour. To their rear, Mayne's vehicle and one other had taken up defensive positions, hammering out a concentrated barrage of fire from their jeep-mounted Vickers-K machine guns, in order to try to buy the rest some time.

Under the cover of their guns, Stirling had ordered an about-turn and, shielded by the lead vehicles' salvoes, most of the jeeps had managed to slip away. Then, with a final blistering eruption of fire, Mayne issued the order for the last of the jeeps to turn tail and run, high-tailing it into the night. But that was just the start of their problems. As the vehicles had raced for the comparative safety of the high ground of the Jebel, the sky had gradually lightened, and so the enemy warplanes had come hunting. The jeeps had run a hellish gauntlet as they tried to make it back into the cover of the hills.

Having learned the worst of the news, it was time for Pleydell and his team to get moving with the wounded. Some forty kilometres further west they'd set a rendezvous point, at Wadi Gamra, another deep ravine that sliced through the Jebel. That was where all would gather, prior to commencing the long drive back towards friendly lines. Night was almost upon them, and as they set out into the gathering darkness, Pleydell reflected upon how things could have been so much worse. Driving into a prepared ambush, Stirling and Mayne were incredibly fortunate not to have lost scores of men and vehicles. As things stood, their chances of getting back to Kufra alive and unmolested were looking reasonably good. Crucially, as far as Pleydell was concerned, they should have the space on the trucks to carry the worst of their wounded.

Even so, that night's drive turned into a 'wretched affair'. The heavy cloak of darkness might hide them from the enemy, but it also masked the worst of the terrain. Every bump and jolt of the vehicles caused a chorus of agonised cries from the wounded, and pleas for a softer ride. It was stop-start all the way, as they halted to administer shots of morphine, or because someone had spied a light up ahead and feared it might be the enemy. Fatigued, plagued by the cumulative lack of sleep over the long weeks gone by, it was a battle simply to remain alert. 'Asleep? Awake? The two had merged together,' wrote Pleydell of the interminable journey.

Finally, at around 3.00 a.m. they reached the Wadi Gamra. There it was a repeat performance: unload the wounded, make them comfortable, set camouflage netting, throw down some blankets and collapse with exhaustion. 'Silence in the wadi,' wrote Pleydell. 'A little breeze that tugged fitfully at the bushes. A deep sigh and a stretch of the legs. Then sleep, dear God, merciful sleep!'

It didn't last long. By 6.00 a.m. all were awake. An uneasy, nervous atmosphere had settled over the camp. A thousand questions crowded into battle-weary minds. Where were the enemy? Where was Stirling? What were their orders? It was made all the worse by a rumour doing the rounds that 5,000 Italian troops had moved in under cover of darkness, throwing a cordon around the British force, to close off any avenues of escape. Sentries were dispatched to the surrounding hilltops, in case there was any truth to this. With ample warning, at least they reckoned they would be able to put up a decent fight.

The worst of the wounded were corralled ever more closely. One, Sergeant Eustace Sque, shouldn't even have been there. He'd taken leave from his parent unit so as to be able to join the raiders as an unofficial attachment, for no one could dictate where he spent his leave, he'd argued. Sque had been shot in the leg, the bullet smashing his femur. Another, Sergeant James Webster, had been injured in a mine blast during the convoy's long approach to the Jebel, and Pleydell had been forced to amputate his leg. He'd done so in the middle of the open desert. 'I gave him two pints of plasma and he lived,' Pleydell noted. 'Not bad, amputating with an officer to help me, and the dust blowing.' Then there was Macleod with his shattered arm, Bailey with his punctured lung, and Bob Mélot, with his legs and torso peppered with shrapnel. Bailey, in particular, had worsened overnight. No matter what Pleydell might try, he feared it was unlikely that Bailey would survive all the way to Kufra.

Bailey's was a particularly vexing case, for he'd only been with the SAS for a short while. A veteran of the June 1940 battle for France, and later that of Greece – from both of which countries he had been evacuated, even as the enemy closed their traps – Bailey had volunteered for the SAS that August, so just a few weeks earlier. Due to his background in the hospitality sector – Bailey had managed a hotel prior to the war – he'd been appointed as the Catering Advisor to MEHQ. Baulking at such a non-frontline posting, Bailey had stepped forward for Special Service. Barely three weeks into his time with the SAS, he had proved himself a popular and capable officer, yet Pleydell feared that his was one life he would not be able to save.

Around eleven o'clock that morning a lone jeep appeared driving at speed. It came to a stop in the wadi, only for the driver to announce that he was looking for Pleydell. A missing man, Corporal Anthony Drongin, had been found, and he was in a bad way. Could Pleydell possibly come to help? The SAS doctor set off, but he was forced to transfer to another jeep halfway, due to his own suffering a puncture. They reached a point where they pulled over into a patch of scrub, and there, in the shade, was the wounded man.

'I'm sorry to have given you so much trouble, sir,' were Drongin's first words, on spying Pleydell, as he tried to force a smile.

Preparing a shot of anaesthetic, Pleydell wondered if anything could more typify the 'fortitude of these men? Could anything more nearly express their spirit?' Having put Drongin to sleep, he examined the man's wounds. He needed urgent surgery, and before they could even think about moving him. Pleydell made a start, but he was just a few minutes in when the drone of an enemy warplane reverberated through the air. Pausing his work, they threw a blanket over Drongin and crawled beneath the bushes, to hide. Once the aircraft had passed, Pleydell went back to his bloody task, but another warplane soon appeared, and so the horrific game of cat and mouse continued.

As he struggled to close the incision, Pleydell thought back to his days as a student doctor. There were no cool, calm wards here, he reflected, ruefully. 'No tidy white coats. No trim white nurses . . . Only the green-brown hill shuddering in the heat-haze; only the hot blue of the sky . . . only the thin trickles of sweat running down our foreheads . . .'

Once he reckoned that they could risk moving Drongin, they laid him crosswise on the jeep, cradled in some camo-netting, and set off. Almost instantly, an enemy warplane swooped over-head and they were forced to pull over. Repeatedly they juddered to a halt, in an effort to hide. Then, from the direction of Wadi Gamra, they heard the most disturbing noise of all: an outburst of bomb blasts and gunfire. Glancing to the heavens, it seemed as if all the enemy aircraft were suddenly speeding in that direction, and shortly a series of thick columns of smoke spiralled into the sky above the wadi. Studying the area via his binoculars, Pleydell could see a swarm of enemy warplanes swooping and wheeling overhead, as the ground below them took a pasting.

For now at least, Pleydell and his patient were stuck where they were. If they got going along the track, they were bound to be seen. Movement spelled death, and even if they made it to the wadi, it looked like the worst of places to be right now. There was no option but to sit tight and sweat it out, but even so it was horrible to have to remain there as 'helpless spectators'. At least Drongin was oblivious to it all, dosed as he was by a powerful shot of morphine. At one stage Pleydell considered carrying the wounded man, but it was fifteen kilometres to the wadi – an impossible distance laden with such a burden.

With dusk, the enemy planes departed, streaming back trium-phantly the way they had come. Pleydell signalled to get the jeep under way. Long before they'd reached the wadi, the silhouettes of burning vehicles stood out 'clear and red against the gathering darkness'. As they drew closer, a figure waved them down. Etched against the angry flames, it was Bill Cumper.

''Ullo, Doc, plenty of work for you to do all right,' he declared.

'Who's hurt?' Pleydell snapped, practically biting Cumper's head off. He was in no mood for levity right now.

By way of answer, Cumper led Pleydell towards the wounded. As he did, the SAS doctor spied his Red Cross truck ablaze. His patients had endured an utterly 'harrowing' onslaught. Unable to run or to hide, they had lain where they were on their stretchers, as first one vehicle and then another were hit and set alight. Time after time they had been strafed. It was a miracle that only one of the wounded men had been hit. Sergeant Sque had been shot through the leg, the bullet smashing into the same one as had already been injured. Typically, Shotton, Pleydell's other medical orderly, had remained with the wounded all through that terrible day, caring for them as best he could under fire.

Shotton, a fair-haired lad from Yorkshire, had impressed Pleydell with his down-to-earth common sense and practical nature. The SAS doctor had come to value him most highly. But this – it was an exceptional example of 'devotion to duty'. Yet there was little time to dwell on any of that now. A first casualty was brought into what remained of Pleydell's medical station, which was lit by the devilish light of the burning vehicles. He was slung in a bloodied blanket, and even as they lowered the burden to the ground Pleydell felt his heart sink. He knew the injured man. It was Germain Guerpillon, better known to all as 'Henri', and as unlikely an elite forces warrior as one could ever wish to meet.

Upon his arrival at Kabrit, Pleydell had envisaged joining a force of supermen; the stereotypical boy's own commandos. He'd worried they would treat him – the newbie and the non-combatant – with outright disdain. Quite the reverse had turned out to be the case. Stirling's outfit was a meritocracy – merit had to be earned, as did respect, and regardless of rank. In fact, as the unit's very first medic – a much-needed addition to their ranks – Pleydell had been welcomed with open arms. He'd found the self-sufficient, open-minded, egalitarian spirit of the SAS training camp immensely refreshing, and in short order he was hungry to join their exalted ranks. Though he'd never once intended doing so – he was the medic, after all – he'd promptly volunteered for parachute training.

That in turn had brought him into the orbit of the Free French SAS, some of whom were likewise being put through jump training. The very worst recruit had been Guerpillon; Henri. Short, rotund, a diplomat prior to the war, he was the foremost duffer of the class. Even so, he simply refused to give in, no matter how many times he landed on his face, getting sand in his eyes and a bloody nose. The rest of the French mocked him mercilessly, crying out: 'Un! Deux! Trois! Sautez!' – one, two, three, jump! – as Henri went to execute a practice leap, landing in a heap like a broken frog.

Yet each time Henri remained undaunted. 'Non. Non,' he would declare, as he picked himself up and dusted himself down. 'Ce n'est pas drôle, c'est formidable!' – It's not funny, it's fabulous!

What had struck Pleydell most powerfully was Henri's sheer gutsiness and his die-hard fortitude. When Pleydell had executed his first real jump from an actual aircraft, Henri had made up the last man – No. 10 – in the stick. That way, if the Frenchman bottled it, no one else would be prevented from executing their leap. As Pleydell had glanced up, counting the 'chutes in the air above him, sure enough Henri's was there. But it turned out that he had smashed his face on the narrow hole in the aircraft's floor, even as he had plummeted through it, and broken his nose.

Pleydell had tried to get a look at it, to see if he could help. Henri had waved him away, dismissively. '*Ce n'est rien, docteur*' – it's nothing, doc – he averred. All that mattered to Henri was that he had jumped . . . and survived. As was so often the case in life, Pleydell observed, those who overcame the most difficult obstacles and hardships turned out to be some of the most courageous and robust of individuals. Yet here was Henri now, wrapped in a bloodied blanket, and Pleydell could tell he was not long for the world. There was nothing he could do for the Frenchman. He was 'beyond any crude help I could provide'.

They wrapped him in a blanket and prepared to dig a shallow grave.

There was no time to dwell on the loss. Pleydell had his hands full. More wounded kept being brought in. But considering the murderous intensity of the attack, which had been sustained all through that long day, the casualties proved mercifully light. Mostly, the men had been able to run and to find good cover. It was the vehicles that had taken the real pounding. Just as Pleydell had finished doing what he could for the injured, a messenger arrived on foot. He was wanted by David Stirling.

As Pleydell made his way towards Stirling's position, there were scores of vehicles either burned out, or still spitting and blazing fiercely. It was a 'very desolate scene', he observed. In fact, something like twenty trucks packed with stores, plus a dozen jeeps had been destroyed. Tonnes of water, food, ammunition and fuel had gone up in smoke, which had to make their return journey even more of a perilous – some might argue impossible – undertaking.

Faced with all of that, Pleydell wondered what Stirling might have in mind, and what on earth might be their plan to escape from such chaos and carnage. He discovered the SAS founder ensconced with Mayne, plus one or two other officers. Catching sight of Pleydell, Stirling flashed his trademark shy smile. 'Hallo, Malcolm, you have had a busy time. You must be absolutely exhausted. How are the wounded?'

By way of answer Pleydell gave a short report on the litany of the injured, outlining the worst of the cases. As he spoke, Stirling's face noticeably darkened.

'I'm afraid we have some very bad news for you,' Stirling ventured, his voice halting and troubled. 'We're moving off in two hours' time, but we simply haven't got the room to take the wounded.' He gestured at the burning trucks. 'I'm terribly sorry.' Pleydell looked blank for a moment, as his mind tried to grasp what the SAS commander was intimating. 'We've hardly got enough space for our fit men . . .' Stirling added. 'Stretchers are just out of the question.'

Pleydell realised then that subconsciously at least, he'd known that this was coming. What other options were there? But internally, he was distraught and wrestling with a 'major crisis'. He had six men who needed constant care and attention, Bob Mélot included. If they *were* to be left behind, they needed to be spirited to a hospital as soon as possible, which could only mean that they would have to be handed over to the enemy. There was no other option. And if they were to do that, one of the medical team at least would have to stay behind to look after them.

Fortunately, they'd captured an Italian medical orderly during the radio station battle, so he could lend a hand. Even so, Pleydell found himself speared on a terrible dilemma. If he chose to stay himself with the worst of the wounded, he'd be deserting his 'duty to remain with the main fighting force'. Yet he could not bring himself to abandon those stretcher cases – men he had done everything possible to save and to care for. Recently, Pleydell had been paid what he saw as the ultimate compliment by one of the wounded, being told: 'The lads'll go anywhere with you behind them.'

Well, right now, he couldn't stay with both parties.

Though he was torn, Pleydell asked if he might remain with the stretcher cases, while accepting that it was up to the unit's commanders to decide. Stirling and Mayne were adamant. A man of Pleydell's calibre – their only doctor – was far too valuable to leave behind, and especially as God only knew what trials awaited them in the open desert, in addition to which there were still the walking wounded that required his care. That decided it. One of Pleydell's assistants would have to stay behind.

Pleydell returned to what remained of his medical station to deliver the grim news. While one man held a torch, the medical orderlies called the toss, Pleydell flipping a one piastre piece – the local currency – into the air. Solemnly, one chose heads, the other tails. Johnson – Razor Blade – lost. Typically, he didn't seem unduly troubled. He hunched his shoulders and, blinking through his thick glasses, as was his wont, he remarked that what he really needed now was 'a decent Red Cross armband'. It was a sensible request, for all the obvious reasons. In attempting to parlay with the enemy, and to gain safe passage for the wounded, being clearly identifiable as a medic, and not a combatant, would be crucial.

Between them they selected the best armband they had and fastened it in position on Johnson's arm. One of the surviving jeeps was chosen, with which Johnson would drive into Benghazi, come daylight, leaving the Italian medic to care for the wounded. Upon reaching the city, he would need to convince the German and Italian defenders to provide an ambulance, with which to return and collect the stretcher cases, and to ferry them to the nearest hospital. The jeep had ample fuel for the journey. Johnson had his compass. What more was there to do or to say?

There was *one* thing. The very worst of all. Breaking the news to the wounded.

Drongin – the man Pleydell had been forced to operate on beside the track, even as they had been hounded by enemy warplanes – seemed beyond caring. Dosed up and dead to the world. In his weakened state, Webster – the man whose leg had been amputated – was never going to make the journey to Kufra, so in a sense he was only learning the inevitable. But others were far less sanguine.

Captain Bailey, whose punctured lung was still holding up, found the dark news 'a bitter pill to have to swallow'. Sergeant Sque, shot twice through the thigh, swore that he was fit to travel, although of course, without space for a stretcher on the few remaining trucks, he was going nowhere. Macleod – with his shattered arm – vowed that come hell or high water he was going to climb aboard a vehicle and get out of there. As for Mélot, he simply refused to be left behind. If necessary, he'd walk the entire way back to friendly lines.

For Pleydell, this was the bitterest of moments. He couldn't help but feel that he was deserting them. He tried to proffer a few last words – an attempt to sound encouraging – but what in truth was there to be hopeful for? Then, he offered each of those who were to be left behind – Drongin, Bailey, Webster and Sque – a brief handshake, before turning to walk away. Mélot and Macleod remained adamant that they would join the convoy, wherever space could be found aboard a vehicle.

The scene was utterly desolate, the black of the night riven with the fires of those vehicles that were still burning; a veil of acrid smoke hanging over all; the stench of scorching rubber lying bitter on the air. Here and there Pleydell could spy the odd group of men sifting through the wreckage, to see what they might salvage for the coming journey. He sought out Johnson one last time. He found the unfortunate medical orderly buttoning up his coat and stamping his feet against the chill.

'Goodbye, Johnson. I'm sorry about all this. It's very bad luck.'

'Well, someone had to stay, sir.'

'Yes.' Pleydell paused. An awkward silence. 'You are quite sure what you have to do?'

'Yes, sir.'

'You've got the morphia and syringe?'

'Yes, sir. Thank you.'

'Well, goodbye, Johnson. All the best.'

'Goodbye, sir.'

They shook hands. Pleydell went to find his jeep. Shaw, his taciturn but ever-reliable driver, was already at the wheel. Before getting under way, Shaw tried regaling Pleydell with a tale about how their vehicle had survived that day's aerial onslaught. He seemed uncharacteristically talkative, and Pleydell didn't doubt that it was all for his own benefit, in an effort to bolster his spirits. But it was a hopeless task. Pulling a blanket over his head, with barely a word Pleydell curled up exhaustedly, seeking the oblivion of sleep.

As the jeep jerked into motion, Pleydell drifted into an uneasy slumber, one punctured by hallucinations and fevered dreams. 'Confused, frightening thoughts swept across my mind and dropped away in the darkness.' At one point, Pleydell jerked awake, convinced that they were surrounded by the enemy, seeing hostile figures dashing out of the darkness. He yelled out a warning to Shaw. In truth, there was nobody there. At another, he was convinced their jeep had been left behind, the rest of the column speeding off into the darkness. And so the nightmare drive – 'cheerless'; 'suddenly terrified'; 'fighting to keep alert' – continued.

As they dropped down from the Jebel, pushing into the open desert, that old enemy – the 'faint glimmer of lightness in the east' – caught up with them. First light revealed an utterly godforsaken landscape. It was as flat as a billiard table in all directions. If they were trapped here come sunrise, they were dead men, for the enemy pilots were certain to find them. Here and there voices cursed at their ill-fortune. Why this, after all that had transpired? The sound carried clearly on the still dawn air. It was bitterly cold, and the situation seemed quite hopeless.

'At this hour, our spirits had sunk to their lowest ebb,' remarked Pleydell.

Then, an altogether different note cut the air – the plaintiff tones of a mouth organ. One of the men had begun to play. At first, he chose a romantic lament, the 'sobbing notes' rising and falling hauntingly. All around the cursing and grumbling died away. All listened. The tune changed, morphing into a Highland reel, and then a Scottish marching song, as one by one men began to whistle along to the spine-chilling cadence, and scores of booted feet began to stamp in time, beating out a rhythm on the footwells and floors of the vehicles. Gradually, but increasing in tempo and passion, sonorous voices rose in song all along the line of battle-worn vehicles, echoing across the empty desert terrain.

It was one of those uniquely special moments wherein the fortunes of a battle – or, as in this case, a desperate escape and evasion – turned.

The long column of vehicles, isolated in the wilderness, pressed on, hope renewed, faith restored. Somehow, all were gripped by a 'strange sense of restoration of endeavour'. Shortly, a patch of cover emerged, seemingly from nothing. It was little more than a paintbrush-splash of low bushes, cut here and there by shallow ditches, but it was enough. Edging their vehicles into its embrace, it felt as if this was an answer to their prayers. Feverishly, the fugitives dragged camo-nets across jeeps and trucks, before scattering clumps of vegetation all over them.

Even as they were doing so, the signature snarl of V12 aero-engines cut the dawn skies. A pair of Me 109s flashed through the heavens, just to the north of their place of hiding, looking 'ugly and full of spite'. The pilots must have failed to spot anything, for they thundered on by. Once they were gone, Pleydell got the wounded carefully hidden, after which he tried to grab some rest. It was dawn on 16 September 1942, and though few could know it, they'd covered barely eight miles from the Wadi Gamra during that long night's drive. The rough country of the Jebel had frustrated their progress, but so too had the sheer weight being carried by the overloaded vehicles.

Rations were painfully short. They had one bottle of water per man to last them through the day, and there would be no food until evening. Worse still, there was simply not enough fuel to get them back to Kufra. Without somehow securing further supplies, they were as good as done for. That being the case, Mayne had volunteered his services. Gathering a few vehicles and men, he had sped on ahead of the convoy, aiming to continue into the desert, in a nonstop dash towards an uncertain promise of salvation. Mayne's intention was to reach the Jalo Oasis, which lay some 500 kilometres further south. While Jalo had been held by the enemy for some time now, a sister force to the SAS had been charged to attack and to seize it, even as Stirling's raiders had gone in to attack Benghazi.

Banking on the fact that Jalo now lay in Allied hands, the hope was that there they might secure those desperately needed fuel supplies, hence Mayne serving as their pathfinder and their trailblazer. At Jalo, he hoped to achieve their deliverance. But of course, if the assault on the oasis had failed, the future would be dark indeed. While Mayne and his column had begun their dash south, Stirling had opted to remain behind in the Jebel, together with three jeeps, one of which was a wireless vehicle, plus a handful of men. Stirling's plan was to search for any stragglers and the missing, in an effort to ensure that they, too, might somehow make it home.

In short, the original Operation Bigamy force was splintered, strung out across the desert, and in dire need of salvation. For Pleydell, the responsibility of caring for the wounded had proved a huge mental strain, not to mention being forced to abandon those stretcher cases, together with his orderly. In time, he would write home to his then sweetheart about how 'bloody awful' it was to lose so many 'good friends'. As for the SAS itself, this was do-or-die stuff. Operation Bigamy had involved pretty much the entirety of their force, and certainly all the senior and experienced commanders. If they failed to make it home, the unit itself would very likely die with them.

From personal experience, Pleydell was well aware of what fate befell those who became marooned in the desert. At one stage his patrol had stumbled upon the wreckage of an RAF Bristol Blenheim that had crash-landed in the empty wastes. The crew had been engaged upon a flight to the Kufra Oasis, which at that time served as the forward base for the SAS, and was the point to which their convoy was heading now, in their desperate bid to reach safety. A 'slight error in navigation' had resulted in the twin-engine Blenheim running out of fuel. The pilot had had no option but to execute a forced landing in the open desert, ending up a huge distance away from his intended destination.

The aircraft had lurched over in the soft sand, coming to a halt all out of kilter. That had allowed Pleydell to clamber into its cockpit. There, he had 'tried to read the notes of the navigator', as a hot and eerie wind had moaned through the aircraft's buckled propellers and her wireless cables. Those scribbled notes told the saddest of stories: a wrong turn, a lack of fuel, the forced landing . . . A rough grave had been dug near by, the final resting place of one of the three-man crew. But where were the others? 'Lost at sea,' was all that Pleydell had been able to surmise.

On another occasion, he had himself become lost, and all due to his own lack of vigilance. He'd wandered off from his patrol to 'relieve himself'. It was night, and while he was gone the men had settled down to sleep. By the time Pleydell was done, and went to rejoin his patrol, he'd realised he had not the slightest clue in which direction they might be. Being lost in the dark like that, and alone, 'created a fear all of its own'. Pleydell had had to force himself not to panic. He'd taken a grip on himself, lit a cigarette and settled down to watch, to listen and to wait . . . Finally, after what had seemed like an age, a distant noise had betrayed the location of the patrol, and he'd found his way back again.

But in truth, Pleydell would far rather face those kinds of hardships and tribulations, compared to the terrible trials that lay behind them, with the wounded, not to mention whatever might lie ahead. The day dragged on, and the enemy came hunting in their droves. Sometimes, the warplanes passed so low overhead that the pilot's face was clearly visible. The sun rose higher. The shade dissipated. The heat crawled and clawed. No one could risk the slightest move. With the approach of dusk their presence had yet to be detected, which seemed like a miracle in itself. But as Pleydell had barely been able to risk the slightest movement during that long, hot day, he had been kept away from his duties with the wounded.

As the skies cleared of enemy warplanes and the sun began to set, he hurried over to his jeep and grabbed his medical kit. First stop was Macleod, who, sure enough, was clinging onto life stubbornly. Helped aboard a truck at Wadi Gamra, Macleod had dragged his shattered arm with him. A quick shot of sedative, and Pleydell was able to cut away the dead tissue from his injuries and to properly splint the arm. This was the first time the SAS doctor had had a chance to properly inspect it. To Pleydell's eye it looked as if two 'explosive bullets' had hit Macleod's arm, for the wounds were horribly torn and ragged.

Even as he was finishing his task, an enemy warplane – hopefully, the last of the day – streaked across the desert to the east. The sedative was wearing off and Macleod came to. The injured man, half-delirious, grabbed Pleydell's arm, and, as he wept hysterically, he begged the SAS doctor not to leave him.

'Let me come with you! Oh, please don't leave me!' Mired as he was in his 'anaesthetic delusions', Macleod's mind was trapped within a horrible loop, reliving the events on the Jebel, when the worst of the stretcher cases had been abandoned to the mercy of the enemy. Finally, Pleydell managed to reassure and to pacify Macleod, and to settle him, after which he headed to the cook's lorry, for the first – and only – meal of the day was about to be served. Rations were a small bowl of porridge and a mug of hot black tea. Even so, it cheered everyone's spirits immensely.

With sundown, the vehicles got going once more, a 'crocodile procession' creeping into the desert, and endeavouring to move at a pace and via a route that would avoid causing the wounded too much suffering. Fortunately, they had an ace desert navigator to lead the way. Willis Michael 'Mike' Sadler was a Brit who'd been working on an East African ranch prior to the war. Volunteering to fight, he'd run into some members of the LRDG, by chance, in a Cairo bar. Deciding to join their ranks, from his very first outing with the unit he'd been fascinated by the craft of desert survival and navigation.

Sadler had gone on to learn the nuts and bolts of how to cross vast expanses of uncharted desert, his instructor being a former seaman then serving with the LRDG. It was most appropriate, for steering a route across the desert had much in common with doing so across an ocean, both of which tended to be vast and featureless – and quite deadly to those marooned within their trackless expanse. Largely a process of celestial observations, married up with rigorous calculations and record keeping, there was also an instinctive gut-feeling that was crucial to such work, with which Sadler seemed uncannily blessed. In time, he had graduated from the LRDG to the SAS. Arguably there was no one better to lead the column bearing the wounded towards the distant promise of safety.

Steering the convoy of vehicles away from the Jebel, Sadler plotted a route by observing the heavens. At regular points he paused to check his position, using a sextant to take a reading of the stars, which gave him a decent fix. He cross-checked that with his 'dead-reckoning' – a set of scribbles noting direction travelled times speed, which equalled distance covered – recording all on his charts. But one of the chief challenges of such tradecraft was the lack of any reliable maps. So much of the desert, bar the fertile coastal strip, was unexplored and uncharted. Even so, Sadler exuded a quiet, understated confidence. He was truly gifted, without ever having to show off or posture.

As Sadler led that long line of vehicles into the wastes, there were well over a thousand kilometres of hostile desert terrain lying before them, and he was guiding an overloaded convoy burdened with the injured, that had nowhere near enough fuel to reach journey's end. Yet Sadler looked as if he were embarking upon nothing more than an 'interesting game', Pleydell observed. While they were still a very long way from home, Sadler would express his overriding emotion as being, 'glad to still be alive ... I think everybody thinks that it is always going to be somebody else who gets killed – you do think you are almost beyond it. But that raid was a pretty close-run thing for most of us.'

Under Sadler's unerring guidance they carved a path deeper into a desert cloaked in darkness, each turn of the wheels taking them further from the reach or the scrutiny of the hunters. Few pilots liked to venture far into the Sahara, for the simple reason that if their aircraft malfunctioned they would be forced to bale out, or to crash-land, amid such inhospitable terrain, where the chances of survival were just about zero.

That night the convoy made good progress, and after lying up in cover the next day they pressed on, the second night's drive turning into a repeat of the first. By then Sadler reckoned they were far enough from the coastal strip to risk pushing on, come daylight. They motored into the dawn of 18 September 1942, and kept driving all through the heat of the day. For the wounded especially, there was a sense that keeping moving was good, for at least it allowed a cooling breeze to wash over the vehicles. Shortly after midday they came across a hugely encouraging sign, proving that Sadler had steered them well and true: they'd found the very tracks that they had made when driving north from Kufra, on the outward leg of Operation Bigamy.

While they'd yet to cover half of their journey, ahead lay the Jalo Oasis, which in turn presented the fugitives with something of a quandary. If all had gone to plan, the oasis should have been captured by the men of the Sudan Defence Force (SDF). The SDF was a British military outfit raised locally, in Sudan, initially as a border defence corps, but one that had increasingly operated in conjunction with the LRDG, especially as the war had intensified. With a heavily armed, camel-mounted warrior as their cap-badge, the SDF patrolled the desert both on camel and horseback, but also boasted squads of armoured cars, plus open-backed trucks mounted with 2-pounder field guns. Their forces were designed to be fast, nimble and wraithlike, being able to attack and withdraw as the vagaries of this kind of fast-moving warfare demanded. They also relied upon the innate desert lore of the Sudanese troops to give them an edge.

For their raid on Jalo, codenamed Operation Nicety, the SDF

had assembled a bespoke unit, christened 'Force Z', with which to lay siege to the enemy stronghold. But had they been successful? If their mission had suffered anything like the same fate as Operation Bigamy, the defenders at Jalo – mostly Italian troops – would have been furnished with ample forewarning. In which case Jalo's defences would have been strengthened and the garrison reinforced, to repulse the attackers. If that had happened, the much-hoped-for supplies of fuel would be beyond the reach of any British forces.

After the losses they had suffered on the Jebel, the convoy carrying the wounded was desperately low on petrol. If there was none to be had at Jalo, very shortly they would run dry. As the shadows lengthened and the column of vehicles edged forward, moving at a dead slow, the first hints of battle reached them from the direction of the Jalo Oasis – the thud of distant artillery, plus the odd 'shuddering explosions' of bursting bombs. By the distinctive crump of that artillery fire, it sounded as if Force Z was still in the process of laying siege to Jalo, and that the battle was very much still in swing.

The column pulled to a halt. The discovery that the battle for Jalo was ongoing – if that was what this signified – 'concerned us all deeply', Pleydell confessed, especially since the condition of the wounded was critical. There was only so much that men like Mélot or Macleod could take, before the constant battering, the burning heat and the lack of sufficient food or water, not to mention proper medical care, would get the better of them. The able-bodied men gathered, listening to the 'thud and boom of cannon' and wondering what on earth they should do next.

Eventually, a decision was reached to send a scouting party on ahead. Two trucks, under the command of Lieutenant Alexander

James 'Sandy' Scratchley, a relatively recent recruit to the SAS, were to be sent forward, with a skeleton crew. Their mission was simple: they were to feel out the way, assess the status of the battle, and try to scavenge enough fuel to get the convoy the remaining 650 kilometres to Kufra. Those jerrycans of petrol, loaded aboard their trucks, would be the life-saver all were hoping for. If, as intended, Mayne and his convoy had been here ahead of them, then very possibly the SAS commander would have been able to sort out and earmark supplies in advance.

'Away they went and were soon lost to sight,' Pleydell noted of Scratchley and his trucks, carrying all their hopes with them.

The rest of the column wheeled away from the sound of battle, seeking cover. They found a grove of stunted palm trees – outliers of the oasis. Closely spaced, dense, with a low-lying canopy of fronds, they provided perfect cover. There they 'hid the vehicles, ate our solitary meal of the day, and prepared ourselves for a welcome night's rest,' Pleydell noted. For the first time in what seemed like an age, he slept the sleep of the dead. While they were still very far from salvation, hope springs eternal. Refuelled, and with one last push to Kufra, deliverance should be well within their grasp.

But all that night and the following morning there was no sign of Scratchley or his trucks. The tension began to mount. There was little to do but wait. No food would be served until the evening. They each had their one bottle of water to eke out with precious care. Short of hospitalisation, there was little more Pleydell could do for the wounded. With their tobacco exhausted, nervous soldiers tried to improvise. Crushing up the parched remains of some dried palm fronds, they rolled it in some paper and attempted to light up. The acrid, choking results proved spectacularly unpalatable.

Increasingly, the question on everyone's minds was this: *what had happened to Scratchley and his team?* As the hours dragged by, their disappearance became all the more worrying. From the direction of Jalo the sound of battle rolled on. At one stage an aircraft flew directly over the column's hidden position, reigniting that horrifying feeling of being hunted, and of being utterly helpless and unable to do anything to strike back. Pleydell began to wonder if they would have to cut their rations still further; less water and less food, to prepare for whatever trials lurked in the desert.

Water, in particular, was the issue. A human could go for weeks without food, but just a matter of days without fresh water. The less that each man was issued as his daily ration, the more nerves would be set on edge and tempers spike. Eventually, it would reach the stage where the very 'sound of someone else drinking could cause envy and fray the temper', Pleydell noted in his diary. This was entirely psychological, of course, for whether a fellow soldier chose to 'eke out their water bottle in sips, or drink it in gulps' had no bearing on another's meagre supplies. But severe dehydration was a terrible thing. Pleydell had seen what it could do to people and dreaded its onset.

Bob Mélot was particularly troubled. The Belgian was assailed by swarms of ants, which seemed to be driven wild by the scent and the taste of the dried blood that caked his injuries. Tiny, voracious, implacable, there was nothing that Pleydell seemed able to do to prevent them from besieging the injured man, and working their way into his wounds. There wasn't even the water to spare to bathe them properly. Compared to what had gone before – carrying out that track-side surgery on Drongin, for example, as the enemy warplanes had swooped and dived overhead – this paled into insignificance, but no one was pretending that the injured could brave such predations indefinitely.

For a moment, Pleydell wondered what fate had befallen those four stretcher cases – those that he had been forced to leave behind, together with the unflappable, phlegmatic Johnson, charged to deliver them into enemy hands. In reality, it was hugely fortunate that Pleydell didn't know their dark and terrible fortunes. He would have been tortured by the truth. Grief-stricken. And right now, Mélot, and the other walking wounded needed him. It was best that the SAS doctor didn't know the full bitter reality. In this instance, ignorance really was bliss, at least comparatively speaking.

By nightfall, there was still no sign of Scratchley or his party. Something had gone wrong, that was for sure. In their absence, one of the SAS's long-experienced officers and foremost raiders stepped forward, a man who had had more than his fair share of epic getaways during the war. Lieutenant Bill Fraser – the commander of the escape from Marble Arch – set off into the gathering darkness, driving one jeep, and with another providing backup. It was vital to discover what had happened at Jalo. Sheer exhaustion was setting in, particularly with the wounded, and the earlier high point in their spirits – triggered by the mouth organist's evocative playing – was fast being forgotten.

Fraser and his jeeps were swallowed into the night. As Pleydell well appreciated, this level of uncertainty – this life-and-death, rollercoaster ride – was 'not good for the morale'. As the wait dragged on, he had time to think. He realised that today was 19 September, his father's birthday. What would his parents be doing to celebrate, he wondered? Would they visit the cinema, to treat themselves to a movie? What had his mother seen fit to give his father as a birthday treat – maybe some gramophone records? The family had a fine collection, but there was always room for more. As he lay back and stared into the heavens, he allowed himself to indulge in a delicious, but bitter-sweet dream about what it would be like to spend just a few precious moments at home.

Three hours after Fraser had set out, Pleydell and the others were shaken from sleep by the noise of approaching engines. Shortly, a pair of Willys jeeps nosed out of the darkness. Amazingly, Fraser was back, and with him the mystery was well and truly solved. Sure enough, he had managed to make contact with the SDF's Force Z, but only by the narrowest of margins. The siege of Jalo, though hard fought, had ultimately proved abortive. The Italian defenders had known the attack was coming, and had stiffened their defences. Failing to seize the oasis, Force Z were poised to withdraw under the cover of darkness. Indeed, they were to do so on the express orders of MEHQ.

A message had winged its way through the ether, from Cairo, to Kufra and onwards to Force Z. MEHQ had been warned that Blair Mayne had reached Jalo, and had sent back orders that the SAS advance party was 'to keep with Force Z who are withdrawing tonight . . .' It was followed up with a second message, to make matters even clearer: 'Tell Mayne that his force is to withdraw with Force Z.' No matter what he might have intended, the SAS commander had been ordered to pull out of Jalo, and Fraser had caught them all just in the nick of time. An hour or so later, and the two parties would have missed each other completely.

As it was, Fraser had been able to get two crucial things sorted. One, he'd solved the mystery over Scratchley and his men. Unwittingly, they had driven into the no-man's-land separating the two warring sides, getting trapped between the opposing parties' guns. Pinned down and taking fire from both directions, they had been unable to move. Secondly, Fraser had managed to secure enough petrol for the convoy to refuel. It was ready and waiting in a cache. While Mayne had been ordered to withdraw, he was determined to leave the means for those Operation Bigamy parties that followed him to reach home.

Having shared around some delicious dates – fresh from the oasis – Fraser grabbed some trucks and set off once more, to fetch in the fuel supplies. Of course, Fraser's was the most 'wonderful news'. Like his close friend, Paddy Mayne, Pleydell was a firm believer in luck and fate. He'd pen a letter to his sweetheart about how, even here in the deep desert, the number thirteen had proved to be a curse. 'I haven't told you, but thirteen has been unlucky for me out here,' he wrote. 'I have been in two attacks launched on the thirteenth, but they were both such utter wash-outs and we only just got away . . .' Operation Bigamy had gone ahead on 13 September 1942, of course.

But right now, with Fraser's news, it seemed as if their fortunes might just be turning. With daybreak, Fraser was back, bringing with him Scratchley and his men. Once the vehicles were refuelled, the party decided to await nightfall, after which the plan was to drive hell-for-leather for Kufra. Once they were past Jalo, there was a flat, hard-beaten track running due south across the desert plains. The men knew it well, for they'd followed it on their outwards journey. If they made it to there in one piece, they should be close to being home and dry.

They set out just prior to sundown. Soon, they were speeding along that 'flat, beaconed track', one marked at regular intervals with stone cairns. Over terrain this level and uniform, even the trucks carrying the worst of the injured could average 30–40 mph, for the wounded 'were not upset by the speed'. Like this they finally arrived at Bir Zighen, a remote waterhole that doubled as the site of a cache of hidden supplies. Sheltered in a depression in the desert, Bir Zighen marked the gateway to the Great Sand Sea, the rolling ocean of sand-dunes that stretched from there south much of the way to Kufra.

Here the convoy paused, and mostly so that those riding in it could gorge themselves on the goodies that were stored at Bir Zighen. 'I fear we all made pigs of ourselves,' Pleydell confessed. The escapees found themselves eating and drinking for the pure pleasure of it, until their bellies grew 'heavy and swollen'. The simple knowledge that there was food and water aplenty felt 'too wonderful' to be captured in words. There was an extra bonus at that waterhole. Force Z was there, the SDF column, and their presence offered some much-needed respite for the worst of Pleydell's wounded.

Force Z had paused, for their column was likewise burdened with casualties. Their doctor was worried about whether his worst cases would make it through the Great Sand Sea unscathed. Hence Force Z had radioed headquarters, seeking to call in an evacuation aircraft to fly the wounded the rest of the way home. Near by, there was a makeshift airstrip that had been carved out of the desert, one that had been used previously by Allied aircraft. Indeed, various signals had been winging their way back and forth, trying to get the extra transport sorted, whether by air, or overland if need be.

One message, stamped MOST SECRET, reported, '15 ten-tonners being dispatched to you earliest. NO, repeat NO more vehicles at present available.' The SAS were driving 3-tonne trucks, so this represented a heavy convoy. Another, dispatched on 19 September, declared that recce aircraft were out, searching for the missing, but that the entire area 'could not be covered properly by single aircraft'. Another, sent shortly after, declared that 'HQ RAF have conditionally authorised use of one Bombay ... RAF to inform Force Z LG [landing ground] selected and time ammunition will be dumped.' The in-bound plane, a Bristol Bombay – an ageing duel-purpose bomber-transport aircraft – would be delivering ammunition ('amm'), in addition to picking up the wounded. Further signals requested 'fullest details casualties', while checking that those on the ground 'know drill for guiding aircraft to land'.

Chatting to the Force Z doctor, Pleydell suggested that he leave his worst cases – Macleod and Bob Mélot – in that man's care. That way, he might save them the trauma of the onwards passage through the sea of sand dunes. The Force Z doctor readily agreed, especially as their convoy possessed covered trucks, which would at least offer some shelter from the beating sun. The SAS's 3-tonners were all lacking in covers, leaving them open to the elements, which for the wounded represented a hellish trial, especially as they were largely immobilised due to their injuries.

With that sorted, Pleydell busied himself one last time cleaning and dressing Mélot and Macleod's wounds. He bade them farewell, explaining that this time, there was no chance of them being abandoned. On the contrary, remaining with Force Z offered them the very best chance of survival, and of a swift, pain-free route out of there. Promising that he would see them back in Kufra, Pleydell joined the waiting convoy as it pulled out, moving south, 'away over the ridged Sand Sea ... with its fierce white glare, its cruel slopes of soft sinking sand ... away, over the desolate, undulating wastes ...'

There was no doubt in Pleydell's mind that Mélot and Macleod were far better off where he'd left them, awaiting the RAF to whisk them to safety. Pushing beyond the far fringes of the Great Sand Sea, that evening's 'fine pinks and mauves' illuminated a fantastic scene of wind-sculpted rocks and cliffs, the twisted moonscape fading into the 'softer shades of distance'. Gradually, the 'barren hills turned to icy blueness' as the evening drew in, Pleydell declaring that at any minute 'one could well imagine some dragon would emerge'. Through such terrain, peopled by dragons and giants, as Pleydell imagined it, their 'small weary procession threaded its way'.

At dawn on the following day, the gathering light revealed a faint green smudge on the horizon – the distinctive signature of the Kufra Oasis, lying far ahead. It was an almost impossible vision, but at last Pleydell, plus the others riding in that battered convoy, allowed themselves to believe that they had made it. That mirage-like apparition, shuddering in the early morning heat haze, signalled that they were home.

The convoy of battered vehicles pulled up beside an ancient white-walled fortress that guarded the northern entry to the oasis. One by one, the dust-encrusted jeeps and trucks filed down into the vast expanse of greenery below, interspersed here and there with palm-fringed lakes and lagoons.

As Pleydell's driver, Shaw, eased their vehicle into motion, so he remarked, cheerfully: 'Home at last!'

Pleydell turned to eye the taciturn figure. Shaw had a faint smile playing on his lips and he was beating out some jazz rhythm or other on the jeep's steering wheel. 'D'you remember when you said that last?' Pleydell asked.

'*Aywa!*' Shaw barked – yes, in Arabic. He laughed, sagely. He knew exactly what the SAS doctor was driving at. 'But not to worry this time.'

The last time Shaw had declared that they were home safely, it hadn't quite turned out that way. It didn't this time, either. Not long after pulling to a halt at the SAS's Kufra encampment, the enemy warplanes came. It was a flight of eight Heinkel He 111 bombers. For forty minutes they swooped low over the oasis, strafing and bombing. To find them venturing this far south was something of a shock, as Kufra was generally seen as being immune to air-attack. To have to shelter beneath the palms, and be hunted from the air again, felt like the ultimate ignominy for those who, against all odds, had made it here.

Fortunately, the SAS patrols remained largely unscathed by both bullets and bombs. The thick cover of the palms hid them well. The anti-aircraft guns dotted around the oasis had also given a good account of themselves. Pleydell figured that around half of those enemy warplanes had been shot down. But their very presence here at Kufra had to reflect how deeply the exploits of the desert raiders had got to the enemy's senior commanders. This was a vengeance mission, and few doubted why those aircraft had been dispatched.

By now the SAS had come to the personal attention of General Erwin Rommel, more popularly known as 'the Desert Fox' to both his own and Allied troops. The Afrika Korps commander was well aware that 'Stirling's commandos' had caused his forces 'considerable havoc', not to mention disquiet. As a consequence, Rommel ordered that a special unit be established, equipped, trained and tasked to seek out and destroy the desert raiders. 'Stirling's commandos' were to be hunted down remorselessly.

Shortly after arriving at Kufra, the SAS patrols were also warned about an intercepted German radio message, which declared that David Stirling supposedly had been taken prisoner. The news spread fast and Winston Churchill himself intervened from London. Churchill cabled Cairo: 'Personal from Prime Minister to Commander-in-Chief, Middle East. Have you heard any rumours that David Stirling is missing?' It was a massive relief when Stirling and his rearguard finally made it safely to Kufra.

Stirling and his party had lingered for as long as they could in the Jebel, attempting to round up some of the dozens of missing men. Writing in the SAS War Diary, Stirling would conclude of Operation Bigamy: 'I lost about 50 three-tonners [trucks] and about 40 jeeps on this raid but fortunately not very many personnel ... It was a sharp lesson that confirmed my previous views ...' In truth, Bigamy had been an unmitigated disaster. As all had known from the outset, the mission was woefully ill-conceived. Imposed on the SAS from on high, many fine men had lost their lives, or suffered terrible injuries.

Regardless, Operation Bigamy and the associated desert raids would be portrayed as a standout success by MEHQ, the originators of the entire plan. Headlines in the British press ran: 'DESERT FORCE STRIKES BEHIND ENEMY LINES: DARING RAIDS ON JALO AND BENGHAZI'. Details of the operations were passed to the press in a 'Joint War communiqué' describing a series of 'daring British raids', which had aimed to 'cause as much alarm and despondency as possible' to the enemy. 'Our desert forces have carried out successful operations over 500 miles behind the enemy's front,' the communiqué trumpeted, concluding that 'our forces have now arrived back at their bases.'

While stretching the truth, one thing was absolutely certain: getting the majority of the raiders back from the jaws of death, and the hell of the desert, *was* an outstanding and incredible achievement. Writing to his sweetheart during the aftermath of the long escape from Operation Bigamy, Pleydell would relate how he had brought back two of the most seriously wounded, plus 'all the minor cases', against all odds. With understandable pride he described Macleod, 'with a shattered arm', and Mélot, 'with multiple wounds', and how both had managed to survive 'the long trek home'. The escape and evasion of those who were uninjured was an incredible achievement; to have got most of the wounded out as well was little short of a miracle.

Evacuated to hospital in Cairo, Bob Mélot would make a full recovery from his injuries. Indeed, barely two months after he had suffered those grenade wounds, Mélot would be discharged into the care of his wife in Alexandria. That same month he was back on active duty. He would continue to serve with distinction in the SAS until late 1944. Tragically, on 11 November, Mélot would be killed in a motor accident in Belgium, when his jeep skidded off a road in wet and muddy conditions. His was a loss sorely felt by all. Mayne, then commander of 1 SAS and a very close friend of Mélot's, would write to his wife in typically moving terms:

I find it impossible to tell you how sorry I am about Bob's death. We find it hard to realise that we will not see him again, there is no other officer or man in the unit who could have been spared less . . . Our Regiment has suffered a very grievous loss: Bob was respected and liked by everyone in the unit and I myself have lost a very good friend and a person whose advice and council meant very much to me . . . Your husband was one of the finest persons I have ever known.

Amazingly, Gentleman Jim Almonds and his crew, riding in the first jeep into the Benghazi ambush, survived the blast that tore their vehicle to pieces, leaping free just before it exploded. Captured by the enemy, Almonds would mount several escape attempts before finally managing to slip the enemy's clutches, breaking out of a POW camp in Italy. He reached Britain in time to rejoin the SAS, and to be deployed in support of the D-Day landings, serving in its ranks with distinction until war's end.

Pleydell would go on to be awarded a Military Cross for his Benghazi heroics, and most specifically for caring for the wounded. During the initial onslaught he had continued to do so, even though 'it was extremely dangerous to move by day owing to the Italian and German aircraft which were searching the area and bombing and machine-gunning anything seen'. Pleydell had acted 'without any thought for his own safety . . . giving morphia and dressing their wounds, paying no attention to the bullets or bombs'. Isolated hundreds of miles from the nearest Allied hospital, he 'undoubtedly saved many lives by his bravery and skill', the citation concluded.

Sadly, none of the stretcher cases that had been left at the Wadi Gamra, to be delivered into the care of the enemy by Pleydell's volunteer medic, would survive. The exact fate of Captain Chris Bailey, Sergeant Arthur Sque, Corporal James Webster and Corporal Anthony Drongin remains unclear. When Pleydell learned of their loss, he was distraught. While he had feared that Drongin and Bailey might fail to make it, Webster and Sque should have stood every chance of pulling through. It was a cause of even greater distress to Pleydell when he discovered that his medical orderly, Razor Blade Johnson, also had not survived. Largely, their fate remains a mystery to this day.

But one thing was for certain, following Operation Bigamy. The enemy's foremost commanders had turned their gimlet eye on Britain's Special Service volunteers.

The SAS were set to pay a heavy price in death and in blood.

Chapter Four

THE PHANTOM RAIDERS

January 1943, Tunisia

On Christmas Eve, 1942, Rommel decided to go hunting. It was a rare treat for the German general to take a day off, but he figured he had earned it, though he would end up pursuing very different prey from that which he originally sought. A gifted diarist and writer, he would pen a letter to his wife, Lucia, that morning, describing in vivid terms the day ahead and the wider, dire predicament that his forces faced in North Africa. The tide of battle was turning, and Rommel's greatest worry was that his supply convoys were being harassed and harried at every turn, more often than not by Stirling's desert raiders.

'Dearest Lu,' he wrote. 'I'm going off very early this morning into the country and will be celebrating this evening among the men. They're in top spirits, thank God, and it takes great strength not to let them see how heavily the situation is pressing ... Kesselring was here yesterday. New promises were made, but it will be the same as it ever was. They can't be kept, because the enemy puts his pencil through all our supply calculations.' General Kesselring, the Commander-in-Chief South of German armed forces, had promised to deliver more supplies, but Rommel feared little would ever reach his frontline troops.

Despite his worries, just after dawn on 24 December 1942 he set out into the open desert, on what was 'a beautiful sunny morning'. Flanked by an armoured car escort, Rommel's small convoy slipped through the 'fantastically fissured Wadi Zem-Zem' – a vast chasm that cut through the desert, stretching 150 kilometres far to the south of the Libyan capital, Tripoli. Hemmed in by the craggy cliffs that towered to either side, Rommel and his party hoped to bag some 'Christmas dinner'. They kept their eyes peeled for any herds of gazelle, a small species of antelope, scattered among the sparse vegetation and dry scrub.

Instead, they came across 'the tracks of British vehicles, probably made by some of Stirling's people', as Rommel noted in his diary. The Desert Fox knew only too well that Stirling's raiders were busy everywhere 'on the job of harassing our supply traffic'. As the tracks looked fresh, Rommel and his party turned their minds to a new kind of prey, keeping 'a sharp lookout to see if we could catch a "Tommy".' A lone vehicle was spotted, and Rommel and his party gave chase, thundering across the dry terrain. But it turned out to be a false alarm. It was actually one of their own patrols.

Rommel had created a bespoke force to protect his highly mobile headquarters. It was named the *Kampfstaffel* – combat echelon – or 'Kasta', for short, and it was equipped with mostly captured British vehicles. His Kasta had been busy in the Wadi Zem-Zem region during the last few days, stumbling upon 'some British commandos' – Rommel's euphemism for the SAS – and capturing maps marked with locations of store dumps plus rendezvous points. As Rommel's focus returned to bagging some Christmas lunch – a herd of gazelles 'trotted up to us', he wrote in his diary – he ordered his *Kampfstaffel* to get busy 'combing through' the area, hoping to track down one of Stirling's patrols.

The German general managed to bring down a gazelle – one of those elusive, 'speedy animals' – so there would be fresh meat for the Christmas pot. Likewise, the Desert Fox just had to hope his *Kampfstaffel* would be equally successful in their endeavours. Barely a month later, Rommel's urgings would bear fruit in spectacular fashion, as those tasked to hunt down Stirling and his band of raiders would truly hit the jackpot.

It was January 1943, and David Stirling – recently promoted, and dubbed 'The Phantom Major' by the British and Axis press alike – was about to launch himself upon the greatest challenge of what had been a singularly dramatic military career. The SAS was not yet two years old, but it had already been granted regimental status (in fact, the unit was in the process of expanding to form two regiments, 1 and 2 SAS). Despite its detractors, it was forging a unique reputation, as tales of the desert raiders' daring exploits were whispered across the British trenches. Even so, Stirling – iron-willed and driven, yet plagued by exhaustion and illness after eighteen months of relentless back-to-back operations – was about to embark upon what was arguably the unit's most grandiose and audacious mission ever, in a history peppered with such ventures.

Stirling's plan was to steer a patrol of Willys jeeps several hundred miles beyond the main SAS squadrons, and way beyond their own frontline positions, advancing west through territory crammed with the enemy, to link up with the Allies' new front, in North-west Africa. In November 1942 a joint American-British force, bolstered by Commonwealth and Free French troops, had mounted what was then the largest amphibious operation ever undertaken by the Allies. Codenamed Operation Torch, a force of over 100,000 Allied soldiers had landed on the shores of Morocco and Algeria, seizing what would become the springboard for the advance into southern Europe.

From their newly established bases, the Operation Torch forces, now renamed 'The First Army', had pushed east in a bitterly fought campaign, even as the Eighth Army had advanced from the opposite direction, in a pincer movement designed to crush the enemy. Stirling's intention in the winter of 1942/3 was to drive right through the desert 'from one front to the other', aiming to link up with the First Army. The mission had a compelling intelligence-driven purpose – to see if it was possible to bypass the Mareth Line, a string of fortifications which constituted one of Rommel's last lines of defence in North Africa. If Stirling's patrol could pioneer a route through the deep desert by which to outflank those defences, that could spur final victory in North Africa.

But Stirling's venture also had a very different, overarching, aim: he sought to be the very first to meet those advancing American and British forces, in a spectacular piece of showmanship. As the SAS War Diary noted, 'Stirling saw the political advantages of . . . being the first to penetrate the enemy lines and connect the First Army with the Eighth.' If successful, such a dramatic gesture would put the SAS 'indelibly on the map', being one in the eye for the unit's detractors, potentially silencing them for good. Hence, on 16 January 1943 Stirling formed up a five-jeep convoy, packed with two dozen men and stuffed with supplies, as he prepared to set forth, once again aiming 'for the stars'.

The prize was glittering – 'irresistible', in Stirling's own words – but the risks were stupendous. Stirling and his small force would have to penetrate hundreds of miles of largely uncharted territory – terra incognita as far as the Allies were concerned – while navigating their way around a series of vast and treacherous salt marshes. The Chott el Djerid – the 'Lagoon of the Land of Palms' – stretched a good 250 kilometres south into the open desert. Lying below sea level, its 7,000 square kilometre expanse was beset by *fata morganas* – shimmering mirages, appearing like fairy-tale castles dancing in the air. Bone dry in the summer months and covered in a glittering but treacherous salt-crust, in winter the vast expanse of terrain flooded, adding further to the perils.

As if that were not enough, their five-vehicle patrol would also need to avoid the mass of Axis forces that were being funnelled into an ever-shrinking patch of territory, as the Eighth and First Armies closed the trap. And finally, they'd need to somehow approach the First Army's positions – presuming they got that far – without being mistaken for an enemy patrol and shot to pieces by their own side.

Stirling absolutely needed his A-Team for a mission of such unprecedented daring and scope. First and foremost, he prevailed upon Mike Sadler to join him, for Sadler's superlative navigational skills would prove invaluable. Sadler had been busy, trying to work out how to carry all the petrol such a journey would entail. In fact, it was quite simply impossible; they would need to scavenge or steal fuel en route. While wrestling with such conundrums, Sadler had been promoted to lieutenant. 'I need

In December 1941 Lieutenant Blair 'Paddy' Mayne (left, above) scored the SAS's first ever success, destroying two dozen enemy aircraft at Tamet airbase, in North Africa. Days later, Lieutenant William 'Bill' Fraser (right, above) went one better, blowing to pieces 37 enemy warplanes. But on his very next mission, Fraser and his small patrol would be trapped hundreds of miles behind enemy lines.

Both Mayne and Fraser had served with the Commandos (pictured above), prior to volunteering for the SAS. They'd trained rigorously, learning how to maintain iron water self-discipline on forced marches across moorland or burning desert. But nothing could have prepared Fraser and his four man patrol for what lay ahead.

A unit of the Long Range Desert Group (LRDG), the reconnaissance specialists, were to collect Fraser and his patrol, after their deep-desert raid. Yet all but one of their vehicles were destroyed by enemy warplanes, leaving Fraser and his men to undertake a death-defying trans-Saharan march in an effort to escape.

In June 1942, an SAS patrol commanded by Major Georges Bergé and Captain George Jellicoe, carried out a spectacularly successful raid on a German airbase on Crete, damaging and destroying dozens of warplanes, plus hangars, ammo and bomb dumps. But during the escape and evasion that followed the raiders were hunted by an enraged and vengeful enemy.

Dropped by a submarine on Cretan shores to execute the raid, the epic journey to their intended pick-up by armed trawler would be dogged by disaster. Jellicoe (above, aboard ship, behind kettle) was the sole SAS raider to make it out of there. All the other raiders were either killed or captured – Bergé and Jacques Mouhot (below, depicted in a wartime article) going on to make a series of daring escape attempts.

In September 1942, the SAS set out in a massive convoy of heavily armed jeeps and trucks, to execute Operation Bigamy, a mission ordered from on high, but which 'sinned against every founding precept of the SAS.' The results were utterly disastrous, leaving scores of men – many of whom were badly injured – to try to escape and evade across the desert wastes.

The SAS's medic, Captain Malcolm Pleydell (centre above, with Bill Fraser, left of photo and troop leader Jim Chambers, right of photo) was left to tend to the wounded, as the raiders were harried by enemy warplanes. That so many survived and managed to get away was a truly extraordinary achievement.

In January 1943, SAS Founder Major David Stirling (right of photo) set out on the SAS's most ambitious mission ever, as his small patrol crossed hundreds of miles of uncharted territory, to link up with the Anglo-American First Army. He took with him ace navigator Lieutenant Mike Sadler (left of photo), to steer them through the desert – terra incognita to Allied forces.

Stirling, in officer's cap (centre right), together with (left to right) Archie Gibson LRDG, Reg Seekings SAS, Jack Crossley LRDG, Johnny Cooper SAS, 'Ginger' Blaney LRDG (standing behind Cooper), 'Scotty' Scott LRDG (behind Stirling), Rose LRDG, Archie Murray LRDG. Stirling's January '43 patrol was ambushed by an elite enemy unit, one charged by German General Erwin Rommel to hunt down 'Stirling's Commandos'. Only Sadler, Cooper and French SAS veteran Freddie Taxis managed to slip the trap and get away.

Above: Sadler, Cooper and Taxis' herculean escape was celebrated by *The New Yorker* magazine, for American reporter Abbot Joseph Liebling was embedded with the nearest Allied unit. He wrote in glorious detail about the heroic trio making their miraculous re-appearance, stumbling out of the sunblasted desert wastes, half-dead from thirst, their feet in tatters.

In June 1944, Captain John Elliot Tonkin (above, right of photo, pictured with David Surrey-Dane, one of his party) lead a daring SAS mission deep behind enemy lines in France, charged to stop Hitler's panzer divisions from reaching the D-Day beachheads. His patrol cut railway lines, ambushed truck convoys, and called in airstrikes on the enemy's fuel trains, flown by the superlative Mosquito fighter-bomber, the so-called 'Wooden Wonder'.

On 3 July 1944, a massive force of Waffen SS surrounded Tonkin's base. What ensued was a desperate escape and evasion, as Tonkin (seated in jeep, left of centre, with pipe) and a handful of men slipped away (pictured). From left to right: Trooper Les Keeble, unidentified, Tonkin, Sergeant Johnny Holmes, Troopers Cummings and Will Smith, Lieutenant Flamm Harper (a downed USAAF pilot), Trooper John Fielding, Signaller Plumb, unidentified.

The survivors joined forces with a French farmer and the ever-willing Maquis, to clear a rough and ready airstrip, using their jeep as a makeshift tractor, towing a chain-harrow to flatten the land. Under cover of darkness on 7 August 1944 a pair of Lockheed Hudson light bombers touched down on the strip, codenamed Bon-Bon, plucking the survivors to safety.

In July 1944, twelve SAS dropped into France, charged to lay waste to a key enemy airfield. Included in their number were Lieutenant 'Rex' Wiehe (left of photo), Corporal Thomas 'Ginger' Jones (second from left), plus Troopers Herbert Castelow (second from right), Norman (right) and 'Jock' Morrison (seated front). Betrayed, only the last three would slip the clutches of the enemy, who lay in wait at the drop zone. Ginger Jones and Serge 'Frenchy' Vaculik (above, left) would later execute a daring escape, as the SS and Gestapo went about murdering the SAS captives in cold blood.

It was Herbert Castelow's solo escape that would become the stuff of SAS legend. Hidden in a village butcher's shop, he fought in the French Resistance, cycled to Paris gathering intelligence (pictured, centre of photo), survived torture and worse to join the American 5th Recon Troop, guiding US forces across enemy lines. After his incredible escape, Castelow, plus Norman and Morrison, would soldier with the SAS across Europe in a jeep christened 'The Comeback' (above).

you as an officer,' Stirling announced. 'Go down to the market and get yourself a couple of pips.' This DIY promotion in the field would end up with Sadler getting accused of 'impersonating an officer', but for now his self-made lieutenant's pips would do very nicely.

Next, Stirling picked Sergeant Johnny Cooper for the mission, hitherto known as the 'The Kid', before Pierre Léostic, the even younger Frenchman, had usurped his place (though of course Léostic had lost his life six months earlier, during the Heraklion raid). A personal friend of Stirling's, John 'Johnny' Murdoch Cooper was the youngest of the SAS originals, having lied about his age to enlist with the Scots Guards. Since stepping forward for the SAS, Cooper had acted as Stirling's right-hand man on any number of operations, most notably winning a Distinguished Conduct Medal (DCM) in February 1942, during the raid on the Libyan port of Buerat. Ambushed by ground forces, it was Cooper's skill and courage wielding the Vickers-K machine guns that had helped blast them through.

Slight of frame, smart and with 'delicate features', Cooper had been educated at Wyggeston Grammar School for Boys, in Leicester. Though he didn't smoke and was more or less teetotal, in January the previous year he'd been obliged to go through the traditional induction in the sergeant's mess at Kabrit, for he'd just won promotion. It had involved downing a pint of cherry brandy in one, with the SAS's sergeant major, the implacable Pat Riley, presiding over the ceremonies, assuring Cooper that the sickly red liquid was 'non-alcoholic'. Cooper had immediately vomited it all up, and he spent the next forty-eight hours in bed with the hangover to die for.

Cooper was still only twenty years old, as he readied himself for departure with Stirling's patrol. With his 'fresh-faced boyish looks' at first glance he resembled a boy scout, but his outer appearance belied an unbending inner toughness, as matters were to prove. Stirling also picked Free French SAS veteran Freddie Taxis, who spoke excellent Arabic; where they were heading it was going to be crucial to be able to communicate with the locals, who were largely an unknown quantity. At thirty-one years of age, Taxis was the self-confessed 'old man' of the patrol, and he was very likely going to have his work cut out for him during the days that lay ahead.

As a radio message from Eighth Army headquarters on 10 January had warned them: 'Information received tribes SE TAR-HUNA [sic] and NALUT area very anti-British. Many enemy agents area SE AZIZIA and area also covered by daily air recces.' Tahuna, Nalut and Azizia were settlements along the path of their route, wherein the locals were not believed to be friendly, plus the skies were abuzz with enemy spotter planes, and the land thick with their agents on the ground. A further message warned that 'enemy force strengthening MARETH Line', while also advising 'SHOTT DJERID crossable on KRIZ–SKEBILE track'. In other words, the massive expanse of the Chott el Djerid salt marsh was supposedly navigable via the route specified – a certain track – although Stirling's men were having none of it. As Cooper declared of the Chott el Djerid, with conviction, it was 'quite impossible to cross by vehicle'.

Stirling had also persuaded Mayne to lend him one of his stalwart officers – the southern Irishman, Lieutenant Bill McDermott. McDermott had more than proved his worth during a string of desert raiding operations, including seizing an enemy railway station, in order to comprehensively wreck it. Plus Stirling's party would have a vanguard. A larger patrol made up of nine jeeps, carrying some two dozen Free French SAS, would act as a spearhead, forging the route ahead. That force was under the command of Lieutenant Augustin Jordan, who, following Bergé's capture on Crete, had taken over command of the Free French contingent of the Special Service volunteers.

Jordan's task was to blaze the trail, pushing ahead of Stirling's party to test the ground in action. But more than that, both patrols – Stirling's and Jordan's – were being urged by Eighth Army headquarters to hit Rommel's convoys wherever they could. Rommel's supply situation was reported to be desperate, and any action that could worsen it might tip the scales of the battle, especially in the areas where they were heading. A 15 January message from Eighth Army headquarters outlined the enemy's shifting positions, stressing: 'Greatest assistance if you could operate against . . .' As Sadler put it, succinctly, 'The orders from headquarters were to attack as often and as quickly as possible.'

Moving into country that was 'previously uncharted', this journey would prove immensely challenging. Accordingly, Cooper would share the task of navigation with Sadler, for both were highly experienced, and where they were going two heads were doubtless better than one. They would be pushing into terrain where the maps 'were completely blank, except for lines of latitude and longitude', Cooper recalled. There was a secondary reason for doubling up on the navigation. If Stirling's party were to succeed in their mission, one man – either Cooper or Sadler – was slated to peel off from the patrol, so as to guide Allied forces 'in a left hook to outflank the defensive positions' of the Mareth Line.

On 15 January 1942, with the patrol about to get under way,

Stirling radioed Eighth Army HQ in an upbeat mood: 'All well here and sport very good.' But as his convoy pushed west, the terrain worsened. Their route lay across the Great Sea Erg, an area of dunes less extensive than the Great Sand Sea, the seat of their earlier operations, and the route via which the raiders had executed their escape from Operation Bigamy. Regardless, crossing the Great Sea Erg would prove distinctly more challenging. The landscape, Stirling noted, resembled 'a rough Mediterranean sea', and there was no clear route through. While the serried ranks of the Great Sand Sea's towering dunes had proved regular and navigable, here the stormy, choppy breakers offered only a chaotic, bruising, bone-breaking ride. It was the most difficult terrain any of them had ever encountered.

Doggedly, the five jeeps pressed on, moving at a snail's pace, the overloaded vehicles rattling and groaning with every turn of the wheels. The one upside to braving the Great Sea Erg was that it enabled them to execute their reconnaissance of the southern tip of the Mareth Line: it could only be reached by such a horrendous, tortuous journey. Emerging from that sandy hell, any hopes the men may have entertained about there being better going ahead were to be dashed. Conditions just seemed to deteriorate still further. As they edged into the fringes of the Chott el Djerid, the first fingers of the salt marsh groped forwards, menacingly, interspersed with plunging chasms and patches of dense, clinging sand. The going was 'atrocious', Stirling remarked, being 'hilly with many ravines', and any flat sections were 'laced with bogs and marshes'. And in every direction the blasted terrain was plagued by shifting, beguiling mirages.

Gradually, the jeeps were nudged ever north, as they tried to avoid becoming mired within the perils of the salt marshes.

Inexorably, the five-vehicle convoy was channelled towards what was known as 'the Gabes Gap', a narrow neck of land sandwiched between the Mediterranean to the north, and the vast expanse of the Chott el Djerid to the south. Likewise, Jordan's patrol of French SAS had suffered a very similar fate, being forced to brave a passage through that heavily guarded five-mile-wide neck of land. Moving a day or so in advance of Stirling's party, Jordan's party, riding in their nine jeeps, had slipped through the Gap apparently without being detected. Yet in truth they had been watched and hunted all the way. While their patrol would sow havoc among the enemy positions lying beyond the Gabes Gap, fighting a series of running battles, most of Jordan's patrol would be injured, captured or killed.

Following directly in their wake, Stirling and his men knew none of this. Eighth Army headquarters had lost contact with Jordan's patrol: 'Cannot contact JOURDAIN [sic] as he has not been on the air,' they reported, by radio. Even as Stirling, Sadler, Cooper, Taxis, McDermott and their comrades prepared to slip through the Gabes Gap, the fate of their forerunners remained a mystery. Just before setting forth to run the gauntlet, a message from the Eighth Army offered a little something to cheer their spirits: 'Password from special source from 7 Jan to 24 Jan FOR-TUNA, repeat FORTUNA, reply FIGARO.'

At least now they knew the enemy passwords for most of January 1943. That might well prove useful, where they were heading.

At dusk the patrol got under way. No sooner had they broken cover than a pair of German spotter planes buzzed the convoy – just the kind of thing they'd been warned to be on the lookout for. Stirling knew they had been seen. The pilots simply could not have overlooked their progress. Yet there was little option but to continue.

'The going was terrible and slow,' Sadler observed, as they pushed on through the gathering night. 'We were all exhausted. I don't think we had slept for 48 hours.' Pressing on, the men had a scare, as they blundered onto what seemed to be a deserted enemy airfield. They only realised that it was an active airbase when they stumbled upon ranks of German warplanes. At another point one of the heavily laden jeeps slid into a ravine, taking hours of back-breaking work to free it again.

In the dead hours of the early morning of 23 January, they slipped through the Gabes Gap, seemingly without so much as a challenge. But a mile or so further on a German unit was camped by the roadside. It was almost light by now, and they could see the Afrika Korps soldiers 'getting up, cleaning their teeth, making coffee, that sort of thing . . .' Opting to bluff it, Stirling and his men decided to thunder on through. With feigned nonchalance – a nod and a friendly gesture – the five jeeps 'sped right past'. With sunrise not long away, they needed to find somewhere to lie up. Near by, they spied a 'series of narrow hills'. A deep wadi sliced through the heart of those dry, ragged folds. With the wadi's walls rising to some four hundred feet, it offered the promise of sanctuary, the depths of the chasm being thick with thorny bush and scrub.

Pulling into its cover, the jeeps were camouflaged as swiftly as possible, before exhausted figures bedded down, craving sleep. Stirling and his party had just completed a non-stop epic lasting several days, and they were utterly shattered. Even so, before settling down to rest, Sadler and Cooper made a point of climbing to a high ridge to get a sense of the lie of the land. A mile away they spied the coast road, clogged with enemy traffic. As they studied it through their binoculars, a line of trucks pulled to a halt, figures leaping down. Although that convoy could have halted for any number of reasons, it was somehow ominous to observe the enemy this close.

Back in the wadi, Sadler and Cooper reported what they'd seen to Stirling. There was clearly no chance of changing position now. As all agreed, they were lucky not to have been detected slipping through the Gabes Gap. There was no option but to remain where they were in hiding, and to try to grab some desperately needed rest. Stirling was determined to launch an attack come nightfall, hitting a nearby stretch of railway and an associated highway. Unless they got some sleep, not a man among them would be capable of mounting any kind of a raid.

There was some confusion about whether a watch had been set. Sadler argued it had: 'We posted sentries and went to sleep.' Others claimed it hadn't, Cooper remarking how 'none of us was in a position to be vigilant'. Either way, if sentries had been posted they didn't turn out to be particularly alert or watchful. Luckily, Sadler and Cooper had pulled their jeep right to one end of the wadi. The French SAS man, Taxis, had opted to bed down beside them. For all three, it would prove the height of good fortune.

The first sign that anything was remotely amiss were the harsh cries of: '*Raus! Raus!*' – Out! Out!

Jackboots thundered up the length and breadth of the wadi, as hundreds of figures in *Feldgrau* flooded it from end to end. Wherever an SAS man was jerked awake, he found himself staring into the barrel of an enemy soldier's gun. In reality, a 500-strong force had tracked Stirling's patrol for some time now, following the jeeps to their hideaway. These were the troops

173

of the *Fallschirmjäger* z.b.V. 250 battalion – elite paratroopers formed into a hunter-force at General Rommel's behest, with the specific task of hunting down Stirling's desert raiders. They'd even trained with captured Willys jeeps, so as to establish just what the heavily armed but nimble 4x4s were capable of, to better counter and confound them.

Moving quickly, the enemy paratroopers saturated the wadi from end to end. Stirling and McDermott – the railway station destroyer – had been sleeping in the shade of a shallow cave. They awoke to the sounds of gunfire, the thump of boots and the guttural cries of German commands. Realising what must have happened, Stirling ordered his signallers to destroy their top secret signals logs and codes, to prevent them falling into enemy hands. Then he gave the order that it was every man for himself. Stirling and McDermott made a break for it, but they were brought to a halt by a 'barking command in German', realising that 'a fantastic array of guns' were 'trained down the wadi'. The enemy had the entire place covered.

In short order the SAS founder, his key lieutenants and his men were rounded up and searched, as the enemy busied themselves dragging the camo-nets away from the patrol's jeeps and heaping up the piles of captured weaponry. Once that was done, Stirling and his party were herded aboard a convoy of waiting trucks, with a heavy guard shadowing their every move. It was dusk by the time the line of enemy vehicles pulled out. As they'd prepared to get under way, the wadi had echoed with sporadic bursts of gunfire, and the occasional grenade blast. Presumably, the enemy were trying to ensure that no one had slipped the net or would escape alive.

The vehicles jolted into motion and set out through the rough terrain. An hour or so later they pulled to a halt at a bare building that resembled a warehouse. The captives were herded inside. The captors were noticeably 'jubilant', and Stirling figured they had to know just who it was they had captured. One, who spoke decent English, told Stirling and his men that they would be getting little to eat, for there was no good reason to feed them. 'It would only be a waste . . . as we're going to shoot you,' he gloated. 'We have orders to execute all saboteurs, as an example to others who might be foolish enough to follow in your footsteps.'

Back at the wadi, three figures stirred. With infinite care, Sadler, Cooper and Taxis crawled out of the patch of camel thorn in which they had taken refuge. Their hideout lay at the very highest point of the wadi's rim, after which the terrain opened out into an exposed ridgeline and a rough, rocky plateau. Their place of refuge was little more than a shallow scoop in the earth, some three feet deep, with that smudge of spiky bush at one end. But, thank God, it had sufficed.

Hours earlier, the three men had been subjected to that harsh wakeup call: the toe of a jackboot kicked into legs or feet, and the chilling yells. Startled into wakefulness, Cooper had stared up at a 'fully equipped German parachutist with his Schmeisser sub-machine gun . . .' Beside him, Sadler was also jerked into consciousness. They'd exchanged glances, both wide-eyed with shock at the realisation that they'd been 'jumped'. They could only imagine that they were all so 'deadbeat' that the patrol's watch had fallen down. In an instant they knew that their only chance was to make a break for it, right away. For Sadler, it was a matter of 'escape or we're prisoners. It was instantaneous . . . There was nothing else to do.'

Just as soon as the enemy soldiers turned their attentions to the ongoing search, the two figures broke away. Taking only the clothes they stood up in, Sadler and Cooper executed a desperate dash for the higher ground. With them went a third escapee, Taxis, as the trio pounded up the 'narrow defile' out of which the wadi descended, at every moment fearing the enemy would catch sight of them and open fire. They reached the top and came to a fork. Taking the left-hand gully, they noticed that two other SAS men chose the one opposite, but there was no time to work out who they might be. On the trio ran, lungs gasping for breath, as the terrain grew ever more precipitous, the ground friable and loose.

They continued climbing until they 'couldn't take another step', the gully opening out into exposed ground. It was there that they'd found the shallow scoop and the patch of bush, crawling into its uncertain embrace. Sadler, Cooper and Taxis had no water, no food and no weapons. But at least they were alive and had escaped capture . . . for now. As they'd been sleeping fully dressed and wearing their boots, at least they had warm clothing and footwear, which was a massive bonus. Without boots, no one was about to make a getaway, and the desert nights were murderously cold. From below, the noise of the hunt echoed eerily, leaving little doubt as to the fate of the others.

'We had no idea if anyone else had escaped,' Sadler recalled, 'but it was fairly obvious it had been a disaster.'

As the enemy troops went about rounding up any 'stragglers', there were blasts of grenades and bursts of fire. Sadler had a bunch of highly sensitive signals stuffed in a pocket. Mindful that they weren't out of the woods yet, he managed to dig a hole and bury them, 'just in case we were captured'. Time dragged. As the afternoon shadows lengthened, the three fugitives began to hope that maybe they had slipped the net. But it was then that a group of German troops appeared. Step by step the searchers came ever closer, until it seemed inconceivable that they wouldn't alight upon the fugitives' patch of scrub. It was such an obvious place to look.

'What the hell's the German word for surrender?' Cooper whispered.

'*Kamerad*,' Sadler hissed back.

Twice the enemy patrol swept the cleft in which the trio had taken cover, until they came to a halt just 'a few feet away'. Even as the three hunted men feared they were about to be forced to give themselves up – 'when the moment would come to stand up and shout "*Kamerad*"' – fate intervened. Out of nowhere an Arab goatherd wandered into view. Appearing oblivious to the German troops, he shooed his flock downslope. They converged upon the fuzz of bush, nibbling away contentedly. In an instant, the three fugitives found themselves 'surrounded by a whole herd of the smelly beasts', their bodies providing a screen of munching, bleating, 'mobile camouflage'.

None of the trio could be certain, but it seemed as if the shepherd had thrown this cloak of animal protection around them on purpose. Either way, not one enemy soldier braved the goatherd and came to search their hideout. Come dusk, the last of the German paratroopers appeared to melt away. Echoing up from the far end of the wadi the three escapees heard the grunt of engines, as the enemy convoy began to move out. They had to presume that was the end of the search. Stiff and cramped, they emerged from their place of hiding, crawling 'out of their hole' into the gathering darkness.

The three men paused to take stock. Between them they

possessed a compass, and had a good idea of where they were. They also had the one map – but at 1:1,000,000 scale, one inch equated to 15.78 miles, so it wasn't overly rich in detail. Yet the main issue was their lack of food and, more specifically, water. Only two options seemed open to them, if they were to try to get back to friendly lines. The first was to retrace their steps the way they had come. The upside was that they'd be moving through territory with which they were familiar. There was one major downside: it would necessitate trying to slip back through the Gabes Gap, which as they now fully appreciated 'was swarming with enemy soldiers'. None of them doubted that it was their passage through the Gap that had alerted the enemy to their presence in the first place.

The second option was to press onwards, towards the First Army's front lines. Sadler figured their nearest positions lay some 200 kilometres south-west of their present position. Of course, that meant moving through territory that was a total unknown, but on balance it was the only course of action that seemed to hold out the slightest promise of salvation. Even so, their present predicament appeared deeply unsettling. 'It was a very depressing time,' Sadler would confess, 'because we assumed they had captured David [Stirling] and all the others – that meant the SAS had lost its commander and we thought the whole future of the SAS might be in jeopardy.'

Despite such worries, the priority had to be to try to save their own skins.

The three men set out, aiming to skirt around the far side of the Chott el Djerid, keeping the salt marshes on their left-hand side, as a kind of a handrail to guide their progress. But shortly they found themselves having to change course, to avoid a large enemy encampment. All through that first long night they were forced to keep doing the same, twisting and turning in their line of march. Beyond the Gabes Gap the terrain was broken and hilly, and peppered with enemy encampments, which raised the question of where they would be able to hide, come daybreak.

At first light they spied an Arab camp, with beyond it the 'salt lake shimmering white in the sunlight'. Just the sight of that alone – chimera though it might be – was enough to remind all of their burning thirst. According to Taxis, in the Muslim holy book, the Quran, it was considered good luck for strangers to approach an Arab camp in the early morning. The inhabitants would be 'obliged to offer us hospitality', he explained. They were desperate, and so the decision was made to give it a try.

They crept closer to the tented camp, the dogs setting up a ferocious barking. Shortly, figures emerged, 'fearsome in their long robes and beards'. Taxis began speaking Arabic, offering a hurried explanation – they were British soldiers 'fleeing from the Germans', and trying to get to the Allied lines. The response – and the welcome – was all they had hoped it would be. Sadler, Cooper and Taxis were invited into a tent and offered fresh-baked bread, dates and water, as the Arab tribespeople did their best to make them feel at home. By the looks of their camp, this was a semi-permanent settlement, as opposed to those of the nomadic Bedouin, which the SAS were far more used to encountering during their desert journeys.

Eventually, Taxis explained that they needed to be getting on, although their hosts seemed reluctant to let them leave. Finally, they thrust a battered old earthenware jug, brimful of water, into the trio's hands, and wished them luck with their onward passage. Well fed, and with that precious pint of water to sustain them, the trio set off. Eventually, as the heat of the day built to an unbearable level, they retreated into the shade of a narrow cave. It was set on the lip of an escarpment, from which the terrain shelved away in a series of sharp drops and precipitous slopes slick with scree.

Utterly spent, sleep claimed them.

Sometime later, Cooper awoke to find himself staring into the business end of a 12-bore shotgun. At the far end was a 'very angry looking Berber tribesmen', the Berber being a fierce warrior race who inhabit much of north-west Africa. The gunman started yelling wildly, his hand gestures punctuating his apparent rage. Taxis, who had been woken by the racket, exchanged a few hurried words in Arabic with the man, who kept his 12-bore pointing right at Cooper's midriff.

'He wants your clothes!' Taxis yelled.

Odd though this might sound, it made complete sense to Cooper. Back at Kabrit, they'd been briefed about how any Berber they encountered would very likely strip and rob them, if they could possibly get away with it. That was what had happened to any number of Allied pilots who had been forced to bail out over Berber country. As it was January and unusually cold in the desert, Cooper was wearing a leather jerkin. With great reluctance he removed it, and threw it towards his assailant.

At that moment, a whole host appeared, 'running over the skyline'. It was a gang of Berber children, and each was hefting a rock. Before Cooper could even think to protect himself, a hail of missiles rained down, one stone striking his forehead. It left him reeling and momentarily helpless, as he felt 'the blood stream down my face making me virtually blind'. The crowd closed in, and Cooper didn't doubt that they intended to stone him half to death, in order to strip him of all that he possessed.

'Help!' he cried. 'I'm blinded!'

To one side Sadler was also being assaulted. He handed over his battle dress blouse, in an effort to placate the mob. As the crowd edged closer, they made it clear to Taxis that they were quite prepared to murder them all, in order to rob them. 'Give us more!' they cried, in Arabic. 'You won't need anything, because we are going to kill you!'

'They want everything!' Taxis yelled out. 'They want us to give them everything!'

'No fear!' Sadler retorted. If they handed over all that they were wearing, boots included, they were as good as dead.

Confused, bloodied, half-blinded, and worried about how badly he was injured, Cooper heard a familiar voice crying out: 'Run this way, Johnny! Protect your head with your arms!'

Homing in on the sound of Sadler's voice, Cooper 'blindly took off', going as fast as he dared, until he blundered into his two fellow escapees. Taxis and Sadler grabbed him by the arms, and the trio took to their heels, making a desperate bid for safety. Choosing a particularly steep and rocky slope, they took their lives in their hands and careered down the scree. It was that which saved them. The Berbers, who were barefoot, simply couldn't match their pace across such rough and punishing ground.

Once they were certain they had shaken off their pursuers, the three fugitives paused. Sadler and Taxis inspected Cooper's wound. He was pretty 'shaken up', Sadler remarked. While he had suffered 'a nasty gash' they figured he should be able to carry on. He would have to. What other option was there?

By ripping off strips of their own uniforms they managed to

cobble together a DIY bandage, in an effort to stem the flow of blood. But Cooper's open gash remained angry looking and horribly painful. The wound needed stitches, and in a sense that only made the need to hurry onwards all the more pressing. There was nothing for it but to gird up their loins, grit their teeth and get moving once more. 'We marched all that night,' Cooper noted, simply, 'and I was in great pain.'

At first light the intrepid trio found themselves wending their way down from the high ground, into low-lying, more open country. The panorama that stretched before them looked unrelentingly bleak. They were passing into a 'flat and arid landscape of almost white sand and salt'. The sun was blinding, and even at this early hour it felt 'burning hot'. As Sadler, Cooper and Taxis ran their aching eyes over the forbidding landscape, they caught sight of what appeared to be an oasis, marked out by a burst of verdant palm trees. It shimmered and danced in the haze of heat. Was this a *fata morgana* – a mirage? Or was it for real? From this distance there was no way of knowing.

They stumbled towards it, their footsteps driven on by the promise of water. Their earthenware jug had been drained of its last precious drops the previous evening. Since then, they'd drunk not a sip, and they had been forced to flee from that murderous Berber gang, after which they'd crossed several dozen kilometres of utterly exhausting terrain. They reached the nearest palms, to realise they were all too real. This clump of greenery had to mark the western fringes of the Chott el Djerid. It being wintertime, just beyond the shade of the palms lay pools of beguiling water that would be thick with salt.

Parched beyond reckoning, they forced their wills not to break; to remain strong, and to fight the irresistible urge to drink. Their iron discipline was to be rewarded. As the evening shadows drew in, they spied a lone figure – an Arab, or possibly a Berber – making his way through the godforsaken landscape. The old and dignified 'grey beard', as Sadler referred to him, was riding on a donkey. Given what had happened earlier, they remained nervous; edgy. But the stranger greeted the trio in a friendly-enough manner, and when they made their predicament clear, he appeared only too ready to help. Unslinging a 'smelly goatskin bag' he handed it to the three fugitives. By its cool, bulging feel they could tell that it had to be full of water.

Having wetted their throats, Sadler, Cooper and Taxis realised what this battered old goatskin signified: it had just become their most precious possession in all the world. Ragged and leaky, it was sorely in need of some tender loving care. Removing their bootlaces – the only things with which they could even attempt to execute some kind of repairs – they strapped it up as best they could, in an effort to prevent any further spillage.

Once that was done, the Arab described to Taxis how there was a further supply of fresh water up ahead, for a well lay some distance away in the direction they needed to travel. Before they left him, the good Samaritan offered them a few words of caution. 'Be careful,' he warned, 'there are some very bad . . . men around.' There were indeed. Sadler, Cooper and Taxis had encountered some of the worst, in that Berber gang, and they were desperate to avoid any further such confrontations.

Moving on, the intrepid trio steered their steps towards what they hoped was that well. They found it, only to discover that two young Arab women were there ahead of them, drawing water. It took just one look at the desperate fugitives, with their 'filthy and unshaven' appearance, and the women screamed and took flight. Sadler, Cooper and Taxis moved in to drink their fill, though the water proved murky and stomach-turning. With their leaky goatskin bag refilled, Sadler took the opportunity to bathe Cooper's wound and to clean it as best he could. It was the first time they'd been able to do so since they'd been set upon by the Berber mob. Cooper seemed made of incredibly strong stuff. Despite his injuries, the young SAS warrior was holding up remarkably well. It was Taxis who appeared to be suffering. Increasingly, he was plagued by hallucinations, and Sadler and Cooper could tell he was 'really struggling'.

Beyond the well lay another Arab camp. Fearful of being set upon once more – this time, they might not be so lucky – the trio decided to try to slip around it undetected. The only way to do so was to brave the Chott el Djerid. Gingerly, they stepped out onto the glittering expanse of the salt marsh. At first, with each footfall the white crystalline crust seemed firm enough to bear their weight. But shortly, the first among them broke through, boots plunging into the dark, sucking gunk that lay below. As they crunched and crashed their way ahead, the noise they were making was fearful. In an effort to try to move more quietly, they decided there was nothing for it – they would have to remove their boots and proceed barefoot.

The trio slipped off their footwear, socks included. It was then that Sadler and Cooper noticed a very odd thing. Taxis had six toes on one of his feet. It struck them as being 'rather peculiar', but there was little time to explore any of that right then. Creeping across the salt pan, bare feet burning and blistering horribly, they hobbled past that Arab camp, step by painful step. On the far side they set up a makeshift base, in the shelter of some palms, and decided to try to get some sleep. They were several days into their escape by now, and the trio were losing track of time. Out here in this sun-blasted wilderness, all the days seemed to blend into one.

The following morning, Taxis appeared to have deteriorated still further. He seemed driven half-mad with thirst. Before Sadler or Cooper could think to stop him, the Frenchman dashed forward, fell to his knees and, scooping up handfuls of the water from the Chott, he proceeded to drink. All that did for the fevered Frenchman was to make him 'violently sick', after which he seemed to 'break down completely'. Taxis collapsed by the lakeside. Lying there under the full sun, he made it quite clear to Sadler and Cooper that, as far as he was concerned, he'd taken his last steps.

'I can't go on any further,' Taxis murmured, whenever Sadler and Cooper tried to get him back on his feet. 'You will just have to leave me.'

As Sadler remarked, this was the Frenchman's 'Captain Oates moment' – the point at which the Antarctic explorer Lawrence Oates had walked from his tent into a blizzard, and certain death, in an effort to save his fellow explorers. But despite their own sorry state, there was no way that Sadler and Cooper were about to abandon their SAS comrade. Instead, they manoeuvred him into some shade, reassuring him that they would press on and find help.

That done, the pair of escapees set forth, stumbling onwards across the beguiling landscape, even though they were fighting the effects of dehydration and hallucinations themselves. After a few kilometres they spied a fresh clump of palms in the far distance. Interspersed between the trees were what appeared to be signs of human habitation. Buildings. The hint of some kind of a permanent settlement. Neither Sadler nor Cooper had any certainty as to who might hold this outpost – friendly forces or the enemy – and to be captured now, after all they had endured, would be the deepest cut of all.

'Nevertheless, we decided to risk it,' Sadler remarked, for in their parlous state they had few other options. It was either chance it or die.

As they approached the settlement, he and Cooper looked utterly piratical – desert castaways driven half-mad by thirst. 'We had long hair and beards,' Sadler remarked of their appearance. 'Our feet were in tatters.' When they were still around half a kilometre short of the oasis, they heard a crackle of rifle shots, and the odd burst of more concentrated fire from a machine gun.

'Oh God,' Cooper exclaimed. 'That must mean the Germans are still fighting . . .'

Some kind of battle did seem to be in train, but they would have to chance it, 'even if it did mean being taken prisoner'. Taxis was in desperate need of rescue. Without help, the Frenchman was as good as dead. Cooper needed urgent medical care. Even Sadler was utterly spent.

The two fugitives crept ever closer, slipping into the shade of the nearest palms, after which they followed a muddy track that snaked into the shadows. It led to a small stream. As Sadler and Cooper bent to scoop up the water, greedily, a figure emerged from out of the trees. It was an elderly Arab and in his hands he caried a *chatti*, a traditional clay pot. He offered it to the two men, and it proved to be full of 'delicious cold water'.

As Sadler and Cooper quenched their thirst, more Arabs arrived, offering them dates and more water. Welcomed by this crowd of locals, who struck Cooper as most likely being Bedouin, he and Sadler sank to their haunches on the side of the path and drank and ate ravenously. Shortly, the sound of running feet echoed through the palms. Boots were pounding along the path towards their place of repose. The moment of truth was upon them.

Around a bend in the track dashed a striking figure – a tall black African man. In his hands he clutched an ancient-looking rifle, with bayonet fixed. As he drew closer, Sadler and Cooper could see that he was dressed in the distinctive uniform of the French military. They felt their hearts leap with joy. This could only be a Senegalese trooper, whose forces served with the Free French, and whose ranks now made up a part of the First Army.

In broken French Sadler and Cooper explained that they were British soldiers, and that they'd left their comrade in a perilous state, a few miles away at the lakeside. The Senegalese soldier disappeared, heading back the way he'd come, and shortly he returned, leading a phalanx of troops. Among them was an utterly striking figure: a French Army sergeant with a massive ginger beard and a smile that split his face from ear to ear. In no time a squad of the Senegalese troops had set forth, returning in due course with Taxis. He was brought in, supported by strong arms on either side.

Together, the three escapees made their way along the path, painfully slowly. It 'opened out on to the finest *Beau Geste* fort I had ever seen', remarked Cooper. The entire scene was like something out of a film set: 'palm trees, blue sky, strange uniforms and the brilliant white paint of the fort'. Out of the entrance strode the garrison commander, who lost no time in making the three escapees feel at home. In short order Cooper had a medical orderly cleaning and sewing up his wound, while a meal was being prepared – goat stew, potatoes, wine and white rum. Simple enough fare, but to the intrepid trio, 'it was a banquet,' Cooper declared, 'a magnificent feast'.

It turned out that their desperate journey on foot had lasted five nights and five days. In no time the surfeit of food and alcohol, after such prolonged privation and abstinence, had the three escapees 'in an advanced state of inebriation'. But they reckoned they had earned it.

The French commander explained that they had reached a frontline outpost, called Kriz, which lay near the town of Tozeur, both of which were within the American sector of operations. Accordingly, he would have to alert the US commanders to the intrepid trio's miraculous appearance. The nearest American outpost was at Gafsa, which lay some 80 kilometres away. He composed a short message, to be sent by radio.

'Today, three gentlemen from the English Army arrived at my location, Tozeur, having escaped capture by the Germans at the Gabes Gap, and we commemorate the meeting of the glorious British Eighth Army with our forces here in Tunisia. One is a French sergeant and two are English sergeants [sic], names and numbers as stated.'

An hour or so later, an American patrol turned up to collect Sadler, Cooper and Taxis. But right away it was clear that all was not well. The US troops marched into the fort and promptly arrested the three escapees, handcuffing them and bundling them into a waiting armoured car. Admittedly, the trio did look somewhat dubious, with Cooper's bandaged and bloodied head, their heavily bandaged feet, and their bodies covered in blisters and desert sores. 'I don't think we looked very much like soldiers,' Sadler confessed. By the close guard placed upon them it was clear that the Americans suspected the trio of being something very different from what they really were.

With little food or water, they were driven practically non-stop to the American base. A French officer had travelled with the convoy, and he went ahead to prepare the ground. His arrival was witnessed by an American press man, Abbot Joseph 'A. J.' Liebling, of the *New Yorker* magazine, plus his Norwegian colleague, Noland Norgaard, of the Associated Press. Both would file graphic reports of the incredible escape of the SAS soldiers, and of the war-winning intelligence they were able to furnish. The two journalists happened to be at the Hôtel de France, which the US commander, Colonel Bowen, had requisitioned as his headquarters, when the convoy arrived.

As no one on reception knew how to speak much French, Liebling dealt with the French officer. He explained in a 'matter-of-fact' voice that he had three soldiers from the Eighth Army, who 'came in from a patrol . . . into our lines at Kriz, on the Chott [el] Djerid . . . If you will show them to Colonel Bowen, I will leave them with you.' With that the Frenchman ducked out through the doorway onto the street without waiting for an answer. A few moments later the three figures were led in, their steps 'mincing', Liebling noticed, their feet 'wrapped in rags', which had to be 'a mass of blisters'.

One had his head shrouded in a 'blood-soaked bandage', Liebling noted, and all had 'long beards'. Their uniforms were ripped half to shreds, from where they'd torn off strips of material to improvise bandages. One still clutched a 'goatskin water sack, with the long hair outside'. To the amazement of Liebling, the entire scene reminded him of something out of *Robinson Crusoe*. The one figure whose appearance affected Liebling the most was Mike Sadler. While all had sunken faces and bulging eyes – 'preternaturally large' – Sadler's were like golf balls. They were 'really protuberant . . . round and sky blue', and framed by a mass of sun-bleached hair and whiskers. The whole thing struck Liebling as being 'slightly dotty', but then Sadler began to speak, offering up some kind of explanation.

'We walked forty miles further than we should have,' he volunteered, half-apologetically, 'because some Arabs told us the Germans had taken Gafsa and that two thousand Americans were prisoners. But we knew the French were at Kriz and Tozeur, so we went around that way. We've been walking for five nights and five days.'

Chairs were brought in. The three escapees sat gazing around 'incredulously', their expressions seeming to reveal how 'they had not really expected to get out of whatever awful scrape they had been in'. The figure with the least facial hair – Cooper had been partially shaved, when having his wounds dressed – ran a hand over his head, exhaustedly.

'Grazed by a bullet?' Norgaard, the Norwegian reporter, ventured.

'No,' Cooper replied, shaking his head ever so slowly. 'An Arab hit me with a stone. They tried to strip us of our clothes, and when we fought they tried to kill us. We ran. We had no weapons, you see.'

'Have many others came in?' Sadler inquired, meaning how many of their fellows from Stirling's patrol. 'Have you heard anything about Big Dave?' Big Dave: at some six foot six inches tall, the SAS founder was seen as more than deserving of that nickname by his men. No one else from Stirling's patrol had made their way to the First Army's positions, one of the American soldiers explained. In fact, Sadler, Cooper and Taxis were the 'first British who've come into our lines'.

Cooper looked distraught. 'Big Dave must have been killed,' he muttered. 'That was all that shooting back in the wadi.'

Sadler, shaking himself out of his own stupor, suddenly announced: 'It's very important that we put out a radio warning to all our people behind the German lines that the enemy may have got our codes. We must change the code.'

Sadler's chief worry was that the enemy might have captured the SAS's top secret signals and codebooks. If they had, they might well be able to intercept and decrypt the SAS's wireless traffic, which would cause no end of calamity and upset. Hence his disquiet.

It struck Liebling as if Sadler was 'trying to carry out a duty, before he too caved in'. 'Are you *really* from the Eighth Army?' Liebling queried.

Sadler confirmed that they were. Faced with the reporters', and the American soldiers', incredulity, the escapees offered up a little more information. They'd been soldiering behind enemy lines since 17 November the previous year, they explained. It was now 28 January 1943, and they'd been living and operating deep inside hostile lands for all of that time.

'We were supposed to stay out four weeks longer, but we had a bit of hard luck,' Taxis remarked, simply.

An American soldier appeared and ordered the three escapees to go up to see Colonel Bowen. Liebling watched as they climbed slowly up the stairs towards the colonel's office, grasping the banister and trying to take as much of their weight as possible on their hands. Colonel Bowen received the intrepid trio with 'a squad of soldiers' standing guard. He issued a caution to his troops: 'Keep these men covered.' As was becoming clear to the trio, the American colonel 'didn't believe we were British soldiers', and harboured suspicious that 'we were Germans or something sinister'.

The escapees did their best to explain, but it got them nowhere. Colonel Bowen just didn't know what to make of them, and he remained convinced 'they might be spies'. They would need to be sent to the 'G2' headquarters, he announced, where the United States Army military intelligence staff were based. Those G2 officers would know what to do with them. The colonel sent for an ambulance, for a long journey lay ahead. The G2 base was at Tébessa, on the Mediterranean coastline, a good 150 kilometres away. As Tébessa was in Algeria, the trio would have commenced their patrol in Libya, crossed over into Tunisia shortly before capture, and were now about to move into a third country, as part of their epic odyssey.

Liebling and Norgaard, sensing the story of a lifetime, rushed to grab their jeep and their US Army driver, insisting that they travel with the ambulance. They got back to the Hôtel de France, to find the three escapees were ensconced in the kitchen, drinking hot coffee as they waited for their carriage to arrive. Liebling asked Cooper to explain just who exactly they might be. They served with a unit called the SAS, Cooper explained, which stood for the Special Air Service. Liebling posed the obvious question: was it something to do with the RAF? Not at all, Cooper replied. It was an 'air service' in the negative sense.

'You see, when we were first formed we used to specialise in destroying German airplanes on the ground,' Cooper continued. 'Get onto an airfield at night – do in a sentry, you know, or something of that sort; it's easy – and then attach pencil bombs to as many planes as we could get . . . We do a bunk, the bombs go off, and all the planes burn. Quite a good idea. Major Stirling, the one we call Big Dave, really thought of it first. Bright chap.'

Cooper took a pensive swig of his coffee. 'One chap in the SAS got a hundred and twenty planes with his own hands . . .' By that, Cooper was referring to Mayne, of course. 'But Jerry got onto that airport dodge. Now there are too many guards and too many booby traps. So on this last trip we stayed away from airfields . . .' They'd focused on hitting road convoys and railway lines, spreading mayhem and confusion instead. 'We made a whole Italian division pull out of one area, frightened stiff. Glorious fun, really.'

Cooper described how they'd alighted upon the American-made Willys jeep as being perfect for desert operations, especially when mounted with an array of machine guns. 'They're the finest combat vehicle developed in this war. When you come to a deep wadi, where you can't progress farther, you can lower them in by ropes and get them out the same way on the other side . . . When your own petrol runs out, you raid an enemy petrol dump, or shoot up some enemy trucks and take whatever they have. You lose all sense of strangeness, really, after a while. It seems as normal to go to an Eyetie dump for your petrol as to one of our own places.'

Sadler joined in, as he and Cooper spoke in an odd, disjointed way, the words tumbling over each other, which Liebling realised had to reflect their recent ordeals. 'Altogether we made a shambles of the enemy's lines of supply . . . We never had a casualty in six weeks, until the thing in the wadi north of Gabes.' To both Sadler and Cooper's minds, they'd been jumped by the enemy for one reason only: they'd become accustomed 'to feeling too safe'.

They'd remained hidden and elusive for so long that they had begun to believe 'it would last forever'.

The ambulance arrived. An American officer appeared at the kitchen door. He was there to escort 'the three suspicious characters' to Tébessa. With that Sadler, Cooper and Taxis got up and hobbled their weary way towards the waiting vehicle. There was a jeep full of American soldiers acting as escort and maintaining a close guard. Liebling and his fellow reporter, Norgaard, jumped into their jeep, and so the convoy set forth. The route lay across high terrain and it proved to be 'the coldest, and it seemed the longest', ride ever. At their one break stop, taken at a mountain pass, Sadler, Cooper and Taxis got down to take a pee, discovering the terrain to be 'sprinkled with snow'.

Their welcome upon reaching Tébessa was to prove equally chilly. Admittedly, they did look something of a 'motley crew', as Cooper readily confessed, but their 'most uncivil' reception at the hands of the Americans was really starting to grate now. They had reached the G2 base at around two o'clock on the morning of 29 January. The situation there turned out to be a picture of red-faced confusion and consternation. Suspicion that they were enemy spies was in the process of being replaced with a deep-seated sense of unease and embarrassment, as the Americans realised just who the trio really were.

A signal had just arrived, confirming that the three suspicious characters were indeed members of David Stirling's SAS. It came from General Harold Alexander himself, the commander-in-chief of Middle Eastern Headquarters (MEHQ), so could hardly emanate from a higher authority within the British military. It was further endorsed by General Mark Clark, the American who served as the Supreme Allied Commander in the Mediterranean theatre of operations. With noticeable reluctance, the trio's erstwhile captors began to execute an about face, and they tried to fete the escapees with all kinds of goodies. To the trio's regret, however, there was 'only Coca-Cola to drink and no beer!'

Far from being suspected enemy spies, Sadler, Cooper and Taxis suddenly became a precious trove of intelligence. Debriefed about their 'penetration of the Gabes Gap' and their wider mission, they explained how they had recce'd a route around the Mareth Line, at which point Cooper and Sadler were in the very highest demand. If one of them could be flown back to Cairo, some three thousand kilometres east of there, he would be able to help guide the British 7th Armoured Division as it headed towards the Mareth Line. They could deliver that much-hoped-for left hook, so outflanking Rommel's defences.

In truth, Sadler had found their epic ordeal 'far more harrowing . . . than anything he had suffered at the hands of the Germans'. Despite this, he volunteered to go, for at least he was free of injuries. Thus it was that via Sadler's herculean efforts, one of the key aims of Stirling's original mission would be accomplished. Sadler was dispatched to join General Bernard Freyberg's New Zealand Division, which was charged with the mission of outflanking the Mareth Line. 'Thus I passed for a second time over the same territory I had reconnoitred with David [Stirling], but in far more comfortable conditions,' Sadler remarked. 'It was good to know that the original journey had not been in vain.'

In fact, Stirling's overarching objective had already been achieved, simply as a result of the intrepid trio's escape. As the news article that Liebling subsequently penned would declare, the SAS had been the first of the Eighth Army forces to link up with the First Army. This historic achievement would be recorded in the SAS War Diary, under the headline 'Bewhiskered Raiders'. It explained how 'three sunburnt ... desert raiders from the Eighth Army who had finished an operation behind Rommel's lines,' turned up at a 'U.S.-held outpost in Southern Tunisia. They were Lieutenant Willis Michael Sadler, of Sheepscombe, Gloucestershire, who formerly lived in RHODESIA, Sergeant John Cooper, 20, of Leicester, and Sergeant A. F. Taxis, a Frenchman.'

With Sadler having departed, Taxis was reclaimed by the French Army, which left only Cooper to further brief the US commanders. The twenty-year-old SAS man was congratulated by General Clark in person on his epic escape, before being assailed by a barrage of questions about all that he had seen. The real focus of interest was the Gabes Gap, and how all enemy traffic had to be funnelled through there. An American Air Force general was paying particularly close attention to Cooper's words. 'Goddamit,' he declared, 'everything has to go through that goddamed gap!' Then he turned to one of his assistants and barked out an order. 'Just bomb that goddamed gap!'

As a result of the intelligence they had delivered, not to mention their incredible escape, the trio would be hailed by the American commanders as the 'Limey heroes'. Both Cooper and Sadler would go on to serve with the SAS until war's end. In Cooper's case he would end up as a captain, though he was still just twenty-three years old, and when the SAS was re-formed he would rejoin the unit, to serve with distinction in Malaya, Oman and the Yemen.

When Liebling's report was published in the *New Yorker*, it introduced an American public to a completely new form of waging warfare, in which piratical-looking British soldiers operated deep behind the enemy's lines, spreading untold mayhem, and seeming to find it all 'glorious fun'. When all went wrong, they executed the most unbelievable escapes and evasions, across seemingly impossible terrain, in territory that was crawling with the enemy. This was the Special Air Service, as Liebling trumpeted, and for them it was all in a day's work.

The capture of David Stirling and most of the patrol would cast a long shadow over the trio's escape. They were 'saddened by what fate awaited David', Sadler remarked, fearing that 'he might be executed'. Despite the death threats, neither Stirling nor his fellow captives were shot, although the SAS founder and one of his deputies had come perilously close. In the hours after being herded into that first place of captivity, Stirling and McDermott had made a break for it. Both were hunted down and recaptured, Stirling in part due to treachery. Seized by a burning rage, he had subjected the Arab who had betrayed him to a beating, 'bashing him into the ground'.

But menaced as he was by the enemy's guns, there was to be no second escape for Stirling. 'They got him at last,' is how his capture is recorded in the SAS War Diary. 'He was caught by the Germans, escaped, and was subsequently recaptured . . .' From there Stirling was spirited across the Mediterranean on a flight bound for Italy, in an effort to prevent any further breakouts. There, he was incarcerated first in a Rome prison camp, before being transferred to Oflag IV-C, Colditz, where he would join the likes of Georges Bergé, to spend the rest of the war in captivity.

Once Rommel had been informed that the Phantom Major had been captured, he was ecstatic, noting in his diary triumphantly how his forces had 'captured the commander of 1st S.A.S. Regiment, Lieut.-Col David Stirling'. Rommel described

Stirling's escape attempt, and how 'the Arabs, with their usual eye to business, offered him to us for 11 pounds of tea – a bargain which we soon clinched. Thus the British lost the very able and adaptable commander of the desert group which had caused us more damage than any other British unit of equal strength.'

In fact, simply in terms of enemy warplanes destroyed, the SAS had caused Rommel's forces far greater harm than Allied units of far greater strength; arguably, more harm than the entire Royal Air Force over the same period. Since their formation in the summer of 1941, the SAS had accounted for 367 confirmed enemy aircraft destroyed, and quite possibly as many as 400. It was some achievement.

But right now the focus of the war was shifting, as would the missions of the SAS. Europe beckoned, as Allied forces headed for French and Italian shores, seeking to drive out the occupiers. With that change of focus came a whole new set of challenges, and a whole new chapter in the fortunes of this elite unit.

As the noose around Nazi Germany tightened, any SAS escapees would face a dark fate indeed.

Chapter Five

ESCAPE FROM THE CAULDRON

July 1944, France

Churchill had laid down his marker: he wanted action, action, action – not perfection. Seeking ideal conditions as a prerequisite for launching raids would 'render operations of this character utterly impossible', he warned his Chiefs of Staff, adding that 'the maxim "Nothing avails but perfection" may be spelt shorter [as] "Paralysis"'. In other words, raiding operations had to continue unabated, no matter what seeming impediments might stand in their way. Indeed, their tempo had to be increased, and even as the fortunes of the war began to turn in the Allies' favour.

Throughout all the vicissitudes of this global conflict, Churchill had kept his hand firmly on the tiller of special operations, and with the approach of Operation Overlord – D-Day – he was determined to up the ante still further, his elite units striking relentlessly, far behind enemy lines. With that in mind, scores of SAS patrols had been parachuted deep into occupied France, even as the D-Day landings took place, charged to harass and harry the German supply lines, and to do their utmost to prevent enemy reinforcements from reaching the vulnerable beachheads.

One such party, commanded by Captain John Elliot Tonkin, a long-experienced special duties officer, had been doing sterling work in the countryside across the Vienne region of west-central France. Tonkin had parachuted into the area on the night of 5/6 June 1944, touching down on the drop zone (DZ) at 1.37 a.m., so a few hours *ahead* of the forces going ashore on the Normandy beaches. Since then, he and his men had spent the best part of a month blowing apart the enemy's rail-transport and road convoys, targeting especially their columns of heavy armour.

The operations of Tonkin and his men had been notably successful, their casualties light. Perhaps it had all come a little too easily. There was a sense when operating in the open French countryside, far from the urban centres or any major enemy bases, that the war almost wasn't for real. At least not here. Not in the way many of Tonkin's men experienced it. Four Willys jeeps had been dropped into Tonkin's force, each slung beneath a clutch of giant parachutes. But with some fifty-five troops under his command, that meant that at any one time a maximum of sixteen men could be out and about on vehicle-borne operations. Other than executing small-scale raids on foot, that left many to kick their heels at base camp, passing the hours as best they could.

At times the war felt as if it were a million miles away, as the SAS traded soap for tobacco with their French comrades, the resistance fighters with whom they had linked up here on the ground. Local tobacco rolled in toilet paper – which was all that mostly remained now, after the long weeks on operations – proved barely smokable. Still, it was better than nothing. Many made a point of regularly shaving and brushing their teeth; good discipline and it served to keep up the morale. Tonkin himself had been out and about on numerous raids, but the toll had proved debilitating, as had the need to keep getting supplies ferried in. A lot of the resupply flights had failed to materialise, or had missed the DZs completely, so necessitating many sleepless nights.

But chiefly, Tonkin was plagued by the worry that the enemy – despite their seeming absence – would discover the SAS base camp, which was positioned deep in a patch of woodland. Their predicament was made all the worse in that the summer of 1944 had proved one of the driest on record, which meant getting access to fresh drinking water was a constant challenge. That in turn constrained Tonkin's ability to keep shifting the location of their base. Too long spent in one place was dangerous, as he fully appreciated. But conversely, moving to a location bereft of a river, lake or a well made no sense whatsoever. 'Choice of camps was limited due to lack of water . . .' Tonkin would report, in the SAS War Diary. 'This proved the main difficulty.'

Tonkin found himself speared on the horns of that dilemma, even as their woodland camp had taken on an ever more homely and settled feel. One of the few daily highlights were the regular BBC radio broadcasts, via which coded messages were delivered to the raiding parties deep in the field. The BBC evening programming would be interrupted by a distinctive song, the first few lines of which would signify that a series of messages were about to be broadcast, and each for the specific attention of any one of the scores of SAS patrols scattered across France. Bizarrely, ironically, it was the opening lines of a French nursery rhyme that all were listening out for:

> *Sur le Pont d'Avignon,*
> *L'on y danse, l'on y danse . . .*
> On the bridge of Avignon,
> They are dancing, they are dancing . . .

There is in fact an ancient bridge in the French city of Avignon, where, by tradition a certain dance is supposed to be performed – the inspiration behind the rhyme. Out of sheer devilment, it was those singsong nursery lines that had been chosen to signify that crucial information was about to be imparted to one or other SAS patrol. As those first stanzas faded out, there would be a slight pause, before the BBC announcer's voice would declare: 'Hello SABU . . . Hello SABU . . .' Each SAS party had been given a 'SABU' codename, the acronym most likely standing for 'Safe All Business as Usual', a set phrase used by patrols to signify that all was well. In Tonkin's case, he was SABU-35; his deputy, Lieutenant Tomos Stephens, was SABU-37. So much had the SABU identity been taken to heart, that one of those summer '44 patrols dropped into France had a dog serving as its mascot, which the men had named 'Sabu'.

Tonkin's camp was located in the Forêt de Verrières, which lay some twenty kilometres south-east of the French city of Poitiers. Set amid a vast and rolling carpet of green, it had the all-important stream running through the heart of it. They had been there since 25 June, so for over a week, and Tonkin was starting to feel unsettled. His unease was made all the worse in that the inhabitants of the nearby hamlet of Verrières had learned of their presence, and a group of curious French girls had made their way to the woods, keen to get sight of the British adventurers. Worse still, one or two of his men, drawn by the promise of drink and female company, had paid a visit to the village. It seemed impossible to stop the villagers from calling at his camp, especially as there was a roaring trade to be done, SAS rations and parachute silk being bartered for fresh provisions, including 'eggs, bread, meat, vegetables, potatoes, cheese, wine and fruit'.

In a sense Tonkin could hardly blame his men. Due to repeated problems with the airdrops, supplies were running low – especially fuel, explosives and fresh provisions. Petrol was 'non-existent' across France, as all supplies had been seized by the enemy for their war effort. Indeed, one of Tonkin's top priorities was hitting the enemy's fuel dumps. In just one spectacular action, his patrol had called in a squadron of De Havilland Mosquito fighter-bombers, to strike at a dozen fuel trains then passing through his area of operations. Each consisted of a line of petrol tankers, towed by a locomotive, their contents destined to fuel Hitler's heavy armour, which was even then making a dash for the Normandy beaches.

It was one of Tonkin's deputies, Lieutenant Richard Crisp, who had executed the daring reconnaissance of those targets, and he'd done so in inimitable fashion. A budding actor, Crisp had won a scholarship to the Old Vic Theatre School at the age of sixteen, being a talented singer and comedian. Being keen to fight the scourge of Nazism, four years after joining drama school he had volunteered for the SAS, in due course finding himself behind the lines as part of Tonkin's squadron. Thespian to the core, Crisp had disguised himself as a French farmer, complete with flat cap and pipe jammed between his teeth, in order to get eyes-on those petrol trains. And so the former drama student had become 'the unusual leader of convoy-harassing parties',

Tonkin remarked of Crisp's remarkable transformation. 'I must have thought he had quite a gift for it!'

Though he had complained of the area being 'lousy with the enemy', Crisp's disguise and his language skills – he spoke good French and German – had got him through. In one fell swoop, the 'Wooden Wonders', as the Mosquitos had been nicknamed, had been called in by radio to hit those fuel trains. Just six hours after Tonkin had sent through the target details, the RAF had struck by utter surprise, taking out what amounted to all the petrol destined for the elite – and soon to be notorious – Waffen SS Panzer Division Das Reich.

'We observed the result of the bombing,' Tonkin would report, as 'a large flame' illuminated the entire horizon. But between such spikes of adrenaline-fuelled high-drama, there had been long stretches of inaction. In a sense Tonkin wasn't surprised that the 'the men tended to forget that they were behind the lines and liable to be attacked at any moment', and that the 'British soldier's aptitude for scrounging' inevitably brought them into close contact with the locals. But equally, he was alert to the dangers, and especially since he had himself been taken prisoner once already in this war.

Educated at King William's College, then an all-boys boarding school on the Isle of Man, Tonkin was a 'classic English public schoolboy', according to his peers, excelling at sports and marksmanship. Yet there was also a deeper, hidden, more individualistic side to Tonkin: he was 'a great practical joker, never unkind', and blessed with a wildly offbeat sense of humour. More to the point, beneath the public schoolboy gloss and charm there was a core of iron-willed determination and an unbreakable spirit.

John Tonkin was known as a hard grafter who never gave up. His sheer dogged 'persistence', and his refusal to throw in the towel no matter what, were qualities that inspired others and made him a 'natural leader in all walks of life'. While still in his early twenties, Tonkin had cut his eye teeth in North Africa, serving with the Long Range Desert Group. Volunteering for the SAS in 1943, with his LRDG experience he was a shoo-in for Stirling's raiders. He was just twenty-four years of age when given command of Operation Bulbasket, as the present mission was codenamed, and it was barely a year earlier that he'd been captured by the enemy.

In September 1943 the SAS (then temporarily renamed the Special Raiding Squadron) had been charged to take Termoli, a strategically important port lying on Italy's east coast. During forty-eight hours of intense fighting, Tonkin had attempted to capture the vital bridge over the Biferno River, one of the key objectives. But while pressing ahead in a daring thrust, Tonkin's patrol had found itself surrounded by a squadron of German paratroopers. Outnumbered, they'd fought until all was lost, Tonkin finally giving the order: 'Every man for himself!' The patrol had scattered, six had got away, but Tonkin, among others, had been captured.

Taken prisoner by the men of the elite German 1st Parachute Regiment, Tonkin was initially treated with the respect such airborne troops tended to extend to each other. But even he was surprised when he was invited to dinner by none other than General Richard Heidrich, a First World War veteran and a paratrooper himself. The German general insisted on dining with all captured Allied parachutists. Though somewhat taken aback, Tonkin accepted the invitation. The conversation ranged over the entirety of the war, including the Termoli attack, which General Heidrich described, admiringly, as 'a beautiful stroke' that had been 'perfectly timed'.

Over cigars, Heidrich confided in Tonkin that Hitler's decision to wage war on Britain was a grave mistake, before leaving him with a parting gift – five further cigars. But there was to be a sting in the tail. As Tonkin was being driven back to his cell, the German escorting officer had issued a grave warning. 'It is my duty to inform you that we have orders that we must obey, to hand you over to the special police. I must warn you that from now on the German army cannot guarantee your life.'

A year earlier, the Commando Order – *das Kommandobefehl* – had been issued, at Hitler's personal behest, a directive emanating from the Führer's legal team and bearing his personal signature. Issued on 18 October 1942, it read: 'Henceforth, all enemy troops encountered by German troops during so-called Commando operations . . . though they appear to be soldiers in uniform or demolition groups, armed or unarmed, are to be exterminated to the last man . . . If such men appear to be about to surrender, no quarter should be given to them.'

German officers were ordered to 'Report daily the number of saboteurs thus liquidated . . . to serve as a warning to potential terrorists.' Any such captives were to be kept alive only for as long as the Gestapo or SD had need, for interrogation purposes. The order ended with a chilling threat: 'I will summon before the tribunal of war all leaders and officers who fail to carry out these instructions – either by failure to inform their men or by their disobedience of this order in action.'

In the aftermath of the D-Day landings, a supplementary clause had been added to the *Kommandobefehl*, just in case any commanders were in doubt: 'In spite of the Anglo-American landings in France, the Führer's order of 18 October 1942, regarding the destruction of saboteurs and terrorists, remains fully valid . . . all parachutists encountered outside the immediate combat zone are to be executed.' In short, by the summer of 1944 the SAS – and related units – had been passed a double death sentence.

Tonkin had sensed right away that the German officer was giving him the nod: either he escaped, or he was facing the very worst. 'When a man knows he is about to be shot, it sharpens his mind wonderfully,' Tonkin would write of the moment. The following evening, he was loaded aboard a truck, to be driven north into the Italian mountains. There were some twenty troops from the Liverpool Irish, a British (territorial) infantry corps, riding in the truck – fellow captives. Two SS guards perched on the tailboard, while a motorcycle-and-side-car combination guarded the rear, with its mounted machine gun. The two-vehicle convoy set off, the truck jolting along the spine of high ground on boneshaking tracks and roads. Not a word had been said about where they were heading.

As the convoy climbed through a remote and frozen pass, it grew increasingly cold. Shortly, snow began to fall. The truck halted, so that the guards could take a smoke break and try to stamp some warmth into frozen limbs. An hour or so later, they did the same again. Each time, Tonkin had noted how he was ordered to make himself known to the guards upon halting, and setting off again – presumably, as a precaution to prevent him from trying to escape. But he'd also noticed that the German troops gathered at the rear of the truck for their smoke-break and conflab. As the truck set forth once more, Tonkin got busy working free the canvas covering at the front, where it joined the vehicle's cab. Once he'd worried the ropes free, the canvas was loose enough to allow a body to slip through.

Tonkin told his fellow captives to count the number of enemy troops getting down from the cab, just as soon as they stopped again. If two got out, the cab should be empty, and they were to follow him in breaking out. With little warning, the lorry pulled over. Sure enough, two figures from the front jumped down, gathering with the rest at the rear. Tonkin knew he had to seize his chance. Slipping under the canvas, he crawled '*very* quietly' across the roof of the truck's cab, and steeled himself to jump. For one horrifying moment a hand snaked out of the side window below him, flicking a cigarette butt away, before that figure got down and strolled around to the rear. There had been *three* riding in the cab, not two, perhaps for the greater warmth it might offer.

Seizing the moment, Tonkin 'was down on to the bonnet and away down the mountainside' in an instant. Slipping further into the darkness, he opted to head south, in the direction of friendly lines. After two weeks moving on foot through the Italian mountains, by luck more than judgement he stumbled upon a British patrol. Having linked up with two fellow escapees, the trio had been creeping ahead at night, when they came across a mystery force advancing towards them. It was only when one of the approaching figures blundered into something in the dark, and let out a curse, that Tonkin realised they were friendly.

Amazingly, barely two weeks after his capture the SAS lieutenant, as he was then, had executed a masterful escape. Dispatched to North Africa for a full debriefing, plus medical and psychological observations – to assess if his ordeal had had any long-term effects – Tonkin wasn't best pleased. There, he met a fellow escapee who was likewise chafing at the bit to return to frontline duties. It was a strikingly fiery Welshman, Lieutenant Tomos W. M. Stephens, better known as 'Twm' due to his initials. Tonkin was immensely impressed by the man. In his escape alone – 'his 500 miles trek, including re-capture and re-escape' – Stephens had shown 'ample evidence of guts, initiative and endurance. He has as genuine and deep-seated hatred of the enemy as anyone I know.'

Tonkin regaled Stephens with tales of derring-do from his time with the SAS, and the Welshman had certainly listened. Upon his return to Britain, Stephens had promptly volunteered for the SAS. In due course, Stephens had come to serve as Tonkin's second-in-command on Operation Bulbasket, and would do so with an utterly indomitable spirit.

Tonkin's escape in Italy, when facing all-but-certain execution, had earned him the reputation of being 'legendary'. It also epit-omised another of his standout qualities: Tonkin was to prove decidedly hard to kill. As Kevin Walton, one of his future fellow adventurers and a close friend, would declare, 'if a cat has nine lives, John was "the cat of all cats"'.

While Tonkin worried about the Gestapo learning of the where-abouts of their camp, he was far more fearful of the Milice Française – 'the real "bastards"', as he called them. 'Having been hypnotised by the Boche in the early part of the war,' he would observe, this pro-Nazi French militia 'was drilled, dis-ciplined, armed and injected with Boche frightfulness.' In the summer of 1944, following the D-Day landings, the position of the Milice 'was most unenviable, as they are traitors to their own country . . . The Milice will hesitate at nothing.'

The battle for the soul of France was proving fierce, dark and deadly. In towns and villages across the nation, posters had been pasted on walls and doors by the French resistance (formally known as the Forces françaises de l'Intérieur; the FFI). 'Patriots, the enemy has eyes and ears everywhere. Frenchmen even sell their brothers to the enemy, every day. Keep quiet! This is not just the way to ensure the FFI's safety, but also your own . . . You can, by your gossip, make yourselves the unwitting accomplices of the Gestapo and the Milice, and, unwittingly or not, we will treat you as accomplices.'

With potential adversaries on all sides, the constant need for watchfulness and to be wary wore on the nerves. Thankfully, in sorting out the 'good French' from the 'bad French', Tonkin had a foremost ally on hand. While Tonkin was the SAS party's commander, the real power-broker on the ground was a remarkable agent of the Special Operations Executive (SOE), codenamed 'Samuel'. Formally, Agent Samuel luxuriated in the name René Amédée Louis Pierre Maingard de la Ville-ès-Offrans. Hailing from an aristocratic background, and being born in Mauritius, Maingard was fluent in both French and English, the two languages widely spoken across that Indian Ocean island nation.

Studying accountancy in London at the outbreak of war, the twenty-four-year-old Mauritian had volunteered for Special Service, being recruited into the SOE. In April 1943 he had been parachuted into France to serve as the deputy to Agent 'Hector', Squadron Leader Maurice Southgate, who ran one of the largest resistance networks in France, codenamed the *Shipwright Circuit*. But upon Southgate's arrest by the Gestapo, three months prior to the Bulbasket team dropping in, Maingard had had to step forward and take over command. By July 1944 he had some 5,000 resistance fighters under him, and he was responsible for arming and training them all, in preparation for rising up against the reviled enemy, in close coordination with the D-Day landings.

Agent Samuel's was one impressive record, and he served as Tonkin's link-man on the ground. Some of his fighters had been assigned to the SAS party, to furnish a screen of protection and to act as guides during their sabotage operations. Maingard's resistance groups lacked for little in terms of training, armaments or security strictures. Following Southgate's example – once he had been captured by the Gestapo, the squadron leader had been sent to Buchenwald, the notorious concentration camp – Maingard had instigated rigorous screening measures, including that any traitors were to be shot.

Across his 5,000-strong force, recruits were 'carefully vetted and questioned before they were allowed to join', Maingard would report. In that way, those trying to infiltrate his network had been found out and liquidated. 'As a result, there was no serious penetration of the Maquis in this area.' ('Maquis' and 'Resistance' were more or less interchangeable terms.) The roles – SAS versus Maquis – were also crystal clear. Tonkin's force was there not to engage in stand-up battles with the enemy; the mission of the SAS party was to mount hit-and-run sabotage operations. Maingard's fighters were to support the SAS in that task, and to fend off the enemy when required.

Maingard's men were in the habit of praising 'the abundance of weapons which fell from the sky, thanks to our Major Samuel'. Between May to July 1944, Maingard had organised 105 separate airdrops, courtesy of the SOE, consisting of 2,510 containers packed with weaponry, explosives and supplies. He'd also alighted upon an unexpected source of funding for his operations. On the night of 3 July he had staked out a DZ, expecting a resupply. Sure enough, an aircraft had appeared and a cannister had floated down from the dark sky. But when Maingard had gone to open it, it proved to be stuffed full of 1,200,000 French francs, not the weaponry and explosives he'd been expecting.

Maingard had radioed SOE headquarters, in an effort to discover what had happened. It turned out that the cash had been dropped to him by accident. It emanated from the Secret Intelligence Service and was intended for one of their agents to finance clandestine operations. As it had fallen into Maingard's clutches, and there was no way of getting it back again, he was told to use it for his own purposes. With funds like that to hand, Maingard was able to set up hospitals to treat the wounded, for he was expecting casualties in the coming clashes with the enemy. Sure enough, in one major battle his men would attack a German convoy, after which 'over three hundred German dead were counted', but they had their own tally of dead and injured too. As Maingard 'frequently led' such high-risk operations, that only served to increase his standing in the eyes of his men.

But such daring actions – and now, Tonkin's repeated sabotage missions – had drawn the enemy's ire. Hundreds of German troops had been dispatched to comb the countryside, hunting for the British saboteurs. Just a few days earlier, Maingard's forces had intercepted one such unit, even as it had converged on the SAS base. 'Jerry estimated 400 strong attacked area of camp,' Tonkin would report. 'Beaten off with losses by Maquis.' At the same time, Tonkin's wireless communications were suffering, as the enemy upped their 'jamming' operations, blocking his radio signals. At one stage Tonkin had resorted to dispatching a carrier pigeon to London, bearing the following message: 'Being chased from area by large German counter insurgent sweep.'

Such close shaves had forced Tonkin to move his base again and again, most recently settling upon the Forêt de Verrières as his new outpost. But even while he was trying to guard against discovery, he remained under fierce pressure to up the pace of operations. Repeatedly, 'HQ SAS Troops' had radioed him, stressing the need to prevent enemy reinforcements from flowing north, and of the 'great importance' of the rail links in his area, which had to be 'kept cut'. Daily the messages kept coming. 'To Tonkin. Infantry Div. passing through your area tonight. May be 277. Try to identify and harass.' Another: 'To Tonkin . . . Infantry Div. moving north from TOULOUSE. Put a brake on it please.' And: 'To Tonkin. CHATEAUROUX–LE BLANC Airfield coming into use again. 30 Stukas parked under trees . . . Can you attack?'

Despite Tonkin's vigilance, the first hints of betrayal were to come from the most unlikely of quarters. On 1 July 1944 Tonkin received an urgent message to meet with Maingard. As he held the SOE agent in the very highest regard, he headed direct to the rendezvous. He reached it, only to find Agent Samuel ensconced with three of his resistance chiefs, and in a dark mood. In short order, Maingard explained to Tonkin the cause of their disquiet. There was a third force active on the ground, in addition to Maquis and SAS. Known as 'the Phantoms' – more formally called the Phantom/GHQ Liaison Regiment – their remit was to serve as signals specialists attached to Allied frontline units. Phantoms were tasked to keep abreast of the fast-moving battle, making Allied headquarters aware of where enemy and friendly units were located, and monitoring radio transmissions.

A five-man Phantom team had deployed at the same time as

Tonkin's SAS party. It was commanded by a Belgian, Captain John Sadoine. Maingard got straight to the point: Sadoine was suspected of being a turncoat. Repeatedly, the Phantom Captain had been instructed to link up with Tonkin's SAS, but had refused to do so. On 24 June an order had been sent by radio: 'To Sadoine . . . join Tonkin.' Sadoine's response: 'Not ready to move.' On the 27th: 'To Sadoine . . . you are alternate W/T [wireless telegraphy] source for Bulbasket.' In other words, Sadoine's team were supposed to form the second radio link for Tonkin and his men. On the 29th: 'To Sadoine . . . must rpt. must be prepared to close [with Tonkin's party] . . . Tonkin has been informed.' To all such urgings Sadoine had replied with unconvincing excuses, while refusing to comply.

Tonkin was well aware of this, and it had struck him as being decidedly odd. Disquieting even. But now Maingard was warning him that Sadoine had done far worse – he'd been actively telling the Maquis to have nothing to do with the SAS. Apparently, Sadoine had become obsessed with the fear that the SAS's high-profile operations would lead to the demise of his entire Phantom team. With Operation Overlord in full swing, the *raison d'être* of Tonkin's raiders was gone, Sadoine reasoned, for Allied forces would steamroller through the enemy's positions. Sadoine had decided that there was only one sensible course of action open to him, Maingard explained – 'the elimination of Tonkin' and his SAS patrol.

Tonkin was speechless to learn of such allegations; stunned. For Maingard, and the Maquis commanders, Sadoine had crossed the line into treachery, and only one possible fate should accrue: execution. They urged Tonkin, as the highest ranking British Army officer then present, and the man to whom Sadoine should be answerable, to act. He should court-martial Sadoine in the field and shoot him. Tonkin baulked. Sadoine was not even SAS: he was a Phantom. They were both captains, though formally Sadoine was under Tonkin's command. Did the SAS captain even have the authority to do as they suggested? Tonkin argued that Sadoine should be placed under close arrest instead, and that justice would be served once they returned to Britain at the end of the mission. 'In retrospect,' Tonkin would later remark, 'it was a stupid decision.'

Of course, hindsight is a fine thing. But Tonkin had little time or space for reflection right then. Orders from London were coming in thick and fast, with repeated target designations. On 30 June: 'Tonkin . . . Inf. Div [Infantry Division] held at BRIVES lacking petrol.' On 1 July: 'For Tonkin. Petrol high priority target. One armoured unit fighting Normandy on foot.' Same day: 'To Tonkin. LIMOGES marshalling yard reported much damaged. No repair time given.' Tonkin's replies reflected how he and his men were busy hitting such targets: 'From Tonkin. Lt. Morris left for CHATEREAUX airfield and VIERZON–TOURS railway . . .' 'Lt. Weaver confirms he derailed train PARTHENAY . . .' 'Lt. Stephens in, job completed.' Plus, in reference to a coming air-drop of supplies, Tonkin radioed confirmation: 'DZ for night Jul . . . Codeword MILTON understood.'

But on 3 July 1944, Tonkin's communications suddenly fell strangely silent. All that day there was nothing. Not one single message. At 7.00 that evening, headquarters sent an urgent message to the SAS commander winging through the ether. His 'MILTON' resupply airdrop, scheduled for that very night, was about to be cancelled, unless Tonkin could radio through final confirmation that all was set on the ground. There was no response from the SAS captain. Far worse was to follow.

Early on the morning of 4 July, a contact codenamed 'Raincoat Blue' radioed SAS headquarters, with alarming news. 'Tonkin attacked morning 3 July at FORET DE VERRRIERS. 100 Maquis dispatched to assist him.' (The identity of Raincoat Blue is lost to time, but it seems very likely it was Captain Maingard's radio operator.) With SAS headquarters desperate for further information, Sadoine, the Phantom officer, was asked what he might know. In response, Sadoine sent a radio report that 'all party captured . . . Unconfirmed Capt. Tonkin captured wounded'.

In truth, at first light on 3 July a 400-strong force of Waffen SS troops had converged on the SAS's Verrières base camp. Earlier that morning, SS *Obersturmführer* Hoffman, the local commander, had mustered his men. The main bulk were made up of troops of the 17th SS Panzergrenadier Division, Götz von Berlichingen, named after a fifteenth-century German Imperial Knight and mercenary of the same name. An armoured infantry unit, the 17th was equipped with mortars, artillery and StuG VI armoured and tracked assault guns, and assisted by a recce platoon mounted on bicycles, among other specialist units. Even as the assault force had closed a ring of steel around the Forêt de Verrières, Tonkin had slipped back into the SAS camp, having just returned from checking out an alternative location for their base.

As *Obersturmführer* Hoffman set his pre-dawn trap, so some forty SAS men, Tonkin included, were at rest in the forest (the remainder were out on operations). There was also Maingard's Maquis at the camp, plus an American pilot who had only recently made it to their treebound fastness. Two days earlier, Lieutenant Lincoln F. Bundy had pitched up at the SAS camp, seeking to join their number. Bundy claimed to have been shot down immediately after D-Day, while flying his P-51 Mustang single-seat fighter-bomber in combat operations. Tonkin had remained suspicious, and he'd radioed headquarters asking for checks to be made of Bundy's bona fides. 'From Tonkin. Reports pilot Lt. Lincoln Bundy USAAF with them and asks for question check on him.'

But there was no time for even the most basic of enquiries to be made, before the enemy trap was sprung. By 0600 hours on 3 July the Panzergrenadiers had ensured that the noose of steel was ready to bite. Shortly after sunrise, two of Maingard's men would be the ones to trigger it. Pierre Lecellier and Marcel Weber were moving in towards the SAS encampment, having spent the night in Verrières village. The first sign that the two Maquisards noticed of anything being amiss was when they realised that the very bushes to their front seemed to be moving.

Moments later, the first enemy troops, heavily camouflaged with sprigs of vegetation, sprang to their feet, ordering the two Frenchmen to surrender. Lecellier and Weber drew their weapons, but, as more and more German soldiers emerged, they decided to make a break for it. Both managed to spring free and to dash back to Verrières, at which point they lost each other, the village itself being full of enemy soldiers. From windows and doorways, the Germans opened fire on the two fugitives. Rushing down a side street, Weber blundered into a group of the enemy, but managed to break free again, 'zigzagging as I ran'. Despite such precautions, the hail of fire found its mark, and Weber 'felt a strong burning sensation' in one thigh, as blood poured down from a flesh wound.

Despite that, and the pain that he was in, Weber managed to press on. He circled back to the SAS camp, whereupon he went about raising the alarm. Staggering into the forest encampment, he began yelling out warnings. As startled figures shook themselves awake and grabbed their weapons, Weber was collared by a Corporal Allan, Tonkin's medical orderly. Allan was instantly recognisable with his Red Cross armband, and he went about dressing the Frenchman's wounds, to try to stem the flow of blood.

One moment Tonkin had been fast asleep. The next he found himself crawling out of his sleeping bag, even as the first heavy shells and mortar rounds screamed down, detonating in the forest thereabouts. Their camp lay at one end of the sweep of woodland, and it was situated above the valley with its freshwater stream. Together with Lieutenant Peter Weaver – one of Tonkin's old hands – plus a Maquis commander, Tonkin dashed to the edge of the wood, to get a fix on the enemy. Gazing out from the cover of the trees, the trio spied a heavy force of German troops down in the valley, creeping ever closer along the hedgerows. The enemy were still a good 200 yards away, but to the watchers this had all the appearances of a well-set trap.

At thirty-two years of age, Weaver was the 'old man' of the SAS party, and was blessed with huge experience, both in and out of the military. Born in India, the son of a First World War regular Army officer, Weaver had been sent to public school in England. But, being dyslexic, his studies had floundered. It was in sport that he'd found his true calling, captaining England at hockey and playing cricket for Hampshire. With war looming, Weaver had signed up, joining the highly secretive Auxiliary Units – otherwise known as the British Resistance Organisation – specially-trained forces that were charged to wage guerrilla-style warfare, should Nazi Germany succeed in invading Britain.

Serving under the motto *Valiant but Vigilant*, the Auxiliaries' creed had been laid down by Brigadier Colin McVean Gubbins, the future chief of SOE. Outlining his plans for a very British form of irregular warfare, Gubbins had stressed: 'Surprise first and foremost by finding out the enemy's plans and concealing your own . . . Break off the action when it becomes too risky . . . Choose areas and localities for action where your mobility will be superior to that of the enemy . . . Confine all movements as much as possible to the hours of darkness . . . Retain the initiative at all costs . . . When the time for action comes, act with the greatest boldness and audacity . . .' When the threat of invasion – Operation Sealion – had receded, many of the Auxiliaries had stepped forward to join the SAS, Lieutenant Weaver among them.

During parachute training Weaver had narrowly escaped death, when the aircraft he was riding in went to take off but collided on the runway with an in-bound warplane. He had gone on to complete his jump training, but typically the stubborn, iron-willed and unconventional former Auxiliary had refused to endorse the new-style red beret, which had been issued to all British airborne forces, and which the SAS were now supposed to wear. Instead, just as soon as he'd been parachuted into France, he'd whipped it off his head, stuffed it into his backpack, and replaced it with the original sandy beret, which had distinguished the men of the SAS since shortly after the unit was founded. As Weaver fully appreciated, there were several former Auxiliaries in the Bulbasket party, and each brought with him the mindset of waging unconventional warfare, something that had been drilled into them in their former unit.

Hurrying back to the main body of men, Tonkin and Weaver

found that the former drama student Lieutenant Crisp, together with Lieutenant Stephens, Tonkin's fiery Welsh deputy, had organised the men into groups, ready to escape and evade. From what they had just seen, it was clear to Tonkin and Weaver that there was little point in trying to stand and fight. They faced a far stronger enemy force, that much was clear. As further salvoes of shells burst in the forest near by, sending shrapnel cutting through the trees, Tonkin gave the order to scatter. They were to disappear deeper into the forest – 'it was a very large area' – for at least that way they might stand a chance of making a getaway. For a brief moment he was tempted to try to use 'the Vickers-Ks on the three jeeps' – the vehicle-mounted machine guns – yet he knew instinctively that 'scattering quietly' was the best bet.

But, by an unfortunate quirk of fate, bad luck and trouble were about to intervene. All of a sudden, a semi-naked figure came running through the camp, yelling out, 'They're coming! They're coming!' It was one of Tonkin's men, seemingly only recently torn from sleep, and for whatever reason panic had set in. Dashing in a 'headlong flight', he made straight for the valley below, which Tonkin and Weaver knew to be thick with enemy troops. Aghast, they saw several others break cover and hurry after the fleeing figure. Tonkin ordered Weaver, Crisp and Stephens to go after them, for this was the very worst thing to do – they were heading into the open and the enemy's guns.

Pausing only to stuff some time-delay fuses into the party's stores of explosives, Tonkin and his remaining men turned west, and, grabbing their weapons, they flitted deeper into the trees. Tonkin hadn't gone far when he was struck by a terrible thought. He couldn't see Corporal Reginald Chick, his wireless operator, anywhere. Though he'd only just turned twenty-four, Chick, a former shoemaker from Tredegar, in Monmouthshire, was one of the old-faithfuls, having soldiered with the SAS in North Africa, in the Sicily landings – Operation Husky – and all through the hard-fought Italian campaign. More importantly, Chick was the custodian of their wireless set and their top-secret codes.

If the radio and codebooks had been left at the camp, and were captured by the Germans, the fallout from that would be potentially calamitous. The enemy might break the SAS codes, leading to horrendous consequences for other patrols. Ordering the rest to press on deeper into the woods, Tonkin turned around and headed back alone. Reaching their now-deserted camp, the clash of gunfire, grenade blasts and the cries of battle rang out from the valley below. He searched everywhere, but there was no sign of either the radio set or codes, meaning that Chick had most likely grabbed them and taken them with him. But as Tonkin turned to leave, he spied two columns of German troops closing in on his position. He was cut off and surrounded.

Heading for the roughest ground he could find, Tonkin burrowed in among the vegetation, taking shelter beside a boulder in an effort to hide. He was only just in time. He 'kept *very* still', as a German armed with 'a Schmeisser' – an MP 40 submachine gun – came into view 'on the top edge of the slope'. The enemy soldier scanned the terrain below, as Tonkin heard blasts of machine-gun fire echoing up from the valley, amid the yells of the German troops. After what felt to Tonkin like 'several hours', but could only have been a matter of 'ten minutes or so', the German turned away and, seizing his chance, Tonkin crept stealthily into the trees.

Meanwhile, Tonkin's key deputies – Lieutenants Weaver, Crisp and Stephens – had found themselves in dire straits, once the ambush had been sprung. Dashing after those fleeing into the valley, they'd reached the edge of the treeline only to be met by an intense fusillade of fire. Heavy machine guns had been sighted in the open ground beyond, ready to rake the edge of the woodlands, just as the German gunners were doing now. Driven back into cover, the three SAS officers did their best to round up as many of the stragglers as they could, while Maingard's Maquis traded fierce fire with the enemy, holding them at bay with volleys of bullets and grenades.

Leading that hastily gathered party, Weaver, Crisp and Stephens steered them in a zigzag procession, as they crossed the stream twice, and tried to steal away into the woods, but at every turn they were met with blasts of fire. It seemed as if the enemy were on all sides now, and eventually, inevitably, they began taking casualties. Lieutenant Crisp – the former drama student – was one of the first to fall, cut down by a burst of machine-gun fire. Wounded in the thigh, he tried to drag himself into cover, driven on by fear and adrenaline. Assailed as they were at every juncture, Weaver gave the only order he could think of right then: they were to split up and try to escape in ones and twos.

Moving in a crouching run, Weaver tried to push west deeper into the woods, heading in the same direction as Tonkin and his party, but he was met with a line of German troops carrying out a sweep through the trees. There was no way through. Weaver turned back, and was forced to risk crawling out of the woodland into a field high with corn. His movements must have been spotted, for in no time blasts of fire ripped through the stalks right above his head. To one side, other figures were trying to belly-crawl through that field of crops, only for mortar rounds to crash down among them, badly wounding one SAS soldier.

Still Weaver pressed on. Reaching the far side of the field he broke cover and dashed ahead, chased by bursts of fire all the way. Vaulting a stile set in the hedge ahead of him, he reached a small stream, pausing for a second to quench his burning thirst. On the far side he spied a dense patch of brambles. A perfect place to hide. Bracing himself against the tearing of the thorns, Weaver wormed his way into the depths of that decidedly inhospitable cover, and taking his pistol in one hand, he steeled himself for whatever else this day of hell might bring.

Back at the woodland's edge, it was Lieutenant Stephens who was about to be among the first to fall victim to the enemy's savagery. Following in Weaver's footsteps, the Welshman had tried to break out through the cornfield. But he'd made it no further than twenty yards when he was targeted by 'withering fire'. Retreating to the woods, Stephens was hit in the thigh. Collapsing at the fringe of the trees, he urged the others who were with him to flee. Bleeding profusely, yet still refusing to give himself up, Stephens attempted to crawl into cover, to hide. But he was set upon by some German troops. They dragged the plucky Welshman to a tree. He was propped against it, whereupon the *coup de grâce* was delivered, with a single shot to the head. As Tonkin would write, in his official report: 'Lieut. STEPHENS was wounded, and afterwards killed . . .'

The enemy began to gather at the edge of the woods now, corralling the dozens of prisoners they had seized – all SAS; all heavily guarded – while issuing loud congratulations to each other on the success of their mission. Unbeknown to anyone, a Maquis member, Denis Chansigaud, was concealed in the bushes nearby, and was able to witness much of what transpired. A half-track roared up, together with a black Citroën car, which disgorged a group of men dressed in dark suits and hats – the Gestapo's de facto uniform. The new arrivals headed directly into the trees. A few moments later there were bursts of machine-gun fire, followed by a volley of single shots. Although Chansigaud didn't know it at the time, this signified that the new arrivals had just executed his captured Maquis brethren in cold blood.

Apart from the thirty-odd SAS captives now herded together, the remainder of Tonkin's force was scattered to the four corners of the wind, as were their Maquis brothers. Ensconced deep in his thorn bush, Lieutenant Weaver actually fell asleep, he was so shattered. Marcel Weber, the resistance fighter who had first triggered the ambush, had managed to drag himself away, his shoe filled with congealed blood, his head spinning horribly. Though he was repeatedly under fire, and hit several further times, Weber stumbled onto a road and managed to flag down a passing car. By stages, his saviours managed to spirit him to comparative safety. But the wounded former thespian, Lieutenant Crisp, had been taken captive, as had Tonkin's signals man, Corporal Chick, plus the American airman Lieutenant Bundy, and scores more.

Though Tonkin was unaware, he would have got just a little solace from knowing the enemy body count, and in learning the full effect of lacing the camp's store of explosives with primed detonators. As German troops had rifled through the SAS camp, the entire stash of charges had detonated, resulting in a powerful blast causing 'enemy dead and wounded'. Apparently, their casualties amounted to '20 killed' and several more injured. But Tonkin had little idea of any of this, for even then he and his handful of fellow escapees were hiding and running in the depths of the woodland.

It was around midday when the German commander ordered

the operation to be brought to an end. Driving back into Verrières, he signalled a halt, only to round up all the able-bodied men of the village, who were herded into the square. Many had heard of the savagery visited upon French civilians who were seen as having aided the Maquis, or worse still the British 'saboteurs', and few doubted what was about to happen. But even as they braced themselves for the worst, the German commanders suddenly seemed to change their minds. In the blink of an eye, they informed the assembled ranks that they were about to depart, and that there were bodies that needed collecting from the forest. While they would need to be buried, the villagers were warned that the fallen were not to be afforded the dignity of a coffin; they were to be wrapped in bare sheets instead. With that, the enemy troops mounted up their vehicles and pulled out.

Those gathered in the square were at something of a loss as to what to make of it. Unbeknown to them, their deliverance was down to a band of daring Maquis – plus some woeful vehicle maintenance. One of Maingard's resistance groups, alerted to the assault on the SAS camp, had mustered scores of fighters. They were loaded aboard the only transport available right then – a convoy of ancient and war-weary trucks. Each lacked the bare semblance of an exhaust. As they roared and snorted their way towards Verrières, they made enough noise to convince anyone within listening distance that thousands of Maquis were on the move. Hearing that cacophony, the Germans had decided that discretion was very much the better part of valour. Opting to avoid another battle, they had hightailed it out of there, with their prisoners – the prize – in tow.

With the German troops gone, the villagers set about doing exactly what they had been forbidden from doing – knocking together coffins in which to bury the dead. But as they were so engaged, without warning a lone figure stumbled out of the forest. By his badges and insignia alone it was clear that he was a British soldier and an officer. It turned out to be John Tonkin, the SAS party's commander, and although he was 'dazed with shock' at that day's terrible events, he was still on his feet and still very much at liberty. The village mayor was summoned, for there was unfortunate business to attend to. Among the dead that were being brought into Verrières, there was one British soldier. The mayor led Tonkin to where the body lay, so he might identify the fallen man.

Tonkin had already been warned that the Germans had carted off some three dozen of his soldiers as prisoners. Now, he was forced to gaze upon the bloodied form of one of those to whom he had been closest in his patrol – Lieutenant Twm Stephens, the fiery Welshman whom Tonkin had basically persuaded to join the SAS in the first place. Scarcely able to speak, Tonkin managed to confirm Stephens' identity, offering the mayor the man's rank and service number. He also handed him a shoulder flash emblazoned with the insignia '1st S.A.S.' and one of the unit's iconic cap badges, completed with its motto, *Who dares wins*. Tonkin asked that both might be placed on Stephens' grave.

By now it was approaching dusk, and a second British soldier arrived in Verrières. This was Trooper McNair, another man with whom Tonkin had a very special bond. All through McNair's SAS training, Tonkin had badgered him to accept promotion, for he was 'a natural'. Tonkin tried to persuade him many times over, but 'he always refused'. Eventually, Tonkin had found out why. Earlier in the war McNair had been a lieutenant, commanding a Matilda – a heavily armoured, but slow and relatively lightly armed tank. Deployed to North Africa, those Maltilda tanks had been no match for the enemy armour. Three of them had been 'brewed up' beneath McNair, who, as the commander, sat in the turret with the hatch open. Three times he had managed to jump free, but his crews had 'burned to death' in those steel coffins. After that, McNair had resigned his commission and volunteered for the SAS as a private (more commonly called a 'trooper' in airborne forces).

McNair had heard that Tonkin was in Verrières, and had come there to fetch him. As McNair led his commander out of the village, he was able to brief him on the wider fortunes of his men. A handful of escapees had gathered at the emergency rendezvous (RV) – the pre-set point at which all were supposed to muster, should the SAS party get ambushed and split up. McNair had brought several of them in. He'd also left notes in pre-set hiding places, to guide any stragglers to the RV. Plus he'd sent out word to the Maquis leaders about all that had happened. As it was late and both men were utterly shattered – Tonkin especially; he had been wandering about in 'a blur' – they headed to a local farmstead. Despite the risks, the farmer and his wife took the two fugitives in, and fed them hot thick soup, before insisting that they take the one bed, while its rightful owners stood watch.

The following morning Tonkin and McNair made their way to the RV, which was situated at La Roche, a remote farm owned by M. Bonnet, who doubled as a Maquis chief under the codename *Baptiste*. There they joined a handful of survivors, including Denis Chansigaud, the Maquis fighter who had hidden in the woods as the Gestapo had executed his comrades. As Chansigaud was uninjured, and could pass as a local, he was charged to make his way back through the woodland, whistling softly the British national anthem, in an effort to flush out any other survivors. In that way, another of the SAS stragglers was brought in. The final figure to appear that day was Lieutenant Weaver. He was greeted by a relieved cry from Tonkin: 'Thank God you got through!' Having slept the night in his thorn bush, Weaver had wandered into La Roche of his own accord.

Altogether, eight SAS had escaped from the ring of steel at the Forêt de Verrières. Apart from Tonkin, Weaver and McNair, there was a Sergeant Holmes, Corporal Joseph Rideout, and Troopers Cummings, Les Keeble and William Smith. Tonkin was particularly relieved to discover that Sergeant Johnny Holmes had survived, for Holmes had been his jeep-driver in the North African desert, and all through Sicily and Italy. But the remainder of his force, thirty SAS – three of whom were grievously wounded – had been captured. The unit's medic, Corporal Allan, had also been seized, as had the USAAF Lieutenant, Lincoln Bundy. Of the Maquis who had been located with Tonkin's party, only four – Weber and Chansigaud included – had escaped with their lives. The rest had either been killed in action or murdered in the forest. While some of the fallen Frenchmen would be returned to their home villages for burial, others were to be laid to rest in Verrières itself, as was SAS Lieutenant Twm Stephens.

Touchingly, the locals wished for the brave Welshman to lie next to the dead of their village, and he was duly interred in a tomb that held the graves of several generations. A simple cross was erected within that small stone vault, which resembled a miniature chapel. Upon that cross was placed Stephens' SAS insignia, as Tonkin had requested. At one point during that long day – 4 July 1944 – Tonkin considered undertaking a desperate escape and evasion, taking his remaining men south through

France, in an effort to cross the border into Spain, which lay some 500 kilometres away. As Spain was officially neutral, from there they should be able to cross into Gibraltar and catch a ship or an aircraft bound for Britain.

The Bulbasket force had been reduced to less than a quarter of its strength, and by rights Tonkin would have had every reason to seek to escape. But the stubborn grafter in him simply refused to quit. Of course, the entire area was awash with wild rumour. There were reports of the SAS being wiped out to a man, which explained why Phantom Captain Sadoine filed the radio report that he did, at 8.45 p.m. that evening, suggesting that the entire SAS patrol had been killed or captured, Tonkin included. In truth, the SAS captain was shaken, bloodied and bowed, but he was certainly not down and out, as events were most powerfully to prove.

Tonkin's incredible fortitude at this juncture – his refusal to step away from the fight – was driven both by rage, and a thirst for vengeance. While on the one hand 4 July would mark the beginning of his and his small group of survivors' long escape, it would also mark the opening of an extraordinary chapter in which Tonkin would seek fitting revenge, particularly for the horrific war crimes that were about to be visited upon his men. Repeatedly, SAS headquarters would try to spirit the SAS captain and his small band of survivor-escapees back to friendly lines. But at the final juncture, Tonkin would have to be ordered out of France, as the anger and the hurt drove him to strike and strike again at those who had so maltreated his brothers in arms.

Those thirty-odd SAS captives were driven by truck to the nearby city of Poitiers, where they were split up. The three most seriously wounded were taken to a local hospital. The rest, including those whose injuries were less life-threatening, were thrown into a military prison, six to a cell. At first, they were left to talk freely among themselves, or so it seemed. In truth, those cells had been fitted with listening devices and secretly their chatter was being recorded. From this, the SS and Gestapo sought to learn the secrets of the SAS raiders – about their signals, the aircraft that flew in supplies, drop zones, timings and so on and so forth. Little of any interest was gleaned. Interrogations followed. Again, they produced precious little intelligence. All the prisoners seemed willing to divulge was that they had been parachuted into France on sabotage operations, which was giving very little away, of course.

Within the first hours after the SAS party's capture, a report had been sent by radio to German Army headquarters, asking what was to be done with the captives. The response that came back to General Curt Gallenkamp, the area commander, made for grim reading. Under Hitler's Commando Order, the prisoners were to be executed at the earliest opportunity. General Gallenkamp baulked at such a draconian and murderous diktat. He tried to argue that the SS and Gestapo should take custody of the prisoners, not the regular military. But when the German general tried to get them to do so, the SS and Gestapo refused. As Gallenkamp and his deputies struggled to find a way to offload the prisoners, or a means to keep them alive, their fate was about to be signed and sealed.

Even as Tonkin and his small group of survivors regrouped and took stock, so the German high command issued a statement to the world's press. That communiqué boasted of how the German Army had captured dozens of saboteurs of the Special Air Service, and that all had been summarily liquidated. They hadn't yet – they were still incarcerated in the cells. But for General Gallenkamp and his deputies this was pretty much checkmate, especially since a signal came in from high command, requesting to know the fate of the prisoners, as well as demanding a 'certificate of destruction of this teleprinted message'. That last phrase – requiring proof that the message had been destroyed – reflected the sensitivity that surrounded such signals, which effectively ordered the murder of bona fide prisoners of war.

Aghast at what he had been ordered to do, General Gallenkamp chose instead to head for the frontlines, supposedly to inspect his troops. It was left to his deputies to agonise over Hitler's Commando Order, and to determine whether they should stand for what was right and just, and refuse to execute the captives, or to follow orders, in order to save their own skins.

Tonkin, meanwhile, gathered his forces. They were bolstered by three more returnees – Troopers Sam Smith, Robert Smith and John Fielding. The trio had been absent from the camp, sabotaging a railway line, so had escaped the carnage. As Maingard had warned, all railroads were intensively guarded by now, with 'sentries every half Kilo [kilometre], patrolling constantly'. Those sentries 'kept in the bushes and shadows', which made sabotage efforts 'distinctly dangerous'. Smith, Smith and Fielding resorted to sneaking through a black pudding and lard factory, in an effort to avoid the enemy, eventually dropping into a deep railway cutting. That stretch of line was guarded by horse-mounted troops and dogs, and the trio were forced to dodge patrols at every turn. Even so, they managed to plant their explosive charges in the depths of the cutting.

'The explosion duly happened,' Fielding reported, 'a very satisfying time!'

As a further boost to Tonkin's spirits, a second raiding party made it into their RV, this one riding in a decidedly battle-worn jeep. Lieutenant Morris was at the wheel, with Trooper Brown manning the Vickers-K guns, and a Maquis figure, Godefroy Koenig, acting as their guide. Days earlier, the trio had been dispatched by Tonkin to raid the airfield at Châteroux, in response to a request from headquarters. En route, their jeep had turned over, throwing those riding in it onto the road. All had escaped with slight injuries, but the jeep was barely drivable. They'd taken it to a nearby farmstead for makeshift repairs, yet shortly Lieutenant Morris had learned of the attack on their Verrières camp, and all that had followed. Right away, he and his men had mounted up their jeep, battered and smashed-in though it might be, and made haste for La Roche.

Lieutenant Morris was a particularly trusted deputy to Tonkin. At one stage the SAS captain had asked Morris to bring in Captain Sadoine, their wayward Phantom officer. That had been in the third week of June, after another message had been sent to Sadoine, ordering him to move to Tonkin's location, to no avail. Morris had driven over to Sadoine's camp, only to have the Phantom commander pull rank on him, insisting that he was still not ready to join the SAS party. Sadoine and his team had been in the field for two weeks, yet an exasperated Morris had been forced to return to Tonkin empty-handed.

With Morris and his party's arrival, Tonkin now had thirteen SAS, himself included, plus that one lone jeep. It was enough. On 5 July, riding in a mixed convoy of civilian cars – operated by the Maquis – plus their jeep, Tonkin and his fellow survivors drove south for thirty-five kilometres. They headed for the Forêt de Plessachere, which lay in heavily wooded and semi-mountainous terrain. With his signaller, Corporal Chick, taken captive, and all his radio equipment gone, Tonkin was in desperate need of the means and wherewithal to re-establish communications with headquarters.

Accordingly, he sent out a force to bring in Captain Sadoine – at gunpoint if necessary – and his Phantom team, with their all-important wireless kit. Tonkin would report of this 5 July move and re-formation: 'Reorganised at U 7828 [the grid reference for their Forêt de Plessachere camp]. Our total strength . . . 18 all ranks including Capt. SADOINE and his party. Could not operate fully until re-equipped, so we continued instructing the Maquis and [with] small scale sabotage. I requested that the SS be bombed.'

That last line – his radio request for the RAF to launch a bombing mission against the SS forces that had attacked their Verrières camp – seems to be Tonkin's earliest move to seek vengeance. In truth, his bringing in Captain Sadoine was the opening salvo in that war. It was the SOE commander, Maingard, who had provided the civilian vehicles to enable Tonkin to move south from La Roche to their new camp. Together, SAS commander and SOE agent, they had gathered at the new base, while Lieutenant Weaver was dispatched with a force of troops to bring in Sadoine. Upon his arrival, the Phantom officer was led into a quiet patch of woodland . . . to be dealt with.

Getting right to the point, Tonkin confronted Sadoine over the allegations of his treachery. As not a word was uttered by an ashen-faced Sadoine in his defence, with no further ado Tonkin delivered his judgement: from now on, the Phantom officer was to be placed under close arrest. He would be guarded round the clock by three of Tonkin's men, operating rotating eight-hour shifts. They had orders to shoot to kill, should Sadoine try anything. That decided, Tonkin took Sadoine's radio operator, Corporal Stephens, to one side and informed him of exactly what had happened. The corporal would now act as the SAS's radio link to Britain, a crucial role, which he would go on to perform admirably.

With Sadoine's guns well and truly spiked, Tonkin could start to focus his efforts on seeking vengeance. Whether Sadoine was guilty or not, Tonkin wasn't entirely certain. In any case, that would be up to the powers-that-be in Britain to decide, once Sadoine was delivered into their custody, and that depended on them all getting out of there in one piece. Although Tonkin couldn't know it, Sadoine had actually sent through reports to Britain, claiming credit for some of the notable successes of the Bulbasket team, including their airstrikes on the petrol trains. But before any of this could be fully investigated, there was business afoot for Tonkin and his rump of survivor-escapees.

On 6 July, Tonkin got a first message through to SAS head-quarters, listing the names of those of his patrol who had survived, and giving details of the attack on their Verrières base: 'Betrayed and surrounded by 200 Jerry incl. SS and field guns. Ordered base to scatter ... Germans now sweeping area for Maquis who have suffered heavy casualties ... Possible PW [prisoners of war] 34 ... Lieutenant Stephens known killed. Codes available through SABU 3 under direct Tonkin control through Cpl. Stephens.' That last sentence signified that Tonkin had put the Phantom signaller under his direct authority. In other words, Sadoine was out of the picture.

Having alerted HQ that 'Germans may well know he [Tonkin] is SABU 35,' and that their signal codes and radio had to be 'presumed captured', Tonkin added a request for 'Jeeps with Vickers and powerful headlamps'. With his men gathered at their new base they were 'free and fit to operate again', he announced. Upon learning of Tonkin and his fellow survivors' escape, the reaction from SAS HQ was immediate. Major Edward Lepine, together with an SAS patrol, was to be parachuted in, to bolster Tonkin and his men. Lepine, recruited to the SAS in December 1942, was a long-standing comrade of Tonkin's. After the terrible misfortune that had overtaken the Bulbasket party – one of the single greatest losses suffered by the SAS in the war – it was hoped that a man of Lepine's standing would help steady the ship, which had to be in dire need of steadying.

But just hours after Lepine and his patrol were stood-up to jump, their mission was cancelled. Instead, Tonkin was instructed to seek out and prepare a landing strip, so that an aeroplane could put down. That aircraft would be coming in to pull out Tonkin and his fellow survivors, signifying an end to their mission. If they could get such a warplane down safely, that was to be the means to execute their escape.

For Tonkin and his fellows this was all too early, and not at all what they had in mind. Typically, at the same time as Tonkin was being ordered to prepare for an air evacuation, he was likewise radioing headquarters asking for the means to continue to wage war: 'IN. From Tonkin. Long list of demands for refits of kit, weapons, food, explosives, petrol, 4 jeeps etc . . . Demands explosives, petrol, oil and food in that priority.' In short, there was a tug-of-war developing between Tonkin and his taskmasters, who wanted him out of there.

SAS headquarters were privy to fresh intelligence, which had proved most alarming. On 27 June 1944, a warning had been passed to them which reported: 'Notices posted in all towns in Brittany stating that parachutists will be considered as Franc Tireurs [guerrilla fighters operating outside of the law] and shot immediately together with any persons giving them shelter.' The memo had been issued by SHAEF – the Allied supreme head-quarters in north-west Europe – so could hardly have come from a higher authority, and what was good for Brittany was presum-ably good for the whole of France.

Little wonder they wanted Tonkin home. If those of his men taken captive were murdered, Tonkin's thirst for vengeance might become unquenchable, and who knew what it might lead to. Tonkin, by contrast, wanted to stay right where he was and to hit back hard. Lord knows, he had his reasons ... On 12 July he'd send a short message to headquarters, suggesting that the fate of those taken captive might be known to him already: 'Unconfirmed Maquis report all SAS prisoners shot in Poitiers.' Tonkin had stated 'unconfirmed', for he'd tried to verify the rumour and had failed to do so. Even so, it fuelled his worries and his fears, not to mention his rage.

A photo was snapped at around this time, as Tonkin mus-tered his survivors at their new base. It is iconic. The men pose before their one surviving jeep – number M5475747. Tonkin perches in the rear gunner's position, jaw set, pipe jammed defi-antly in his mouth. Sergeant Johnny Holmes stands directly in front of Tonkin, balding head to the fore, and with what can only be described as an irreverent, vengeful smile creasing his features. While other figures do appear noticeably battle weary – some are shirtless, all are bare-headed – what is utterly striking is the degree of level-eyed determination in each man's gaze. Immortalised in various French reports, that photograph bears the title '*Les rescapés de Verrières*' – the survivors of Verrières.

Tonkin and his men fully intended to do more than simply *survive*; payback was coming. The first blow was struck just days after they had moved to their new base. 'Railway LA ROCHELLE–NIORT–POITIERS bombed ... excellent results.' Tonkin and his fellow survivors were back in business. But what they hungered for most was the means to hit those who had decimated their patrol, for they feared for the lives of all taken captive.

At the end of the second week of July 1944, Tonkin launched his big gambit. He reckoned he had discovered the location of the headquarters of the SS unit that had attacked his camp, and murdered at least one man, Lieutenant Twm Stephens, in cold blood, while also liquidating any number of Maquis. Some 20 kilometres north-east of Poitiers lay a German base at Bonneuil-Matours, a settlement set on the bank of the Vienne river. The majority of the SS troops that had ambushed the SAS were quartered in the barracks block and sleeping accommodation. Tonkin wanted it hit, and hit hard.

On 12 July a detailed targeting message winged its way to Britain: 'Request bombing of HQ Boche Colonel commanding repression column ... Situated Bonneuil-Matours. 15 km south of Châtelleraut. Chateau 450 metres southeast of crossroads east of village.' That same signal warned of the known defences around the target, including German armour and anti-aircraft guns. The chief bombing point was actually the Château de Marieville, a white-fronted edifice complete with a dozen pointed towers. This fairy-tale castle was perched on a hill overlooking the Vienne river, just upstream of a bridge, the Pont de Bonneuil-Matours, making it stand out noticeably from the air.

The château housed the senior German commanders responsible for the 'repression column' – the troops that had pounced on the SAS's Verrières base. The soldiers of the 17th SS Panzergrenadiers were housed in the barracks on the opposite bank of the river, set amidst woodland. Of course, no one yet knew the true fate of the thirty-odd SAS and other captives, but that German communiqué trumpeting their 'summary liquidation' remained deeply troubling. In response to Tonkin's radio message, an SAS intelligence officer based at headquarters, a Captain Michael Foot, put a call through to RAF 2 Group, speaking to his regular liaison officer for such missions.

By the summer of 1944, RAF 2 Group was operating North American B-25 Mitchell and Douglas DB-7 Boston medium bombers, plus the Wooden Wonders, the Mosquito. It was the latter that the SAS wanted scrambled, and in a similar fashion as before, when they had thundered in low and fast to take out those dozen petrol trains. For much of June and July Allied forces had been endeavouring to break out of the Normandy beachheads, but the battle had proven bloody and hard-fought, the Germans giving not an inch of easy territory. As a result, 2 Group's commanders faced relentless calls to fly missions, striking against enemy targets in and around the area of the landings. Many feared the fate of Operation Overlord was hanging in the balance, and the request for a bombing mission some 500 kilometres to the south of Normandy might have appeared to some as a sideshow. But not to those at the helm of 2 Group.

The commander of 2 Group, Air Vice-Marshal Basil Embry, had compelling reasons to back such a call to action; to strike deep and hard in the cause of vengeance. In May 1940, Embry had been shot down over France while flying a Blenheim. Taken prisoner, he suffered a short spell in captivity, before breaking out and executing an extraordinary escape, finally reaching British shores. While making that daring getaway, Embry had been forced to kill three enemy soldiers, and in response the German high command had placed a price on his head. Consequently, he knew exactly what it felt like to be hunted, and to be condemned to a death sentence when none was justified or called for.

Embry had fought tooth and nail to win 2 Group as many Mosquitos as he could, for he believed the Wooden Wonder to be the most capable aerial war-machine ever designed and built by Britain. An absolute touch of genius. The results of their summer 1944 bombing raids had proved Embry right, as would the coming strike on the targets that Tonkin had identified. Despite the death sentence hanging over his head, Embry often flew on such missions, using a false identity in case he was shot down. Regretfully, he couldn't join the present one, which was to be flown by the aircrew of 140 Wing. They operated out of RAF Thorney Island, situated near Portsmouth, on the south coast of England, so lying directly opposite the Normandy beaches.

While he couldn't fly the mission, Embry made a point of being there at its departure. Making a beeline for Thorney Island, he made sure to brief the aircrews in person. Fourteen Mosquitos would fly in the attack, aiming to strike at dusk, which had the added advantage of very likely catching the SS troops sitting down to their evening meal. Embry pointed out another crucial point about the mission, as far as he was concerned. Scheduled for that night, when the weather would be calm and clear, conditions were ideal for such a precision air-strike. As Embry was at pains to point out, it just happened to be 14 July, which is Bastille Day, the national day of France. The date was auspicious, not to mention deeply symbolic: they would strike a blow on the national day of the nation that they were fighting to liberate from Nazi tyranny.

Normally, a detailed scale model would be made of the target, the close study of which would better orientate the aircrews, imprinting a picture in their minds of the route of attack and what the target might look like as they thundered in at low level. With the time-critical nature of the SAS intelligence, there was no chance for any of that now. Instead, Embry chose to quicken the appetite and hunger of the aircrews, by explaining just what motive lay behind the present mission. Of course, no one could say for sure that all of the SAS captives had been murdered. But what he did know was that one British officer, Lieutenant Twm Stephens, had been finished off in cold blood, and that many more brave Maquis had likewise been shot out of hand.

As Embry made clear, this was a reprisal mission. He even went as far as to describe how the Gestapo had 'bashed somebody's head in'. With his aircrew suitably fired up, they ran through the plan of attack, which was to target the barracks first with a mixture of high explosive and incendiary bombs. That would serve to blow apart the buildings and set them aflame. Embry's exhortations to his air crews left little to the imagination: they were to 'let the bastards burn'. At the same time, he cautioned his men as to what they should and should not do, if any aircraft was hit and they had to bale out. The one thing to avoid was any talk of this being a vengeance mission.

'If you get shot down and taken prisoner, don't shoot your mouth off about retaliation,' he warned them. 'You can't out-piss a skunk!'

While the barracks were to bear the brunt of the attack, there was no mention made of the role of the SAS in initiating the mission. Indeed, none of the aircrew had the faintest idea that small bands of extraordinarily courageous men were operating so far behind enemy lines, and that it was thanks to their efforts that the present trove of target intelligence had been delivered . . . Shortly before sunset the fourteen Wooden Wonders took to the skies, forming up with an escort of P-51 Mustang fighters. Maintaining strict radio silence, the Mosquitos dropped down to tree-top height as they sped across France, before pulling up to attack, just minutes out from Bonneuil-Matours.

Flying at a few hundred feet of altitude, the fourteen warplanes streaked along the valley of the Vienne, as wild stabs of small arms fire arced skywards, and a lone 20mm cannon barked defiance from a rooftop position. But the speed and surprise of the Mosquitos' approach proved overwhelming, and within seconds the first bombs plummeted down upon the barracks block, which was instantly wreathed in a thick cloud of roiling smoke. As the final aircraft unloaded their munitions, some of which were a new phosphorus-based incendiary bomb, the entire target area was wreathed in fierce flames, pillars of angry smoke billowing skywards.

Even as the surviving SS troops fought their way out of the chaos and carnage, their ordeal was far from done. Moments later, the throaty, high-pitched snarl of the Mosquitos' twin Merlin engines announced that they were back. As the aircraft executed a series of about-turns above the river, to begin their flight home, they passed over the target area once more, cutting through the smoke and raking the length and breadth of the barracks with cannon and machine-gun fire. Setting a course for Thorney Island, the RAF aircrew were still on the hunt. En route, they spied three trains, and tore into them with long bursts of fire. Two were seen to judder to a halt, emitting thick clouds of steam from their punctured boilers. Only one aircraft was hit by enemy fire during the mission, and even that returned to Thorney Island with minimal damage.

The fourteen aircraft touched down at 0045 hours on 15 July. Mission accomplished. Back at Bonneuil-Matours all was chaos. The Mosquito squadron had included one aircraft that was fitted with aerial cameras. It had captured the bombardment in full swing. In the stunning photos the entire scene below the warplane was blanketed in thick white smoke. Fittingly, one of those photos would take pride of place in the SAS War Diary. In his official report on Bulbasket, also filed in the War Diary, Tonkin would state of this day: '14 July. SS Barracks at 6588 bombed, about 150 killed.' Notably, it wasn't only SS troops that had been based there. So too was a contingent of the hated Milice.

On 15 July Tonkin received an urgent follow-up message from headquarters: 'RAF requests report results bombing of barracks . . .' At the same time, the RAF were able to get a reconnaissance aircraft over the target, to secure photos. Together – Tonkin's on-the-ground reports, plus the aerial photos – painted a compelling picture of vengeance requested, and vengeance delivered. On the evening of the attack some 400 soldiers had been present at the barracks. They had just returned from an operation to hunt down a group of Maquis. As intended by Air Vice-Marshal Basil Embry et al., the SS troopers had been sitting down to their evening meal – lamb stew – when the Mosquitos had swooped to attack. Estimates of the number of dead ranged from 80–200, with many more injured.

Fearing terrible reprisals, the townsfolk of Bonneuil-Matours had cowered in their homes, but no such savagery would be visited on their heads. The enemy were simply too busy ferrying their wounded to hospital in the nearby city of Poitiers. Indeed, while scores of residents were rounded up, they were not to face beatings or executions. Instead, they were ordered to help carry the injured into waiting trucks, and to extract the bodies of the dead. While the barracks had borne the brunt of the bombing, the Château de Marieville had suffered a near-miss, giving the senior officers there a real fright. The warning had been sent. Ten days after the attack on the SAS base camp, Tonkin's vengeance had been served.

At his new base, numbers were swelled once more – this time by the arrival of half a dozen American airmen, all of whom had been shot down over France. Brought there by the Maquis, two of the fugitives were keen to contribute to far more than simple camp duties. Lieutenants Bill Bradley and Flamm Harper demanded to join Tonkin's raiding operations, one exclaiming: 'I see no reason why the lack of an aeroplane should stop me fighting.' Tonkin, thrilled by such sentiments, promptly added the US airmen to the list of SAS under his command and ready for operations against the enemy. But the burning question at SAS headquarters remained this: following the evisceration of the Bulbasket party, should Tonkin and his small band of survivors be pulled out, or were they fit to continue the fight on the ground?

In an effort to resolve that issue, the commander of 1 SAS, Lieutenant Colonel Blair 'Paddy' Mayne DSO, signalled that he was flying out to speak to Tonkin direct. Due to his senior position, and because his name and role were known to the enemy,

Mayne was actually forbidden from deploying on active combat missions, not that he would pay any great heed to such strictures. On 15 July a message was sent to Tonkin, warning him: 'Night 16/17 Col. Mayne going over have S Phone ready. Nothing dropping. No jeeps.' In other words, an RAF warplane would execute an overflight of their base, so that Mayne could speak to Tonkin via an 'S-Phone'. This was a state-of-the-art radio-telephone device perfected by the SOE. It allowed a man on the ground to speak to someone in the air, as the aircraft orbited overhead.

On the night in question, Tonkin stood in an open field – the designated location – as an Allied aircraft droned through the dark skies. But try as he might he could establish no contact with Mayne. The commander of 1 SAS was forced to return to Britain, having exchanged not a word with an officer that he knew well, for he and Tonkin had served together during eighteen months of some of the toughest SAS operations. Mayne was none the wiser as to Tonkin's state of mind or his readiness, and Tonkin was none the wiser as to what SAS headquarters intended for him and his surviving men.

Even so, Tonkin was determined to keep busy. Gathering together their one 'battered but working' jeep, plus four civilian cars, his mixed force of SAS, Phantoms and USAAF airmen began sallying forth to hit key targets in the area. In this way they blew up several railway lines, planting devices known as 'fog signals', which used a pressure trigger to detonate explosives as a train was passing, so causing catastrophic damage to both locomotive and track. If triggered, the fog signal – another SOE invention – was guaranteed to cause a derailment, which generally meant that a large stretch of track was torn up, as the careering train ran off the rails.

Tonkin's DIY war convoy was led by a Ford V8 saloon car with its windows removed, and with a single Vickers-K machine gun mounted on the passenger side's dash, poking out where the front windscreen used to be. One of the American airmen, Lieutenant Flamm Harper, proved a dab hand on the Vickers-K. He duly became the Ford V8 battle wagon's front gunner. Striking a poignant note, even as Tonkin got his men out and about causing mayhem, he sent a message to headquarters, asking: 'OK to submit personal messages for families . . . If OK, messages to be preceeded by the code word "Crumpet".' Understandably, Tonkin and his men were worried that their loved ones might have heard rumours of the dire fate of the Bulbasket party, and would presume that all had been captured or killed.

On 21 July those messages for 'next of kin' were duly dispatched. But shortly, Tonkin received the order that he had been most dreading. He was told to 'cease all further operations'. On one level, it hadn't come as a massive surprise. His repeated requests for replacement jeeps had fallen upon deaf ears, and despite the DIY battle convoy he had assembled he'd sensed that their days were numbered. There were reports that some 2,000 mixed German troops and Milice were readying themselves for a massive sweep through the countryside, so it made perfect sense to execute their final escape. Those enemy forces were known to be commandeering cars and trucks, in order to quarter the terrain far and wide.

Communications to Britain were also proving challenging, with headquarters warning: 'Night emergency frequency now no good. Heavy static and jamming. We can hear your call but get no reply.' Increasingly, messages were being sent by pigeon. But even that means could prove risky, headquarters reminding

Tonkin and his men of how to recognise 'friendly', as against 'hostile' pigeons. 'Warning on enemy carrier pigeons. All pigeons dropped by RAF are accompanied by a that-day British newspaper, and a questionnaire in French. Please warn all Resistance groups.' In other words, the danger was of the enemy dropping pigeons to SAS patrols, in a deliberate effort to get them to dispatch their signals direct into their own hands. The inclusion of a 'that-day' newspaper with a bona fide British pigeon drop, was designed to prove they were the genuine article, for the Germans would be hard pressed to do the same.

It was one thing to order Tonkin and his men to cease raiding operations, and to execute their escape via a makeshift airstrip; it was quite another to pull off such an unprecedented means of extraction. The RAF were used to dropping supplies and equipment, plus personnel *into* hostile territory. They weren't accustomed to *landing* on DIY strips in the heart of enemy territory, and neither were the SAS trained for such a means of extraction. But there was one outfit that had set itself up to cope with this kind of eventuality, preparing for it extensively – the SOE. Indeed, SOE agents like Maingard were very often ferried to and from the field by the Westland Lysander, a light aircraft with an excellent short take-off and landing capability. All across Nazi-occupied Europe, remote fields had been marked out as rough-and-ready landing strips on which the 'Lizzies', as they were nicknamed, could put down and take off again.

But the Lysander was a two-person aircraft, pilot included. Something far larger would be needed to extract Tonkin and his Bulbasket survivors, and that would require a much more substantial landing strip. The answer to this conundrum lay in a young SAS officer named David Maurice Surrey-Dane. Towards the end of July 1944, Surrey-Dane prepared to parachute in to join Tonkin and his men. On the night of 28/29 July, he took to the skies in a Short Stirling, the first four-engine heavy bomber to see service with the RAF. Ruled largely obsolete by this stage of the war, the Stirling had acquired a new lease of life, dropping raiding parties and SOE agents into enemy-occupied lands. Riding with Surrey-Dane was Captain Mike Sadler, who carried with him an S-Phone unit. Sadler – whose epic escape had been executed across the North African desert some eighteen months earlier – was there to speak to Tonkin, to sound out how he might be faring.

Bang on cue, the lone parachutist plummeted into the darkness, along with twenty-eight containers and panniers packed with supplies. Even as those twenty-nine parachutes floated to earth, so Sadler was able to make voice contact with Tonkin on the ground. 'Tonkin and men in good spirits,' he would report of their conversation. 'Surrey-Dane dropped O.K. . . . Purpose of Surrey-Dane mission to get residue of BULBASKET team out.' In one of those resupply containers was stuffed a vital piece of equipment right then: a pair of 'size 10 boots'. The SAS commander had requested the footwear by radio, for his own were in tatters, and so the replacements had been added to the load.

Once Surrey-Dane was down safely, Tonkin led the twenty-two-year-old lieutenant to their camp, where he was 'warmly received and given a cup of tea'. Only after the new arrival had been suitably refreshed did Tonkin reveal how worried he had been. Gazing skywards, Tonkin had watched anxiously as Surrey-Dane's parachute had 'breathed', alternately closing and opening as it struggled to find equilibrium and stability. For long moments Tonkin had feared it might do a 'roman candle', at which point the 'chute would collapse, bunching up like a bag of damp washing, as the jumper plummeted to a horrible death. Fortunately, not only had Surrey-Dane made it down safely, but he'd remained blissfully unaware of how his parachute had been playing up, even as he'd drifted towards earth.

At age eighteen Surrey-Dane had volunteered for military service, turning his back on a place at Clare College, Cambridge, and enlisting as a private in order to sign up. Educated at Charterhouse – a top public school – Surrey-Dane was soon singled out for officer training, volunteering first for the Parachute Regiment in 1943, and the SAS thereafter. He'd joined Paddy Mayne's 1 SAS in April 1944, so only just in time for the D-Day operations. In short, Surrey-Dane was young, fresh into the unit and inexperienced in combat. This was his first ever operation with the SAS, which begged the question – what made him the potential saviour of the 'residue' of 'the Bulbasket team'?

In truth Surrey-Dane also played a secret cloak-and-dagger role. Superficially, he was a lieutenant in the SAS. Covertly, he doubled as an agent of the SOE, codename *Dodo*. Agent Dodo was slated to link up with the SOE's Shipwright Circuit in France, which was, of course, Agent Samuel's – Maingard's – Maquis. More importantly, during training with the SOE, Surrey-Dane had been instructed in the art and craft of choosing, preparing and operating covert airstrips, and how exactly to call in aircraft to land. Indeed, he'd been polishing off that very instruction, even as Tonkin and his men had parachuted into war. Having missed the initial thrust into battle, this mission – to rescue the remnants of Operation Bulbasket – was the chance he was longing for to get into the war.

Shortly before boarding that Stirling aircraft for the flight out,

Surrey-Dane had been rushed to London, to receive a special briefing at the SOE's Baker Street headquarters. There, he had been handed a dossier of highly sensitive intelligence. The SOE had proceeded to share with Surrey-Dane the locations of three landings zones (LZs) in Tonkin's immediate area, which were already in use. These were some of Maingard's clandestine strips, and their location was a closely guarded secret, for obvious reasons. If the enemy discovered their whereabouts, they could stake out one or more of those LZs, waiting for a Lysander to land, and for its agents and top-secret messages to fall into their clutches.

Twenty-four hours after dropping in to join Tonkin, Surrey-Dane set off, seeking out those three airstrips. The best Tonkin had been able to offer him in way of transport was one of their civilian cars – a war-scarred Citroën, which lacked a starter motor, and whose clutch was on the blink. The only way to get moving was to bump-start the vehicle and to leap aboard. Fortunately, Surrey-Dane had Lieutenant Morris at the wheel, who proved a dab hand at dealing with the vagaries of their irascible, unpredictable war wagon. Checking his maps to navigate their way to the SOE's first airstrip, Surrey-Dane unwittingly steered them right onto an enemy patrol. Making a spur-of-the-moment decision, Lieutenant Morris figured they would have to front it out and act as if they were Milice, who did tend to travel about in such a fashion.

Fortunately, the bluff held good.

Of the three strips visited, it was the last that held most interest for Surrey-Dane. The man who owned the land there at Foussac farm explained how SOE agents had been ferried to and from his field, seemingly without the enemy being any the wiser. When Surrey-Dane was shown the makeshift strip, it was immediately obvious that it was too small for their purposes. The plan was to fly in a Lockheed Hudson to pick up the SAS escapees. This was a twin-engine light bomber that was actually a conversion of a pre-war airliner, the Model 14 Super Electra. A Hudson would require a strip of around 1,600 metres to land and take off again. The farmer led them to another of his fields, and Surrey-Dane sensed that this was it. With a little trimming of the hedges and trees, plus some flattening of the ground, it should pass muster.

Even as Surrey-Dane had set about checking out those LZs, so the threat from the enemy search columns kept growing. Tonkin sent a warning to headquarters – 'developing enemy threat . . . now serious'. As with the strike on the Bonneuil-Matours barracks, he sent requests for a bombing mission to be flown against those enemy that were gathering, plus their headquarters, which was 'the concentration point for large body of MILICE and German troops'. But the tempo of operations being flown by the RAF was at fever pitch, and any chance of such a mission seemed remote.

Surrey-Dane had codenamed their prospective new airstrip Bon-Bon – sweet in French. It would take two Hudsons to extract all the Bulbasket survivors, as each could carry no more than ten passengers. In case Tonkin might have entertained other ideas, SAS headquarters had made it clear that he was to be 'in first load, and no rpt. no discretion is allowed here'. In other words, Tonkin had to be among the first men to be extracted, scuppering any hopes he might have nurtured of somehow remaining in the field. He was ordered to bring with him Sadoine – the Phantom officer held under close arrest – and also Maingard, who was needed back in London.

Orders were orders, and Tonkin duly radioed headquarters: 'Get BONBON accepted immediately. Landings might become impossible very soon owing to expected large scale sweeps of this area. Anti-Maquis forces gathering . . .' At the same time as Tonkin and his men had been ordered to pull out, they were sent a coded warning as to what might have happened to their captured comrades, and what the wider fallout might be. Even as he prepared to get the Bon-Bon strip ready, so Tonkin was asked to double his vigilance, and to keep sending updates on all he might see or learn.

'Cases are preparing against war criminals,' read a 30 July message from headquarters. 'To . . . substantiate mounting mass of evidence you must forward to England by any secured means the names of enemy units, their formation officers and their responsible commanders where atrocities occur.' The Germans were guilty of terrible war crimes against French villages – that much Tonkin and his men knew. But likewise, the fate of the thirty-odd Bulbasket captives was looking grim. Tonkin had heard nothing further, since his 12 July 'unconfirmed' report that all had been shot. No credible reports and little rumour. It was as if the men of his patrol had been swallowed up without a trace.

Possibly due to the mounting evidence of atrocities, Tonkin and Maingard finally got the airstrikes they'd been asking for. On 1 August a flight of twenty-four Mosquitos from Embry's 2 Group struck the Caserne des Dunes barracks in Poitiers, at which the enemy were mustering a fresh repression column. Just before setting out to sweep the countryside, that column was hit in a devastating air strike. This action took pride of place in the SAS War Diary, as being one of the last hurrahs of Operation Bulbasket.

'Target C.94 [its formal designation] attacked by 24 Mosquitos of 140 Wing (2Gp) . . . POITIERS MILITARY

BARRACKS – CASERNE DES DUNES ... Damage assessment:– Over 150 troops – mostly MILICE – were killed and many more wounded. All the MT [motor transport] – about 50 vehicles – were destroyed and the barracks wrecked . . . accompanying photograph shows ambulances outside the main entrance 12 hours after the attack.'

Post-attack air recce photos showed the rectangular barracks compound devastated from end to end. Each image was annotated with numerous strike points, at which the Mosquitos had caused the maximum damage. Tonkin's report, radioed in on 2 August, confirmed much of what those photos intimated: '150 killed and many wounded by bombing of CASERNE DES DUNES.' He added that the entire barracks had been abandoned, and that the surviving troops and Milice were 'digging in to wait help from ANGOULEME enemy forces'. Angoulême, a city lying over 100 kilometres to the south of Poitiers, was being asked to lend reinforcements to bolster their devastated numbers.

On the following day, a second airstrike was called in by Tonkin, this time to hit the Château du Fou, a fifteenth-century fortress lying on the western bank of the Vienne. Tonkin had fresh intelligence that his old enemy, those SS who had attacked his Verrières camp, had relocated there. Seventeen Wooden Wonders swooped in to strike, with a Mosquito from the RAF's Film Production Unit added to their number, fitted with a 35mm cine camera in its glass nose cone. This time, vengeance, sweet vengeance, was to be captured live on film. Some thirty bombs slammed into that ancient edifice, all three wings of the château being torn asunder and left wreathed in flames.

But this time there was to be no battle damage report from Tonkin and his men on the ground. Instead, they were busy readying their final escape. At the Foussac farm, the Bulbasket survivors, together with their US airmen comrades, were hard at it. Their remaining jeep, doggedly refusing to give up the ghost, was saddled with one final task: it had been harnessed to the farmer's chain harrow, so as to drag it back and forth along the 1,600-metre strip, levelling the ground. The SAS War Diary includes several photos of the airstrip under construction. One shows the jeep chugging across the field, vegetation up to its wheel-arches, with a distinctive figure, Lieutenant Morris, at the wheel, and the Vickers-K gun temporarily unheeded. Two men in shirtsleeves stand in the wake of the jeep, legs braced astride the harrow to better guide its progress, coated in a thick layer of dust.

Under the careful eye of Surrey-Dane – the SOE-trained air-strip expert – bit by bit the landing ground took shape. As it did, the spirits of the men began to brighten. Lieutenant Weaver would later confess that he had given up all hope of ever seeing home again. He had written himself off, convinced he would die in France. Many others had felt likewise. But, as the men stripped to their waists under the hot August sun, and bent to the task of ripping out hedgerows and trimming trees, they began to nurture a hope that what had once seemed impossible might come to pass; that escape and survival were within their grasp.

As a big bonus it turned out that Trooper McNair – the former tank commander – was a farmer's son, and he proved a dab hand at handling their jeep-mounted harrow. Surrey-Dane, mean-while, had one, somewhat sensitive, issue to deal with. A large tree lay bang in the flight path. It was a walnut, so a valuable crop species, and it happened to be owned by the neighbouring farmer. Surrey-Dane had to strike a deal to pay the farmer 'the equivalent of £40, before he would agree to cut it down'. That was a princely sum, amounting to around £1,500 in today's money. Luckily, Surrey-Dane had come prepared. 'I had been sent to France with an emergency supply of Francs, so this did not present a problem.'

Even as the Bulbasket survivors toiled away, so the fortunes of any possible rescue flight waxed and waned. On 3 August the scheduled pickup was called off, headquarters signalling Tonkin: 'Dakota cancelled night 4/5. Will try to send it night 5/6. Sorry only one aircraft available.' The Douglas C-47 Skytrain – called the 'Dakota' when in British service – was the redoubtable twin-engine transport aircraft and workhorse of Allied airborne operations. Right then, it was the only aeroplane that might be available, no Hudsons being free, and even that Dakota was busy with other tasks.

To pile on the pressure still further, Tonkin received reports of a horrific war crime. He sent a signal through to headquarters: 'Inhabitants of village LE VIGEANT massacred by MILICE and Germans ... including women and infants. VIGEANT is ... some 11 km. NW of base.' Reeling from a battle with the Maquis, German troops had set upon that nearby village in a paroxysm of rage, burning and looting houses, and murdering forty resistance fighters and locals with a '*brutalité certaine*' – with shocking brutality. A toddler had been killed in his mother's arms; an elderly lady was slaughtered with an axe; an old man was dragged along, even as he was dying, and finished off in his garden. In short, the enemy were increasingly desperate and wreaking horrific vengeance on all sides.

After four days of sweat and toil, the Bon-Bon strip was declared ready. Satisfied with their handiwork, Surrey-Dane messaged as much to SAS headquarters, as all prayed that an aircraft would be available. 'Landing strip now prepared . . . When a/c [aircraft] heard, a bonfire beacon will be lit on East of strip. This will be extinguished when flare path lit . . . Tonkin demands three planes and asks for confirmation. These Yanks have helped us operationally.' Typically, Tonkin was determined that the USAAF airmen who had stood shoulder to shoulder with the SAS, both on sabotage operations and in readying the airstrip, would be pulled out at the same time.

The reply from headquarters was unequivocal: 'Your instructions, rpt. instructions on priority are Tonkin, wounded, SAMUEL, Phantoms, SAS troops, Yanks. Demand confirmation that landing ground is O.K. Recognition signals – Ground to air Y. Air to ground K.' Unpacking that a little, Tonkin was to be the first to board any aircraft that made it to Bon-Bon, followed by Maingard – who was needed in London on urgent SOE business – Sadoine the suspect traitor, then the rest of Tonkin's Bulbasket survivors, and finally the American airmen.

On the evening of 6 August, Tonkin tuned into the BBC, awaiting the first lines of that nursery rhyme, 'Sur le Pont d'Avignon', and the message they all longed to hear. Sure enough it came, amid a long sequence of coded signals for other SAS patrols: two Lockheed Hudsons were to fly in that night, to pluck out the waiting party. In response, Tonkin and his men erupted into wild cheers of joy. If their makeshift strip proved good, and the aircrew suitably resolute, salvation was so very close at hand now.

It took a very particular sort of pilot to attempt such a rescue mission. Fortunately, a specialist unit had been developed for flying such operations – the RAF's Special Duties flights, and more specifically 161 Squadron, operating out of RAF Tempsford. Tempsford was a clandestine airfield disguised as a farm, which was so secret it became known as the 'Ghost Airfield'. Formally called 'Gibraltar Farm', Tempsford was situated in rural Bedfordshire and was accessed via a side road marked 'Closed to the public'. During daylight hours, RAF Tempsford had all the appearances of being a ramshackle farm, but come nightfall the secret aerodrome emerged, as seemingly run-down farm buildings, barns and sheds were transformed into hangars, storerooms and control towers. It was from there that the sneaky-beaky flights of the SOE operated, being the nerve-centre for the resistance armies operating across Europe.

At ten o'clock on the evening of 6 August, the pair of Hudsons took off from Tempsford and clawed into the darkening skies. The Bon-Bon landing zone lay some three hours' flight away. At the controls of the first aircraft, codenamed 'M', sat Flying Officer Ibbott, followed by Wing Commander Alan Boxer, riding in aircraft 'P'. Boxer was an old hand at such clandestine operations, but Ibbott was a comparative newbie, as were his aircrew. Even so, with unerring skill Ibbott steered a path direct to Bon-Bon, arriving shortly before 0130 hours on 7 August. As that lone Hudson began to approach that untried and untested landing strip, so four pairs of eyes scanned the dark terrain below, searching for the agreed recognition signals.

Hearing the in-bound warplane, Surrey-Dane signalled the fires be lit. The hearts of the waiting party leapt, as the distinctive form of the lone Hudson appeared, silhouetted 'against a moonlit sky'. Having flashed by torchlight the agreed recognition code, the makeshift runway lights were switched on – five torches, arranged to form an inverted L shape, so marking out the strip.

Moments later Hudson 'M' swooped in to land, 'switching on its landing lights at the last moment', to flood the scene with intense illumination. For a horrible moment the warplane 'bounced high into the air . . . and then disappeared into a cloud of dust,' Surrey-Dane reported, being lost to view.

Having only ever called in a Lysander during his training days with SOE, Surrey-Dane was worried sick that he'd messed up. Even as they'd been busy preparing that rough-and-ready airstrip, Maingard – Agent Samuel – had snapped some photos of the work in progress. In one, thirteen figures toil beside their ever-faithful jeep, wielding an assortment of rakes and hoes. Maingard captioned the image: 'British SAS prepare the field on which the Hudsons would have to pick them up and bring them back to England.' Now was the moment of truth: had these men done their job sufficiently well? Was the airstrip fit for purpose?

Thankfully, after 'anxious minutes' the Hudson emerged from the all-enveloping dust cloud, coming into view again and taxiing to a standstill. Unbeknown to the waiting figures, the aircrew would conclude that Bon-Bon was far from suitable as a Hudson landing-strip. Indeed, they would demand that all future flights into there be executed by the Dakota, which was renowned for its rugged durability. But right now that first Hudson had landed safely, far behind enemy lines, and the priority was to get the evacuees loaded into her hold.

'Very soon half our SAS party were aboard,' Surrey-Dane would report of this moment, 'and the Hudson was starting down the "runway" for take-off.' Swallowed into a storm of dust, its twin Wright Cyclone radial engines howling as she went, there were 'more anxious moments' for Surrey-Dane, before he spied the warplane 'climbing away safely'. The second Hudson came in directly on her tail, and within twenty minutes all who could fit aboard had taken to the skies.

Surrey-Dane had remained behind to oversee future air operations. He reckoned it had taken no more than twenty minutes for both aircraft to rotate through the makeshift strip, and he remained 'fairly confident that the operation had passed unnoticed by our enemies'. The two Hudsons had spirited away Tonkin and his twelve Bulbasket survivors, plus Maingard, Sadoine and three USAAF pilots. There had only been one worrying moment for those crammed aboard the aircraft during take-off – when the trees at the far end of the airstrip had loomed large in their vision, but thankfully they'd slipped past beneath the belly of the lumbering warplane.

Apart from a little flak and machine-gun fire, both Hudsons had a trouble-free run back to Britain. But as they were running low on fuel, and with RAF Temsford fogbound, they put down at RAF Tangmere, near Chichester, on the south coast of England. So it was that Captain John Tonkin, the great survivor, and the remnant of his SAS patrol were finally brought home. Tonkin himself would report of this moment: '2 Hudsons landed successfully and took off with 17 happy SAS and 3 delirious Americans.' Four days later a Dakota landed at Bon-Bon and pulled out the last stragglers – Surrey-Dane included – and the few remaining American aircrew (and honorary SAS).

With that, Operation Bulbasket was brought to a close.

In its place came Operation Moses, with Surrey-Dane flying back to Bon-Bon a few days later, to deliver several dozen Free French SAS, plus their arms and equipment, into the field. With him rode Agent Samuel, fresh from being awarded a Croix De Guerre avec Palmes, a high valour French medal. During his short stay in Britain, Maingard had reported having 12,000 Maquis ready to fight, hence his being rushed back into the area. Surrey-Dane would remain at his side, serving as the 'Dakota and weapons expert' for Maingard's Shipwright Circuit. Overall, Surrey-Dane would bring in five Dakotas and two Hudsons, to keep the ever-expanding circuit supplied with weapons and ammo.

Once the entire area was liberated by Allied forces, Maingard would return to Britain, to be promoted, and to be decorated with the DSO. His citation would read: 'Throughout June, July and August, groups organised, trained and frequently led by this officer constantly attacked the Germans, in their barracks as at Magnac-Laval, in the open as at Jousse, and in ambush as at Lussac-les-Châteaux.' Meanwhile, Phantom Captain Sadoine was being thoroughly investigated due to the allegations of treachery that had dogged his return. Though the results proved somewhat inconclusive, Sadoine would go on to have something of a break-down after the war. He would end up in a Belgian mental asylum having adopted the name and identity of none other than ... former SAS Captain John Tonkin. When Tonkin went to visit the ailing Sadoine, he viewed the man's deluded adoption of his own persona and war record as a tacit admission of his wartime guilt.

The real John Tonkin would be awarded the Military Cross for his role on Operation Bulbasket, and for getting those who had survived out alive. He would serve with the SAS until war's end, also earning a Mention in Dispatches. Following the summary disbandment of the SAS in October 1945, he, Blair 'Paddy' Mayne and Mike Sadler would head to the ends of the earth, taking part in a year-long Antarctic survey expedition. Like

Mayne, Tonkin was restless and haunted by the war years. He would follow a tortuous path, alternately prospecting for oil in the Brunei rainforests and searching for uranium deposits in the Rum Jungle of Australia's Northern Territory. He finally settled in Australia in 1961, where he would live out the rest of his days.

Of course, it would be wonderful if the Bulbasket story ended with the extraction from Bon-Bon of the escapees. Sadly it did not. In mid-December 1944, with that part of France having been liberated, a pre-Christmas hunt for wild boar got under way in the Forêt de Saint-Sauvant, a remote woodland lying to the south-west of Poitiers. There, the hunters stumbled upon a mass grave. It contained the bodies of several dozen males, all of whom were dressed in what was clearly Allied uniform. As the French authorities launched an investigation, the identity disks of two were uncovered, plus the names of several embroidered on their battle dress.

By June of 1945, SHAEF had investigated more fully, and had issued its own report on the massacre, which was sent to HQ SAS Troops, for the attention of the Commanding Officer of 1 SAS, Colonel Blair Mayne. The SHAEF report concluded that thirty-one SAS soldiers had been murdered by the enemy, constituting those men of operation Bulbasket who had been captured at Verrières. At that time, only seventeen had been conclusively identified, although the other fourteen were listed as almost certainly being the remaining Bulbasket men. The report concluded by stating that 'the Germans responsible for the murders are not known . . .'

These grim discoveries and that SHAEF report would spawn an epic war-crimes investigation, one that would last beyond the end of the war, as the guilty parties were identified, hunted down and where possible brought to trial. That story remains outside of the scope of the great escape told in this chapter. But suffice to say that of the hundred-plus SAS men that were captured by the enemy after D-Day, only six would ever be returned to Britain at war's end. Facing the brutal diktats of Hitler's Commando Order, the remainder would be murdered.

Indeed, it would take boundless resolve, courage and tenacity to avoid such predations, as our final great escapee would prove.

Chapter Six

THE BUTCHER SHOP ESCAPEE

July 1944, France

Spread out across the moonlit sky below, a string of eleven para-chutes blossomed ghostly white in the ethereal light. For tonight's drop, Trooper Herbert Castelow was serving as jumper number twelve, so going as the tail-end-Charlie. Little did he know it, as he hurled himself out of the Stirling's bomb bay, but being the last in line would prove to be an absolute life-saver. As his 'chute crackled open in the air above him, making that distinctive snap, like a mainsail catching a gust of wind, all seemed as it should be, a dozen figures drifting silently towards earth.

The objective of the present mission, Operation TOBY 3, was Étampes aerodrome, which lay just a little to the south of Paris. These twelve jumpers were returning to that airbase, having executed a dramatic raid on the very same target just a few days earlier. They had good reasons to be sent back in and so swiftly. They knew the place intimately, having planted charges among its warplanes, after which they'd executed one of the most dramatic escapes of the entire war – being plucked off the airstrip in a daring mission flown by the RAF in an unarmed Dakota transport plane. Having been spirited back to Britain, the commander of 1 SAS, Lieutenant Colonel Blair Mayne, had asked them to return right away, for Étampes aerodrome had just taken on a very particular significance for the Allied war effort.

Étampes actually consisted of three separate aerodromes: Étampes-l'Humery, a dummy airfield, designed to draw Allied bombing raids away from the real target; Étampes-Bellevue, an emergency landing ground; plus Étampes-Mondésir, which was the real McCoy. Étampes-Mondésir came complete with four cavernous hangars, plus workshops, barracks, storage bays and thirty-one reinforced aircraft shelters. Flak positions ringed the base, which also boasted radar stations, a demolitions detachment, plus refuelling, signals and ambulance units.

The elite Luftwaffe squadron, *Kampfgeschwader* 51 – KG 51; Battle Wing 51 – was based there. Having fought in the Battle of Britain, the Blitz and on the Eastern Front, KG 51 had been pulled back west to counter the D-Day landings. Commanded by *Oberstleutnant* – Lieutenant Colonel – Wolf-Dietrich Meister, KG 51's most recent success had been against the Nuremberg raid in March 1944, during which RAF Bomber Command had lost more than 100 aircraft, accounting for 545 aircrew, or more than the entire number of RAF Fighter Command pilots killed during the Battle of Britain.

Meister and his men were held in high regard by German senior command. Accordingly, KG 51 had been one of the first Luftwaffe units to be trusted with the Messerschmitt ME 262 *Sturmvogel* – Stormbird – the world's first jet-powered aircraft to enter active service. Sleek, powerful, revolutionary in design, the *Sturmvogel* boasted a top speed of 900 kph, and was faster and more heavily armed than any Allied fighter. It was one of Hitler's much-vaunted *Wunderwaffe* – the Nazis' so-called super-weapons – which were trumpeted as being so far in advance of the Allies' that they would enable Nazi Germany to turn the tide of the war.

The mission of these twelve SAS parachutists – call-sign SABU-70 – was to hit Étampes-Mondésir, and to blow to pieces as many of those ME 262s as they could lay their hands on. They were to be aided in that task by the local French resistance, for the SOE had arranged for a reception party to be waiting at tonight's DZ. Linking up as one united force, the SAS party and the French patriots were to wreak havoc at Étampes, sabotaging all.

In June 1944 a document entitled 'Progress Report – SAS Operations' had been issued, stressing the need for such patrols to be 'dropped to reception so that guides and information about enemy dispositions and targets can be supplied'. SAS parties were to be parachuted in complete with container-loads of arms for the Maquis. In exchange, the locals would pinpoint enemy positions and strengths, plus they would stiffen the SAS's ranks whenever undertaking raids.

Tonight's SAS patrol was dropping into a DZ near the tiny hamlet of La Ferté-Alais, which itself was just a dozen kilometres short of their target. Situated deep within the Forêt de Fontainebleau, a vast expanse of mixed woodland, heath and wetlands, this should be an ideal base from which to strike at Étampes, and to which to withdraw once the chaos and carnage had been wrought. The details for tonight's mission had been delineated in a report entitled 'SAS/SOE Plans', which called for extensive 'sabotage, disruption of communications, individual guerrilla actions etc.', and all delivered in hit-and-run strikes that gave the enemy 'no organised forces to take action against'.

Swift-moving, ephemeral and striking by surprise, the SABU-70 raiders would melt away into the Forêt de Fontainebleau once they had attacked, disappearing to fight another day. That report, 'SAS/SOE Plans', had a slew of security stamps emblazoned across its cover, first and foremost among which was a massive red 'X' covering the entire front page, plus the words: 'BIGOT. MOST SECRET. TO BE KEPT UNDER LOCK AND KEY . . . It is requested that special care may be taken to ensure the secrecy of this document.'

That security classification, 'BIGOT', supposedly stood for 'British Invasion of German Occupied Territories'. In theory, there was no higher clearance level, for the so-called 'Bigots' were privy to the plans for Operation Overlord, one of the most carefully guarded secrets of the war. As Churchill had famously stated, the plans for the D-Day landings had to be concealed from the enemy at all costs – a precious truth that needed to be shielded by a 'bodyguard of lies'. Bigot clearance was rigidly enforced. To check if someone was on the 'BIGOT List', the following question was supposed to be asked: 'Are you a bigot?' Anyone with the proper clearance was supposed to answer, 'Yes, I'm a bigot, by Neptune,' Neptune being a cryptic reference to the coming amphibious landings.

Operation TOBY 3 emanated from that same BIGOT stable, and was surrounded by a similar level of secrecy, for taking out those ME 262s was seen as being crucial to the fortunes of the Normandy landings. A state-of-the-art jet fighter, the ME 262 was typically armed with four 30mm cannons and a complement of twenty-four R4M *Orkan* – Hurricane – air-to-air rockets, for blasting apart Allied warplanes. In short, it could out-fight and out-fly any comparable Allied fighter aircraft, and those Orkan rockets were specifically designed to take down the Allies four-engine heavy bombers, in a one-shot-one-kill scenario.

Hence the vital nature of tonight's SAS mission.

As Castelow drifted to earth beneath his parachute, a series of faint calls cut the night: phrases in French, yelled across the DZ. '*Vive la France! Vive la France!*' – long live France. Nothing so alarming there. Presumably, that was their reception party crying out a greeting, as jumper number one in the stick, Captain Patrick Bannister Garstin MC, touched down.

By rights, Garstin – who had already been awarded a Military Cross during the summer 1940 battle for France – should not even have been there. Enlisting in the Royal Ulster Rifles just before the outbreak of war, Garstin had suffered a series of extensive injuries, first in June 1940 in France, and thereafter in East Africa, after which he had been sent back to Britain, ominously for 'treatment and final disposal'.

Deftly sidestepping a medical discharge, Garstin had somehow managed to volunteer for the Parachute Regiment, only to be injured once again, this time on operations in North Africa. Hospitalised once more, he'd demonstrated truly Herculean fortitude by volunteering for the SAS. The commander of 1 SAS, Colonel Blair Mayne – already the recipient of two DSOs (DSO and bar), plus a Mention in Dispatches – was known to 'cast a favourable eye' on any Irishman stepping forward to join his unit. As a fellow Ulsterman and veteran of the Royal Ulster

Rifles, Garstin was welcomed by Mayne unreservedly, despite his having dodged various medical discharges.

Incredibly, Garstin's second-in-command for tonight's mission, Lieutenant John H. 'Rex' Wiehe (pronounced 'Veehay'), equally should not have been there, and for very similar reasons. A Mauritian, Wiehe was one of the all-important French speakers on the patrol. Two years into the war, Wiehe had volunteered for parachute training, but had injured himself badly during a jump. Taken before the unit's doctor, Wiehe had been told that his career as a parachutist was over. Refusing to be beaten, two years later he'd 'volunteered for any special duty where my knowledge of French would be useful'. Busy preparing for their D-Day operations, the SAS had welcomed Wiehe with open arms, conveniently overlooking his injuries and the supposed prohibition from airborne duties.

Captain Garstin, typically, had led the first half of tonight's patrol out of the Stirling, with Corporal Serge Vaculik, a Czech-French parachutist, serving as one of his deputies and his dedicated French-speaker. Lieutenant Wiehe had led the second stick of six out of the Stirling, with SAS original Corporal Thomas 'Ginger' Jones serving as one of his deputies, and with Trooper Castelow being the backstop to the entire twelve-man party. Jones and Castelow had much in common. Both were the proverbial 'rough diamonds', and both would be promoted up the ranks and busted back to trooper (private) several times, due to various high-spirited infractions.

Some two years earlier, Castelow's then only son, Dennis, had been born, but the four-month-old infant had fallen ill and died. Castelow, the son of a steel worker from Stockton-on-Tees, was serving with the Highland Light Infantry. He had promptly absconded so he could be at his grieving wife Laura's side. Castelow had married his childhood sweetheart, and would often sing to her the song, 'Tell Laura I Love Her'. Shortly, the Military Police (MP) had arrived at the front door of the family home. Castelow had promptly darted out the back and dashed to the nearby station, arriving just as a train was pulling away. With the MPs in hot pursuit, he'd jumped onto the train's roof and raced along its length, in an effort to make good his getaway.

Despite his diminutive five foot four and three-quarter inch frame, and the fact that he weighed under ten stone, Castelow had earned a reputation for being one of the 'real bad boys'. He wore it almost as a badge of pride. Repeatedly since his enlistment in March 1940, he had been busted for being 'A.W.O.L.' – absent without leave – at one point earning '84 days detention', and at another being 'convicted of desertion', and at others being 'CB' (confined to barracks), suffering 'forfeiture of pay' or being held under 'close arrest'. Regardless, none of this seemed to have imperilled his ability to qualify for Special Service.

In February 1944 Castelow had volunteered for the SAS, qualifying for his jump wings that March. This was just his second active mission with the unit. Three times he'd flown into France under Captain Garstin's command. The first drop had been aborted, as no reception party awaited on the ground. The second mission had gone with a bang, Castelow and his comrades blowing up a train laden with war materiel, plus ammo dumps, and finally being plucked out of Étampes airbase. Now, it should be third time lucky – for if they could take out those ME 262s, they would have truly hit the jackpot, striking a powerful blow for the Allies.

Even as the Stirling had circled the Ferté-Alais, so the correct recognition signal – B for Bertie – had been flashed up from the dark field below. Just a few hours earlier, that code-letter had been sent by wireless from the SOE's London headquarters to those on the ground, serving as a last-minute check, and lending an added layer of security. It had given those riding in the Stirling a greater sense of certainty that all was as it should be. There were more reasons to feel confident, including the record of previous drops. The first to this DZ had taken place in early 1944, container-loads of weapons being parachuted in, plus a liaison agent from the SOE, complete with radio kit. Since then, half a dozen further drops had taken place without incident.

It was via that SOE agent's wireless link that much of tonight's operation had been organised. This included the song to be broadcast over the BBC to signal to the local Maquis that the drop was on – '*Son chant me dit tout*'; His Song Tells Me Everything – plus the mission's French codename, which was *Corine Sabot*. As the wireless signals had flitted back and forth, the drop had first been green-lit for the night of 3/4 July 1944. A group of Maquis had headed for the DZ, but unbeknown to them the flight had been cancelled, and it was a no-show. On the following night that song had played over the BBC once more, and the reception committee had made their way to La Ferté-Alais, little knowing what calamity awaited.

As Castelow drifted towards earth, the Short Stirling executed a second fly-past, this time disgorging the containers that were to be released along with the human cargo. That done, the pilot set a course for home. Riding in the Stirling was a thirteenth SAS man, Captain Mike Sadler. Now serving as part of 1 SAS's intelligence corps, Sadler was there to observe the drop, in order to better refine such missions in future. But even as the aircraft pulled away, he sensed that all was not as it should be. He was certain he'd caught the glimpse of a muzzle flash at ground level. Of course, the French resistance were known to let off the odd burst of fire in high spirits, and he just had to hope that might explain it. Otherwise, Garstin and his men looked to be in trouble.

Barely had Sadler entertained such thoughts, when the Stirling ran into what felt like another aircraft's turbulence, which shook the massive warplane from end to end. It was ominous, for only a hostile aircraft was likely to be braving such skies. Sure enough, moments later an enemy night fighter pounced, a Messerschmitt Bf 110 *Zerstörer* coming at the Stirling head-on, its 20mm cannons and machine guns blazing. 'We dived down pretty rapidly into the clouds . . .' Sadler recalled, as the Stirling's pilot tried to take evasive action. 'I thought the wings were going to come off.'

With the night-fighter hammering out bursts, the Stirling's pilot kept weaving dramatically, desperate to shake off his tormentor. By the time he'd succeeded, the four-engine warplane had taken a serious pasting. Still, the redoubtable aircraft managed to limp home. Sadler could only imagine that the *Zerstörer* had been waiting at the Ferté-Alais DZ and primed to pounce, which surely had to mean that the entire SAS operation had been compromised.

For Castelow, the first sign of trouble was the eruption of gunshots from below. In the SAS War Diary, the moment the fortunes of the patrol turned was recorded thus: 'Immediately they hit the deck, Jerry opened up on them with automatic weapons.' Captain Garstin, hailed by a Frenchman whom he believed to be one of the reception party, was led towards a nearby fringe of trees, only to be set upon by a party of German troops. As he'd tried to break free and to yell out a warning, the enemy had opened fire, riddling Garstin with 9mm rounds. Struck in the shoulder, neck and arm, he had been knocked to the ground, grievously wounded.

Garstin's deputy, Vaculik, realised in that moment that 'we had dropped into an ambush. The Germans were expecting us.' Returning fire, he'd dived into the cover of a cornfield and tried to crawl away, but the enemy fire seemed to be coming from all sides. Behind him, further figures had touched down and were strung out across the open expanse of the DZ: Lutton, Walker, Barker, Young, Jones, Varey, Wiehe. The third in that line, Paddy Barker, another Irishman, was one of the first to be hit, even as the Mauritian, Lieutenant Wiehe, had his feet blasted out from under him, 'instantly losing the power of his legs'.

From Castelow's vantage point, he had seen each of their 'chutes slung across the sky. He had little doubt that the enemy would likewise have counted the number of jumpers. They had to know exactly how many men had dropped, which meant that every one of them was now a target. Hearing the cacophony of fire, mixed with grenade blasts and the cries of the wounded, Castelow steered his 'chute as far south as he could, aiming for a patch of woodland shaped like a crooked crocodile's head, with the open 'jaws' stretching out in an easterly direction. Ahead of him, jumpers number 10 and 11 – Troopers Morrison and Leslie 'Titch' Norman – plummeted into the dark trees, but being the last in line Castelow made it further into the woods than anyone.

As muffled cries and yells, plus bursts of machine-gun fire, reached him through the thick vegetation, Castelow cut himself free of his 'chute, hiding it as quickly as he could. If spotted, that flash of white amid the dark trees would be a dead giveaway.

That done, he crashed about trying to locate the means to fight. Stumbling upon a container, he wrenched it open, grabbing a Sten sub-machine gun, plus a handful of magazines and grenades. Alone in the depths of the Bois de Bouray, which was the name of the patch of woodland in which he had landed, he could only imagine that the very worst had befallen his comrades. Most of the sounds of battle were unmistakably German: the bark of 'Schmeissers' – the MP 40 – and the buzzcut-whir of MG 42 machine guns, which were joined by the banshee howl of mortar rounds, and the clanking rumble of a tracked armoured vehicle.

Stabs of muzzles blazing away reached Castelow through the gloom, as did the bark of their fire. One thing was utterly clear to him, as he hunkered down in the woods. This was a well-set, premeditated ambush. Somehow, their mission had been betrayed. He could only imagine it was some among the French who were the traitors, for how else could this have transpired? In fact, tonight's dark turn of events was all down to a double-cross executed by the Gestapo, in what they termed their *Funkspiel* – radio-game – operations. Over the long months of the war, the Gestapo had captured a number of SOE agents, complete with their wireless sets and codebooks. Achieving mastery of all of that, they had composed and dispatched false, but seemingly genuine, messages to SOE headquarters, to make it appear as if their agents were still at liberty and operational. In short, Garstin and his men had been called into La Ferté-Alais on a Funkspiel deception.

Earlier that day the DZ had been staked out by a force of Waffen SS soldiers, with the Gestapo acting as their taskmasters and guides. They had lain in wait for the first prey to blunder into their trap. It had come in the form of the local resistance. At dusk a group of Maquis had travelled to the DZ. Their arrival had been met with a hail of gunfire. The first to fall had been André Branche, a thirty-six-year-old hailing from La Ferté-Alais village itself. In trying to go to Branche's aid, a second man, twenty-four-year-old Georges Heren, was also cut down and killed. A third Maquis member, Gilbert Berlet, had managed to crawl into the woods to hide, and he would remain there all night long, acting as an eyewitness to much of what transpired.

The rest of the Maquis had managed to get away. Being unaware, of course, of the Funkspiel operation, and that the Gestapo had managed to learn the exact recognition code that the Stirling's aircrew were expecting, they presumed no parachutists would drop that night. Normally, without the code being signalled from the ground, no such operation would ever get the green light. But of course, the Gestapo were one step ahead in the game.

Castelow knew none of this. As the night wore on, and the chatter of gunfire died down almost to nothing, he could only imagine that all his SAS comrades had been captured or killed. All he was sure of, as he burrowed deeper into the night-dark vegetation, was that he was utterly alone and could trust absolutely no one. Marooned in a foreign country, able to speak barely a word of French, and surrounded by hostile forces, a lesser figure than Castelow might have crumbled or baulked. But there were hidden depths to the former painter and decorator, and father of two. More importantly, he was driven on by a burning anger against those who had ambushed and cut down his brothers in arms. He simply had to survive.

Beneath the fear, Castelow hungered for vengeance. Yet right then he had little idea how he might escape, let alone strike back against the enemy. Castelow also had others to live for. Married in August 1937, his two daughters, Doreen and Yvonne, were five and four years old respectively. A hard-working family man, he was the breadwinner in the household. Born and brought up in a large working-class family, he was happy to turn his hand to anything. He'd taken that can-do attitude into the military, completing a Gas Course, a Driver and Vehicle Maintenance Course, and training as a Motorcycle Messenger. One of his senior officers would conclude of Castelow: 'splendid type; modest, intelligent, hard-working, adaptable'. He would need all those qualities and more if he was to get out of the present dark predicament.

In the deepest of ironies, that very day a letter would be dispatched from 1 SAS Regimental headquarters, addressed to Mrs Castelow. It read: 'The following information is available regarding your husband, Tpr. T Castelow. He was dropped by parachute into France on 4 July '44 and up to the time of writing was quite safe and well. You may take it for granted that he is safe unless you hear to the contrary from us. He will not be able to write to you for some time, but will be able to receive your letters, so please keep writing. Cheerio, keep smiling, and don't worry.' It was signed by the 1 SAS Regimental Sergeant Major (RSM).

In fact, the first attempt to communicate the extent of the disaster had already been made, by one of Castelow's comrades. Even as he had been chased by enemy fire, Corporal Vaculik, the Czech-French member of the patrol, had readied a pigeon for dispatch to England. Four pigeons had been dropped with the patrol, contained in specially designed tubes and strapped to one of the jumper's chests, complete with supplies of bird food. That man, Lance Corporal Howard Lutton, had been one of the first to be hit once the ambush was sprung, and he would die from his injuries. Salvaging a pigeon, Vaculik had scribbled a hasty note and sent the bird winging into the night sky.

His message read: 'Hard luck. Germans were waiting for us. God help us. Dupontel.'

'Dupontel' was Vaculik's cover name; a name he'd been given in case of capture, which was what he feared he faced now . . . Sure enough, by dawn Vaculik, along with most of the rest of the patrol, had been rounded up and spirited away into captivity – the badly wounded Garstin and Wiehe among them. While the worst of the injured were taken to a Paris hospital, the remainder ended up at the Gestapo's notorious Avenue Foch headquarters. There, Vaculik was confronted with the final cut, as he saw it: the failure of even his carrier pigeon to get out of that well-set trap.

'You had carrier pigeons,' one of Vaculik's Gestapo captors announced. 'We've got four of them.' That had to mean that Vaculik's message had failed to reach home. Shortly, his interrogation in earnest and his torture would begin.

As first light began to filter through the Bois de Bouray, Castelow spotted a lone figure moving through the trees. An old lady, she bent every now and then, gathering up a bundle of firewood. Presumably she hailed from the nearby village. Having no idea who had betrayed them, or of what the wood collector's allegiances might be, Castelow remained stock still and did his best to avoid attracting attention. By the time she was gone, the old woman had shown not the slightest hint that he had been seen. In truth, Madame Annette had spied the mystery soldier. Nothing escaped her eagle eye. She had simply pretended not to, for obvious reasons.

Having dumped her wood at home, Madame Annette did what was for her the only sensible thing. Normally, the local resistance was very active. One of their high points had been in September 1943, when a Boeing Flying Fortress had crash-landed nearby. They had rescued the survivors, after which they had successfully dispatched the aircrew to Britain. But they were found out, and René Léger, one of the masterminds of that operation, had been seized, tortured and sent to Dachau, and from there to Bergen-Belsen. With Léger gone, Louis Moreau had taken over the network, but on 21 June 1944 – less than two weeks before the SAS raid – Moreau himself had been arrested and carted off to Buchenwald.

Moreau's arrest had come about via a 'denunciation'; someone – some informer – had reported him. Accordingly, Madame Annette felt she would be better placing her faith in a figure not directly connected to La Ferté-Alais. Just after dawn, she set out to speak to Michel Leduc, who was based in Vert-le-Petit village, some ten kilometres north of there. Knowing that some kind of Allied air operation had been foiled at La Ferté-Alais, and that treachery was again in the air, Madame Annette reasoned Leduc was the man in who to place her trust.

Leduc ran a resistance network consisting of some two dozen members. It turned out that he knew all about the ambush, including that two British parachutists had been killed and more captured. He had his suspicions as to just how the British troops had been betrayed. But as he listened to Madame Annette's account, and her description of spotting 'movement in the trees', and spying the survivor, he realised right away that time was of the essence. Sooner or later, that lone parachutist was bound to make a break for it. If he slipped away, he might be beyond Leduc's reach or his help.

Pausing only to arm himself with a pistol, Leduc jumped on a bicycle and pedalled hell-for-leather southwards. He reached the Bois de Bouray, and with Madame Annette's careful attention to detail he was able to locate the lone fugitive. Perhaps not surprisingly, whoever the parachutist might be, his means of greeting Leduc wasn't overly welcoming. 'He had me in his sights,' as Leduc would later describe it. Though he was menaced by a Sten gun, using hand gestures Leduc managed to placate the frightened gunman, and to signal that he was a friend and had come to help.

Though he spoke only a few words of broken English, and Castelow next to no French, gradually the two men reached some kind of accommodation. Eventually, Castelow felt able to lower his weapon. In an effort to indicate that he'd flown into France thrice, but jumped only twice, Castelow held up three fingers, and then two. Leduc, misunderstanding the gesture, presumed that Castelow had to mean that he 'was a veteran of thirty-two missions without a hitch', and he was suitably impressed. Once Leduc had convinced Castelow of his bona fides, he stressed how he must remain hidden, while Leduc went about seeking a way to fetch him to his own village.

Having reached that understanding, Leduc cycled away, hurrying back to Vert-le-Petit. Of course, the Germans were everywhere, for they knew full well that not all of the parachutists had fallen into their hands. But Leduc had the perfect cover, which helped him to slip through their checkpoints unmolested. A champion at swimming and judo, Leduc was actually an industrial chemist by trade. Before the war he'd worked for Groupe SNPE, an explosives and propellent manufacturer. He was also a reserve officer in the French Army. But shortly after the invasion of France, his Groupe SNPE credentials had brought him to the unwelcome attention of the enemy.

Arraigned by the Germans, Leduc was ordered to ready himself for deportation, as he would be joining a work gang destined for the German chemicals industry. Slipping his captors' clutches, he had returned to his home village, where his father-in-law ran the local butcher's shop. He promptly gifted it to Leduc, for the profession of 'butcher' was sacrosanct. A butcher was seen as being an 'essential worker', and exempt from being dispatched on a labour party. Leduc had promptly set himself up as the village butcher, ostensibly becoming a 'good Frenchman' in the eyes of the occupiers. Shortly, he had become the preferred supplier of meat for the local German garrison, which was based in the neighbouring village of Vert-le-Grand. It was perfect cover.

Secretly, of course, Leduc was playing a dark and dangerous game. His resistance network embraced a grouping of five villages that hugged the west bank of the Essonne river – Vert-le-Petit, Vert-le-Grand, Saint-Vrain, Leudeville and Écharcon. Crucially, some of his recruits actually worked on the nearby Luftwaffe base, and they began to pass him information on 'the number of German trainee pilots ... and the anti-aircraft batteries'. Gradually, such intelligence-gathering had evolved into guerrilla operations. His men started 'cutting out radio masts, and sometimes even sabotaging enemy aircraft'. Leduc kept each village's resistance group entirely separate, so only he knew the details of what each was up to. In that way, unless he was captured and forced to talk, penetration of any one group could only take the enemy so far.

Twenty-eight years of age, Leduc now faced the greatest challenge of his clandestine career: how to spirit that lone British parachutist to safety. He could only think of one option: despite the dangers, he would have to hide him in his butcher's shop. As

German troops visited daily, in order to buy their meat rations, the fugitive would somehow have to hide in plain sight. As he spoke no French, they would need to concoct some kind of a story – some ruse – as to why. Maybe he could be deaf and mute? Unable to speak, due to a medical impediment? There would be time to decide all of that once he'd got the man to the village.

There was another factor playing on Leduc's mind. Was that lone parachutist really who he claimed to be? The Germans had captured a great deal of British military equipment. What was to stop them dressing one of their own as a British parachutist, and planting him in the forest? What better way to lure out the local resistance? There were two Gestapo agents based permanently in Vert-le-Petit. They were forever asking questions as they prowled the streets, seeking to winkle out those who secretly supported the Allies. In short, the risks of harbouring the fugitive were legion, but Leduc could not, of course, turn him away.

The next day dawned unseasonably grey and damp. A summer's rain started to fall. It was just what Leduc had hoped for. Climbing aboard his bicycle, he threw over himself a voluminous cycle cape, ostensibly to shield himself from the damp. In that fashion, he pedalled back to the Bois de Bouray. During the previous day's confrontation, he had noticed Castelow's diminutive size. He should fit well beneath such a cape, perched on his handlebars. Leduc arrived at the forest, to see that Castelow had done pretty much as he'd asked, but not quite. He'd told him to bury all his kit, weaponry included. Most was gone, but Castelow had stubbornly held onto several items: chiefly, his Sten, his pistol, and his distinctive, double-edged Fairbairn-Sykes 'Commando' fighting knife.

Leduc had wanted Castelow to ditch all his weapons, so they

could move relatively light and fast. But the British parachutist clearly didn't trust his saviour completely yet, and Leduc could appreciate why. Without further ado he loaded Castelow onto his saddle-bar, spread the cape over them both, and set off. In that way he pedalled them both back to his village, slipping past the checkpoints with a cheery, rosy-faced smile and a butcher's ready wave. All knew Leduc, their prize meat-supplier. He was beyond suspicion or reproach. Upon reaching the village, Castelow was spirited into the butcher's shop and straight to the attic. This constituted the first place of relative sanctuary that he had enjoyed for over thirty-six long and lonely hours.

Later, Castelow would write of how the villagers would become his 'very best friends', to whom he 'owed his life . . . for if it had not been for Michel and . . . the old lady who . . . found me in the wood, I would off [sic] been shot like my pals who dropped with me'. But of course, such sentiments were a little premature right then. At that moment, Castelow was under something of a cloud, not to mention close guard. He was joined in the butcher's shop attic by the village English teacher, the redoubtable Madame Andrée Méry. She proceeded to grill him for days on end as to his bona fides.

By the end of that first week, the French teacher from Vert-le-Petit and the SAS parachutist from Stockton-on-Tees had become firm friends. Madame Méry actually towered over Castelow, and in a photo from the time she stands with one arm around his shoulders, her bright summer frock contrasting with the dark slacks and T-shirt that Leduc had provided, to replace Castelow's British army uniform. Both were smiling. Both looked very, very young. By her own admission, she would become like a big sister to 'Bert', as she nicknamed Herbert Castelow. She would finally declare of Castelow that he was not a German spy, but 'in fact Scottish, and he did not speak a word of French'. In fact, Castelow's home town lies over 150 kilometres south of the Scottish border, but such niceties were clearly lost on Madame Méry.

Finally 'cleared of suspicion', Castelow's purdah came to an end. Leduc's solution to his surprise appearance in the village was to paint Castelow as a distant cousin. In the forged ID card that Leduc procured for Castelow, his name was given as 'Hubert Louis Leboulenger'. Cannily, 'Hubert' was close enough to 'Herbert' so that if anyone might cry out his name, the real Herbert Castelow should be able to respond in a fitting manner. That ID card was a careful blend of Castelow's real and fake identities. Like all good covers, it was based in large part on truth. For his profession it gave '*Charpentier*' – carpenter – not so far from a painter and decorator, of course. His date of birth was recorded as 27 July 1917; not so far from 27 July 1916, his real birth date.

Supposedly due to a bad speech impediment, Hubert Louis Leboulenger could barely talk. Crucially, in the section of his ID card detailing '*Signes particuliers*' – distinguishing characteristics – there was written '*Très fortement bègue*'; very strong stammer. That would become Castelow's foil, whenever German troops came to the butcher's shop. The Leducs – Michel and his wife, Suzanne – had a much-loved infant daughter, Danielle, plus a boisterous dog, Bobby, and theirs was a busy family home. Castelow was supposed to be a part of their family. It wasn't seemly for him always to hide. If he ran into visiting enemy troops, he had to nod and smile and act 'dumb'. He'd even go as far as shaking hands with the visitors, although once the enemy troops had left, the first thing he would do was to scrub his hands vigorously, to remove what he saw as the stain of the enemy.

From the first, Leduc understood how Castelow hungered to hit back against the enemy – those who had wounded, killed and captured his SAS comrades. But he asked the British parachutist to make a solemn promise – that he would never kill or harm any Germans in the immediate area, not until Leduc gave him clearance to do so. Castelow agreed. He allowed his weapons to be hidden in the family cellar, as he went about posing as a 'normal' member of the village. Or at least he did so during daytime. Come nightfall, he and Leduc began sallying forth with resistance business in mind.

By the way Castelow would speak of it, with his characteristic modesty, he helped the local resistance in a number of 'minor engagements against the enemy'. Leduc would describe it somewhat differently, as he recalled the two of them sharing 'many difficult moments . . . as dangerous as they were exciting'. On one night they would ambush a German military convoy. On another, they would target the nearby airbase, sabotaging aircraft based there. An official report would state of this time: 'for six weeks he [Castelow] worked with the Resistance in VERT LE PETIT, mainly ambushing transport'. As Leduc would conclude of his redoubtable British comrade, Castelow was fearless. Despite his diminutive stature, 'Herbert was a hard man!'

With the Allies breaking out of the Normandy beachheads, Castelow could have opted to escape and evade, making his way back to British lines – as so many had done before him, including the crew of that downed Flying Fortress at La Ferté-Alais. But he made no effort to do so. Instead, he focused all his efforts in remaining right where he was, undercover – posing as

Hubert Louis Leboulenger – and very much still in the fight. It was almost as if he had taken on the SABU-70 mission single-handedly; as if he could not let their objective, or his vanquished comrades, finally go.

As the weeks trickled by and the frontlines drew closer, so Leduc was able to make contact with some of the nearest Allied commanders. Speaking by telephone from Vert-le-Petit to the nearest Allied lines, Leduc was faced with ever more onerous requests to garner intelligence. The Americans appeared especially demanding, as they sought details of enemy defences, numbers, strengths and their morale and intentions. In time, those intelligence-gathering forays took Leduc north to Paris, which lay just a few dozen kilometres away. Typically, Castelow – sensing adventure – refused to be left behind. As they would be cycling into the city, and Castelow had a habit of riding on the left, as opposed to the right as they do in France, Leduc called in an extra pair of hands.

His cousin, Gilbert Leduc, volunteered to ride on one side of Castelow, with Michel on the other. That way, sandwiched between two Frenchmen and pedalling three-abreast, and with their trouser bottoms tucked into their socks, to keep them free from snagging in the bike-chains, the trio set forth for the City of Light. But as Michel Leduc was starting to appreciate, Castelow had a tendency to 'flirt with danger, even after having just escaped from it'. The SAS soldier-turned-resistance-fighter insisted on stopping at the historic Roman Catholic church of Sacré Coeur de Monmartre. Out of sheer bedevilment, Castelow skipped up the grand flights of steps and parked himself next to a squad of German troops, demanding that Leduc snap his photo.

But Castelow couldn't keep hiding in plain sight for ever

and hope to escape all notice. At Vert-le-Petit's school, Suzanne Leduc's sister, Rolland, began fielding difficult questions. Kids are curious by their nature. Rolland's friends were keen to know who the stranger was they'd spied in and around the Leduc family home. Rolland was under strict instructions not to breathe a word, but even so the rumour mill had started churning. In part, it was Castelow's down-to-earth, easy-going attitude that was his greatest foil. His very joviality seemed to belie any possible suspicions that he could be anything other than what he claimed to be. He just seemed far too at home and at his ease to be an elite British parachutist and a fugitive in hiding from the enemy.

In Britain, meanwhile, the ill-fortune that had befallen Captain Garstin's patrol seemed to have passed without notice. Weeks after they had made that calamitous landing, dropping into that murderous ambush, SAS headquarters again wrote to Castelow's wife, offering the following assurances: 'We are in constant communication, and are glad to say that up to the time of writing he [Castelow] was safe and well. He is still unable to write to you . . . but will be able to receive letters from you, so please continue to write to him. Please don't worry.' Again, it was signed off by 1 SAS's RSM.

Castelow certainly hadn't risked breaking cover or tried to make contact with Britain. If he had, the letters sent to loved ones would have read very differently. Only via an ongoing Funkspiel operation could such a misconception of the fortunes of Captain Garstin's stick have been maintained. From their Avenue Foch headquarters, the Gestapo had to be cranking out the fake radio messages, which, dispatched to SOE's headquarters in Baker Street, London, were finding their way from there into the SAS's hands.

The first hints that anything was amiss came in mid-August, with the successful escape of two of Castelow's comrades. Slipping across France, Troopers Norman and Morrison, jumpers number 10 and 11 in the stick, finally made it to friendly lines. As a result, all bar those two individuals were listed as Missing in Action (MIA), Trooper Castelow being recorded as 'Missing from 5 July'. Finally, a little of the dark and bitter truth about the SABU-70 raiders was starting to emerge. Shortly, the British newspapers would carry the story, under the headline 'GERMANS MURDERED SKY-MEN', reporting that 'some of our airborne troops who landed in France in July were murdered by the Nazis'. The article explained that Garstin and his fellow captives were feared to have been 'shot by firing squad', under Hitler's notorious commando order.

Perhaps inevitably, Castelow's true identity, and Leduc's role in helping him, was about to be betrayed. An 'unknown collaborator' penned a denouncement and sent it to the Gestapo. Due to a friendly local postman, who'd intercepted the collaborator's letter en route, plus an equally friendly gendarme, Leduc got a few precious hours' prior warning. It was the third week of August, and a search and cordon operation was about to start at Vert-le-Petit, combing the village from end to end. He and Castelow would have to run. Dumping all incriminating evidence – including Castelow's SAS silk escape map, his commando knife, his lanyard and even his dog-tags – the two fugitives prepared to set off.

Sadly, this was to be the parting of the ways. Leduc was heading in one direction, seeking to link up with the American forces, those with whom he had been liaising over the past weeks. They were advancing on La Ferté-Alais, so were no more than a few dozen kilometres away. Castelow was heading in the opposite direction, for that way lay the nearest British lines. Making one last attempt at safeguarding him, Leduc managed to persuade the local gendarme to hand over one of his spare sets of uniform, for Castelow. And so, in that guise, and utterly sanitised of any documents or pieces of equipment that might mark him out as a British soldier, Castelow prepared to set out by bicycle, in an effort to be reunited with his countrymen.

Before leaving Vert-le-Petit, he asked Leduc for one last favour. As they were about to flee, might he finally be allowed to kill the two Gestapo agents who were based in the village? Castelow hated them with a vengeance, for they were the brethren of those who had lured so many of his SAS comrades to their deaths. Leduc relented. The war here was all but over. What harm could come of it now? Taking a knife from the butcher's shop, Castelow went about his deadly work. First one and then the other Gestapo man was lured to one of the many boggy lakes surrounding the village, and knifed to death, after which the bodies were dumped in places where the quicksand was thickest, so it would suck down the corpses with barely a trace.

That done, and dressed as a French gendarme, Castelow got on his bicycle and set off. He'd covered just a few dozen kilometres when he stopped for a break. He happened to be passing close to Étampes, the airbase that his patrol had been sent in to attack in the first place. As sod's law would have it, when he returned to the road to continue his journey, he found that his bike had been stolen. Without thinking, he let out a string of curses. Involuntarily, he'd done so in his thick Stockton-on-Tees accent and in English. A squad of German troops happened to be passing. On overhearing his swearing, they pounced on Castelow and he was duly arrested.

Facing the very worst, Castelow seemed remarkably unrepentant, not to mention sanguine: 'Unfortunately, upon discovering this [his bike being missing], I swore in English,' he would report of the moment. Those who'd seized the renegade soldier threatened him with immediate execution as a 'spy'. But shortly, a senior German officer arrived. He decided that Castelow should be sent further into German-occupied territory, under close escort, for proper questioning.

In theory, having waged his solo war from Vert-le-Petit, Castelow faced a triple death sentence. The first, for being an SAS parachutist deep behind enemy lines. The second, for having swopped his British Army uniform and his true identity with that of a supposed French villager. And the third, right now, for changing his guise once more, to that of a bicycling French gendarme. If he talked, and revealed his true nature, Castelow knew he was dead. His only chance, slim though it might be, was to stall and to keep the truth from his captors to force them to keep him alive as they sought to discover his real identity. But that process would prove long, and replete with terrible pain, suffering and trauma.

From the site of his capture near Étampes, Castelow was dispatched further away from the Allied advance. Brought to a private house that doubled as a Gestapo detention centre, the horror began. Though he would rarely if ever speak of what transpired there, Castelow's torture included being burned with irons and having electrodes attached to his chest, to deliver powerful shocks. Day after day the unspeakable terror and pain continued, but Castelow knew that if he cracked, he was a dead man. He also understood that with all that he knew about the Resistance, the lives of Leduc and so many others lay in his hands. He stubbornly refused to break.

After a week or more of such treatment, the Gestapo decided to ship their captive east, towards Germany, for the Allied front was drawing close. Castelow was loaded aboard a truck, and transported under close guard several hundred kilometres, ending up in Verdun, one of the last French cities before the German border. There his ordeal began all over again. Finally, as August 1944 bled into September, he was thrown aboard another vehicle to be dispatched into Germany. By now, Castelow was in such a sorry state that his captors believed him to be finished. Though he hadn't yet talked, they figured it was only a matter of time, and that all the fight had gone out of their suspect spy.

On the evening of 9 September, Castelow arrived in the city of Metz, on the banks of the Moselle river, just a short drive from the German border. If he were spirited into the Fatherland itself, Castelow feared, he was done for. Throughout all this time, he had refused to reveal to his inquisitors 'what I had been doing or that I was a paratrooper'. It was all that was keeping him alive, of that he felt certain. That night he was left alone in a room, with the one SS guard. It was now or never, he realised. He would have to keep vigilant and seize his chance.

At the approach of midnight, Castelow noticed that his lone guard appeared sleepy. As the SS man nodded off, Castelow struck. Killing the guard with his bare hands, he took his rifle, stole silently out of the house in which he had been held, scaled the walls and walked calmly into the night. Metz was a heavily garrisoned city, beyond which lay the German frontline, which was delineated by the Moselle, a tributary of the Rhine. German troops were dug in all along the eastern bank of the river, with American forces facing them across the waters. Intensively fought over, the Moselle was the line that enemy forces had been ordered to hold at all costs.

Several attempts by the Allies had been made to bludgeon a way across the river and to establish a viable bridgehead. So far, all had failed. The fighting had proved savage, bloody, and costly in human lives. The second week of September 1944 had brought driving rain and biting winds. The American lines had been churned into 'a morass of mud boding no good for the assembled armor [sic] and adding to the discomfort of the battle-weary infantry'. Some of those Allied units ranged along the western bank of the Moselle had been 'reduced to 50 percent of their original strength', and both trauma and 'battle fatigue had become a real problem'.

Moving like a wraith, Castelow managed to slip through the night and evade the massed ranks of enemy troops, taking hours to reach friendly lines. In the process, he had somehow to ford the river, all the bridges being heavily guarded, of course. Having no other option, Castelow had 'swum the Moselle and walked towards the Americans', as a report on his escape would record, 'whose forward units he met on 10 Sep. 44'. Finally, Trooper Herbert Castelow had made it back to friendly lines.

Having dropped into France on the night of 4/5 July, Castelow had been on the run and serving with the resistance, or being held prisoner by the enemy, for just shy of ten weeks. During that time he had been ambushed, seen his comrades killed and captured, been rescued by the Maquis, had undertaken repeated sabotage operations, killed several of the enemy at close quarters, and been tortured horrifically. By rights, he would have had every reason to wish to catch a ride on the first truck heading west, and to head for Britain. Instead, and not for the first time, he opted to stay and fight.

This time, as opposed to the Maquis of Vert-le-Petit, Castelow 'attached' himself to the US military's 5th Reconnaissance Troop (Recon), an elite unit charged to scout the route ahead. It formed part of the US Army's 5th Infantry Division, under XX Corps, whose overall commander was General George S. Patton. Of course, Castelow had just slipped through the very terrain on which the American military had expended so much blood and toil, as they tried to cross the river and conquer its far bank. His eyewitness account and his experiences would prove highly useful for what was coming.

Before setting out with the 5th Recon, Castelow paused to write a letter home. It was the first time that he had risked breaking cover since he had parachuted into the ambush at La Ferté-Alais. In a letter address to his 'Darling wife', he wrote: 'I have been picked up by the U.S. Army somewhere in France and I hope to see you soon. The boys I am with now are a good set of guys. They give me everything I want. Please let my father know I am alright. Well darling I will close now for the Germans are running that fast we cannot keep up with them. From your loving husband, Herbert.'

Forty-eight hours after Castelow had reached US lines, the 5th Recon moved out. It was first light, as the unit slipped across the Moselle into a narrow sliver of terrain on the far side. Moving south, they were stopped in their tracks by 'intense enemy shellfire'. With XX Corps' tanks bogged down in 'deep mud', the fighting descended into horrific close-quarter combat, as the American forces attempted to storm Hill 325, the enemy's key vantage point. In a savage, seesaw battle, it was taken, seized again by the enemy, and finally wrestled back into friendly hands.

On 14 September the 5th Recon were probing further south, slipping through Arry village, before they came under intense mortar fire. It wasn't until the following day, when thick fog blanketed the war-scarred terrain, that a ferocious artillery barrage from the Americans' field guns seemed to crush the enemy's will, and the breakout finally began. Within hours the town of Vittonville was taken, followed by a string of key objectives, including the village of Lorry-Mardigny, and Hills 396 and 400. On the 17th the Germans launched a counter-attack, but it was repulsed, and what became known as the Arnaville Bridgehead was firmly in Allied hands.

But the cost to XX Corps had been high. One unit alone, the 10th Infantry Regiment, had lost 725 men, with many more injured. At all stages, the 5th Recon had been at the forefront of the fighting. On 17 September the advance towards Metz got properly underway, but the battle to seize the city would last for a further seven weeks, before it was finally declared clear of enemy troops. The fall of Metz opened the way into the Fatherland itself.

Castelow would not share the next stage of the campaign with his adopted unit. On the day the march on Metz got under way, a letter was penned by 'Headquarters, 5th Reconnaissance Troop', addressed to the 'Commanding Officer, 1st SAS Regiment'. The subject concerned a 'Certificate of Service'. It read: 'This is to certify that Trooper Herbert CHATELOW [sic], 3321164, 1st SAS Regiment, has served with the 2nd Platoon, 5th Reconnaissance Troop . . . He joined the organisation . . . and elected to operate with this troop. His conduct has been honorable and [he] was held in high esteem by the men and Officers of this Troop.' The letter was signed: 'For the Commanding Officer, Louis R Morris, 1st Lt. Cavalry, Exec O' – by the 5th Recon's Executive Officer.

By now, Castelow had been absent from his parent unit, 1 SAS, for well over ten weeks. In Britain, he was listed as MIA, presumed dead. In truth, for most of that time he had been waging war against the enemy, just not with the British military. Indeed, during all of his summer '44 actions against the enemy he had actually been soldiering for foreign powers – first for (Free) France, and then for the United States of America. As his return to Britain loomed large, Castelow felt he might be in need of a little 'top cover' – some kind of official documentation to explain away why he had declined to return to British forces for so long. That letter from the 5th Recon was it.

In truth, he needn't have worried – or at least, not as far as 1 SAS's commanding officer was concerned. Shortly after the end of the war, Colonel Mayne would give a speech to the Royal British Legion, outlining some of the key achievements of the men that he had led. Though Mayne declined to name him in person, he singled out Castelow for particular mention, describing how, when the rest of his patrol had been ambushed, 'he lived in a butcher's shop on the top floor. At night, however, he went out and did some sabotage work.' Mayne further described how Castelow tried to bicycle his way to Allied lines, but was captured, and 'simply killed the guard – and went off with his rifle'. As far as Mayne was concerned, this was vintage stuff, and just the kind of behaviour he would expect from the kind of self-possessed, independently minded warriors he liked to draw to the SAS.

With that letter from the 5th Recon in hand, Castelow finally began his journey home, presumably dressed in US Army fatigues. It seems likely that he had been injured, for his youngest daughter, Avril, born after the war, noted a bullet wound that her father carried in his left side, which is not recorded on any of his British military records. More to the point, Castelow's means of return to the UK was highly unusual and suggested that he may have undergone a quiet, below-the-radar medical evacuation.

On 21 September, Castelow was flown from Paris, in a USAAF warplane, direct to London. In a dispatch marked 'PRIORITY IDENTIFICATION CERTIFICATE', he was listed as 'Repatriation Ex-POW, 1 SAS'. The dispatching officer further declared on the Air Transport form: 'I hereby certify that the movement of this passenger is necessary and essential to the successful prosecution of the war and that the mission of this passenger is of such urgency that transportation by air is necessary.' Whatever the truth behind Castelow's highly unusual means of returning to Britain, he seems to have attracted no obvious opprobrium as a result of his long, and unusual, absence.

On 22 September 1944, he was listed as 'Rejoined from missing', so apparently back with his parent unit.

Indeed, Castelow would be duly awarded a Military Medal (MM), the citation for which praised all of his actions over the past three months, including his '"evading" immediately after being dropped at LA FERTE ALAIS . . . as he had landed in a trap and lost the rest of his party'. It further praised his work with the Vert-le-Petit resistance, his attempt to escape disguised as a gendarme, his dogged resistance to interrogation, his killing his guard and daring escape at Metz, and his finally linking up with US forces. Notably, the citation was signed off by none other than Colonel Blair 'Paddy' Mayne.

The day before Castelow's urgent flight from Paris to London, Mike Sadler had arrived in France, charged to uncover the truth about the fate of Captain Garstin and the missing men of his patrol. To Sadler would fall the horrendous task of exhuming those bodies that had been buried in the grounds of a large country estate, the Château de Parisis-Fontaines, which lies a few dozen kilometres to the north of Paris. Sadler was led to the grisly site by one André Lenain, the chief of the local Maquis. As Lenain knew well, a group of British parachutists had been gunned down in the nearby woodlands. Captain Garstin and his fellow captives had been taken there and murdered by their Gestapo and SS captors, on Hitler's personal orders, after which their bodies had been buried in the château grounds.

Sadler was there to identify the bodies, and to have them interred in a nearby French cemetery, with full military honours. But he also sought a reckoning, as did the higher echelons of the SAS. This was to be the first step in seeking out the culprits and bringing them to trial, a process that would last for several years after the end of the war. As matters transpired, two men had escaped from the execution squad in that dark forest – Czech-French SAS man Serge Vaculik, and SAS original Thomas 'Ginger' Jones. They had broken away even as the gunmen opened fire, and both would survive. When the guilty parties were finally brought to trial, Jones and Vaculik would be there to give powerful eyewitness evidence, ensuring that most would face stiff custodial sentences, and that some at least would hang.

Trooper Herbert Castelow would return to the SAS ranks shortly after his arrival back in the UK. He would soldier with the unit until war's end, serving on Operation Archway, among other missions – the SAS thrust into Germany itself. With the disbandment of the SAS in October 1945, Castelow returned to Stockton-on-Tees, and took up life where he had left off, providing for his family. He would never speak about his wartime experiences, and when the time came to receive his MM, Castelow declined the invitation to meet the King and to be given it in person. As so many of his comrades had been lost, he didn't feel he was worthy or deserving of such an accolade.

He received a short letter from His Majesty the King, enclosing the decoration. 'I greatly regret that I am unable to give you personally the award which you so well earned,' wrote the King. 'I now send it to you with my congratulations and my best wishes for your future happiness.' While Castelow had not felt able to accept such an honour in person, he was keen to reach out to his comrades in France, and particularly to the villagers of Vert-le-Petit. Shortly, he would pen a letter to 'Michel and Suzanne', offering his heartfelt thanks. 'You and Suzanne are my very best friends,' he wrote, 'not forgetting all my other friends in Vert-le-Petit, for I owe my life to you all ...'

In the letter, Castelow explained how he had started working in the local steel mill, and how he was 'saving up so I can come over to see you all again for I miss the good times we had together'. Castelow firmly intended to visit Vert-le-Petit with his wife – that much is clear from his letter. Neither of them would ever manage it. For whatever reason – most likely the pressures of raising a young family – neither he nor Laura would ever visit France. Indeed, Michel Leduc would write several times, seeking news of his British comrade and friend, but they were never to see each other again.

In June 1945, the then overall Commander of SAS Troops, Brigadier Mike Calvert, had written to Leduc, on the announcement that the Frenchman was being awarded the King's Medal for Courage in the Cause of Freedom. The citation for that honour praised Michel and his wife, Suzanne, for hosting Castelow in their home for six weeks, 'in spite of the fact that Germans entered the house every day to buy meat. They knew that his presence in the area was known to the Germans ... Had he been discovered ... they would certainly have suffered brutal reprisals ... The district was well-populated by the enemy, there being a battalion of Luftwaffe troops in the neighbouring town of Vert-le-Grand.'

Calvert's accompanying letter is so extraordinary it deserves to be quoted here in full:

Now that the war with Germany has been victoriously ended, I wish to express to you something of the gratitude which all men and officers of the Special Air Service Brigade who took part in the campaign of France, 1944, feel toward you for your selfless devotion and memorable courage with which you aided them in the accomplishment of their tasks. The help you gave contributed in a large measure to any success we achieved, and we are full of admiration for the disregard of danger and the generosity of spirit with which that help was given.

All men who were involved in the bitter conflict of 1939–1945 grew to recognise the importance to victory of civilian loyalty, steadfastness and determination. We realise that in no country and at no time did the practice of those virtues demand greater firmness than in France under German occupation, and that nowhere was that firmness more abundantly forthcoming. Your individual acts of patriotism as they affected our operations have been brought to the notice of the British Government and will be preserved in the official records of the British War Office.

Those of our men who had known France before returned to England with renewed faith in the destiny of your country to which the civilisation of the world owes so much; those that had not known France before have now an impression of a great people of indomitable spirit. All the British troops under my command have been most deeply touched by the sentiments and comradeship with England which their allies of France have expressed to them in words, and so valiantly proved in deeds. It is our fervent hope that the unity of purpose and ideals between Great Britain and France which we have realised in war will be maintained triumphantly in peace.

On behalf of the Special Air Service Brigade, I wish all good fortune to you personally and to France and offer you our most sincere thanks.

Scribbled on the top of the note was a handwritten message, from none other than Jim 'Gentleman' Almonds, who was now a captain in the SAS: 'M. Leduc, With very many thanks for his kindness to the SAS during July–Aug '44 in taking care of Tpr. Castelow.'

In November 1945, Major Edward Lepine wrote a letter to Castelow, at his Stockton-on-Tees address, triggered by the demise of the SAS. This freewheeling, at times piratical and maverick-spirited unit had never been popular with many in high command, and the naysayers had finally got their way, the SAS being disbanded. Notably, while Lepine had ended up as a major in the SAS, the letter was sent from a private address and was entitled: 'Subject:– S.A.S. Museum'. In it Lepine stressed how 'it is important that a Regiment such as ours, with its brilliant record, should not die a natural death. It is sincerely hoped that the spirit of the Regiment is maintained always and this [a proposed SAS Museum] may prove to be that spirit in reality.'

The letter contained an appeal for any items of interest – 'Documents ... Photographs ... Small items of kit. Personal equipment belonging to you or the enemy that has a "War Story". Any Maps of past operations ... Any letters of Congratulation ... Humorous episodes, cartoons or accounts ...' – to be sent to Lepine's private address, in Carshalton, Surrey. There is no record of Castelow ever responding. A further letter from SAS circles was dispatched to him some five years later. Penned by a Major A. Grenville-Bell DSO, it sought to entice Castelow back into a unit which had seemed to have been dead in the water until then.

Marked 'PERSONAL AND CONFIDENTIAL', Grenville-Bell's letter was written on 'Headquarters, 21 SAS Regt (Artists) TA' headed paper, and sent from a Duke's Road, London address. Quietly, the SAS spirit and identity had been kept alive within that territorial unit, even as the regular SAS had been done away with. Now, Grenville-Bell was busy looking at resurrecting the SAS proper, as his letter so eloquently explained. 'Dear Castelow, There is a possibility that a small SAS unit will be formed soon for operations overseas. It will be raised from ex-members of 1st and 2nd SAS ... I hope to be commanding it and would be very glad if you would consider joining ...'

Grenville-Bell went on to add a note of caution: 'Whatever you feel about this, you must treat this letter as confidential and remember you are now bound by the Official Secrets Act in regard to its contents ... To summarise, this is what you should do: First – Let me know whether you are prepared to join. Second – If you are, do nothing more until you get an order to attend for a medical examination. Third – After the examination, remain in your present employment until you get an order telling you to report somewhere for duty.'

Before long the SAS would be reformed, but Herbet Castelow MM would play no further role in it. Though he was a dedicated family man, Herbert Castelow was nursing his demons. His youngest daughter, Avril, realised this from an early age. On moonlit nights her father would awake, screaming and thrashing in his bed. She got into the habit of going to his aid, taking a damp cloth to mop his brow. Of course, SABU-70 had dropped into that ambush during the 'moon period', as the SAS termed it, when there was enough moonlight to navigate by and to find the DZ. In fact, all of his parachute missions had been executed under the light of a full moon. While Avril's father almost never spoke about the war, while coming out of those nightmares was one of the rare exceptions. He would make a point of showing his daughter his scars, and explaining the burn marks across his chest from the torture, and the bullet scar on his side.

Troubled by his memories, Herbert Castelow MM had no desire to return to war. Perhaps that was why he never again contacted Michel Leduc, or any of those who had helped him in Vert-le-Petit village. Either way, when he died in 1974 – aged just fifty-eight, and from an illness that he had stubbornly refused to get treated – he left four grieving daughters and a widow. And he left not the slightest means for any of them to trace those who had so helped him during his long escape and evasion in France.

In 1995, almost quite by chance, Michel Leduc managed to track the Castelow family down. He had been searching for his friend Herbert for many years. Leduc travelled to Britain for a memorial service and he was able to meet the family, although Laura, Castelow's widow, had died four years earlier. In due course the children paid a visit to Leduc's village and were able to pay their respects at the numerous memorials the French had raised to the fallen of that ill-fated SAS mission. It was hugely touching to see how that memory was cherished and kept alive. But more emotional by far was the tour Michel Leduc gave them of the cellars at his Vert-le-Petit home. There they found their late father's Sten gun, his dog tags, his lanyard, plus the heavy butcher's knife with which he had dispatched those two Gestapo agents.

When Leduc handed Avril her father's original Colt pistol, it was found to have a round still in the chamber. Leduc apologised profusely, deftly removed the bullet, and handed the weapon back to her to study and admire. Leduc also showed her Castelow's old escape map, which he had thought to have framed. Being a well-ordered, methodical type, Leduc had had the rear of the frame labelled thus: 'War 1939–1945. Map of France rendered on natural parachute silk. Arrived on the 5th of July 1944, at La Ferté-Alais, with Herbert Castelow, paratrooper of the 1st SAS (his . . . parachute companions were captured and shot by the Germans). Herbert was saved and collected by LEDUC Michel, from the French Forces of the Interior (FFI), and hidden in Vert-le-Petit until liberation, where he also took part in certain actions of the Resistance.'

One thing Michel Leduc had been totally unaware of – as that caption to the SAS silk escape map makes clear – was how Castelow was captured and tortured by the enemy, after he had bicycled away from Vert-le-Petit village dressed as a gendarme. Upon learning this from Castelow's daughter, Michel Leduc was visibly moved. He realised then that if Herbert Castelow MM had not been a man of such immense courage and fortitude, and had he broken under interrogation and talked, the people of Vert-le-Petit would have paid a terrible price, the Leduc family first and foremost.

In short, as much as Herbert Castelow owed his life to them, they also owed theirs to him.

Acknowledgements

First and foremost, thank you to my esteemed readers. You go out and buy my books, in the hope that each will deliver an enjoyable, rewarding, illuminating read; another work that brings a story to life in vivid detail. I am most grateful and I hope I have managed to deliver that kind of reading experience in this book. Without you, there could be no author such as myself. You enable individuals like me to make a living from writing. You deserve the very first mention.

A huge thank you to Maryann Byrne, and her siblings, for the correspondence and the conversations and for allowing me the kind permission to quote as I have done from your father J. V. Byrne's wonderful book. He was a truly exceptional man with an extraordinary wartime story.

Enormous gratitude to Nick Jellicoe, whose father Earl George Jellicoe's wartime story of martial exploits and escape is so compelling, and who gave me kind permission to quote from his book on the subject, and for the extensive correspondence and discussions on same.

Heartfelt thanks to Alison Smartt for allowing me to use the private papers from your father, Dr Malcolm Pleydell MC's war years, including his diaries and letters written home during the time. Incredibly detailed and moving, these have proven invaluable in rendering that escape story in such rich and compelling detail.

Huge thanks to the family of Amédée Maingard de la Ville-ès-Offrans for sharing with me the private archive of the Maingard family, pertaining to his wartime service as an SOE agent, and especially to Jan Maingard, for the correspondence and conversations regarding same. I am also enormously grateful to Xavier Marrier d'Unienville, for sharing insight, recollections and connections regarding Amédée Maingard's wartime story.

Great thanks to James Irvine, military veteran, whose grandfather was one of those who served on the SAS's post-D-Day operations. James first alerted me to the oustanding heroism of Captain John Tonkin, during Operation Bulbasket. 'Tonkin was another Paddy Mayne in terms of bravery and luck,' James told me, adding that while some might have blamed him for the July 1944 losses of most of his patrol, he deserved praise for a mission that achieved so much, and for getting the survivors out alive. That piqued my interest in Bulbasket and the writing of their great escape flowed from there. I also must thank Scott Hackney, who shared with me his grandfather Charlie Hackney's unpublished wartime memoirs and archive, from his service in 1 and 2 SAS. These provided invaluable further insight, for which I am most grateful.

Massive thanks to Avril Deehan for sharing with me your recollections about your father Herbert Castelow's wartime service and the fabulous Castelow family archive. Your visit to Vert-le-Petit and environs, during the writing of this book, added layers of meaning and richness to that story and I am immensely grateful. I'm also hugely grateful to Avril's husband, Brian, for all the correspondence, conversations and boundless help and assistance you provided me during the writing of your late father-in-law's great escape.

Enormous thanks to Christophe Muller for your correspondence over your grandfather André Lenain's wartime resistance work, and his recollections regarding the Garstin patrol, and for sharing with me his archive, documents and photos from the war years. I also would like to thank Eric Lecomte, for corresponding with me so generously over various aspects of the SAS service in France, as covered in these stories. Special thanks to Thomas Liaudet and all at the AFPSAS, for your kind and generous help in my research into the French aspects of the story as told in these pages. Thanks also to Anthony Watrin, for your correspondence and insight into SAS operations in France.

Thank you to Peter Abbott for corresponding with me over the escape told in Chapter Four of this book, and for sharing with me a copy of the original *New Yorker* article that reported this incredible tale. Huge thanks also to Andrew Atherton, Glenys Atherton and Norman Jones and their families, for corresponding with me over the wartime story of Corporal Thomas 'Ginger' Jones. Thank you also to Paul Norman, for your correspondence and assistance with telling the wartime story of your father, Trooper Leslie Norman, for which I am most grateful.

I have benefited greatly in the research for this book from the resources that the British, French and other governments, and related institutions, have invested into preserving for posterity the archives from the Second World War era. The preservation and cataloguing of a mountain of papers – official reports, personal correspondence, telegrams, etc. – plus photographic, film and sound archives is vital to authors such as myself, without which books of this nature could not be written. Devoting resources to the preservation of this historical record, and to making it

accessible to the public, is something for which these governments and other institutions deserve high praise.

I extend a special thank you to the Imperial War Museum
(IWM), whose archives are a treasure trove of some wonderful
oral histories and the collections of private papers, without which
I would not have been able to render the stories told in this book
in such rich and compelling detail. The IWM archivists, likewise,
deserve special mention, for reaching out to the families of those
whose archives they hold, to secure the kind permission that I
sought to quote from their private papers.

Thanks as ever to Julie Davies, ace researcher and translator, for
your fine translations that I relied upon to tell some of these stories, and your astute and pertinent observations, assessment and
guidance regarding the stories told in these pages; but most of all
for your heartfelt enthusiasm that these stories deserved to be told.

All at my publishers deserve the very best of praise for their
committed, enthusiastic and visionary support of this project
from the get-go. In the UK, Richard Milner, my long-standing
editor, provided seminal guidance and feedback. The wider
Quercus team also deserve the highest praise, and especially
Hannah Robinson, Dave Murphy and Jon Butler. Fabulous to
be working with Sophie Ransom, and her great team at Ransom
PR, once more - absolutely the professionals at getting a buzz
going and spreading the word. In the USA the publishing team
at Kensington Books were superlative, as always. Thank you to all
of you, but especially to Wendy McCurdy, Anne Pryor, Rebecca
Cremonese, Barbara Brown, John Son, Elizabeth Trout, Lynn
Cully, Jackie Dinas, Steven Zacharius and Adam Zacharius. My
gratitude is also extended to my literary agent at Curtis Brown,

Gordon Wise, and to my US literary agent, George Lucas at Inkwell Management Literary Agency.

Finally, of course, I need to extend my deep thanks and heartfelt gratitude to my family – Eva, David, Damien Jr and Sianna – who once again had to put up with 'Pappa' spending far too long locked in his study trying to do justice to this story. That I have – if I have – I owe to you all; to your forbearance, your love and support and kindness, and for putting up with me through it all.

Acknowledgements On Sources

I am indebted to the following authors (and/or estates), who have covered some of the aspects of the story I have dealt with in *SAS Great Escapes Two* in their own writing. I extend my gratitude to all those who kindly granted me permission to quote from their material. For those readers whose interest has been piqued by this book, these authors and their titles would reward further reading:

Nicholas Jellicoe, whose biography about his father, entitled *George Jellicoe SAS and SBS Commander*, is a fine tour de force, being a detailed chronicle of the life of this extraordinary warrior.

Jan Maingard, whose history of SOE agent Amédée Maingard's wartime exploits is told wonderfully well, in the richly illustrated volume *Agent S.O.E. Ils l'appelaient SAMUEL* (available only in French).

The late Malcolm James Pleydell, whose book *Born of The Desert: With the SAS in North Africa* is a brilliant evocation of the time he spent serving alongside the SAS originals in the desert of North Africa.

The late J. V. Byrne, whose book *The General Salutes a Soldier* tells of the time he spent as an SAS original, soldiering in the desert of North Africa and his series of escapes.

The late Blair 'Paddy' Mayne, whose wartime compilation/

diary/scrapbook, the *Paddy Mayne Diary* (the *SAS War Diary*), constitutes a fine record of this regiment's wartime history.

I am also grateful to the following publishers, authors and estates for granting me permission to quote from their works (full details in Selected Bibliography):

Lorna Almonds-Windmill, *Gentleman Jim*, 2011 – all rights reserved.

Lorna Almonds-Windmill, *A British Achilles*, 2008 – all rights reserved.

Virginia Cowles, *The Phantom Major: The Story of David Stirling and the SAS Regiment*, 2010 – all rights reserved.

Paul McCue, *SAS Operation Bulbasket*, 2009 – all rights reserved.

Patric McGonigal, *Special Forces Brothers In Arms*, 2022 – all rights reserved.

Gavin Mortimer, *The SAS In Occupied France,* 2020 – all rights reserved.

Sources

Material quoted from the UK archive files listed below, is by kind courtesy of the UK National Archives. This book contains public-sector information licensed under the Open Government Licence v3.0.

Material quoted from the French archive files, and other sources listed herein, is by kind courtesy of the Service Historique de la Défense/Ministère des Armées (France).

Imperial War Museum

IWM 13039 – Jellicoe, George Patrick John Rushworth (Oral History)

IWM 18045 – Bennett, Robert ('Bob') (Oral History)

IWM 22099 – Documents of Major S. Beckinsale MC (Private Papers)

IWM 337 – Private Papers of Captain M. J. Pleydell MC

The National Archives

CAB 103/586 – Loan of Field Marshal Rommel's war diaries to the Enemy Documents Section (EDS)

CAB 106/603 – Battle of Leros
PREM 3/330/9 – Combined Operations
WO 218/102 – Signals
WO 201/2836 – Raiding Forces
WO 373/46 – Citations
WO 373/185/19 – Citations
HS9/976/9 – SOE
WO/373/26/79 – Citations
WO 201/727 – Raiding Forces
WO 373/46 – Citations
WO 201/748 – Middle East Forces
WO 201/765 – Raiding Forces: Signals In
WO 208/5402 – POW debriefs
WO 218/114 – HQ SAS Troops
WO 218/115 – HQ SAS Troops
WO 218/187 – SAS/RAF liaison
WO 219/2329 – SHAEF liaison SF HQ
WO 219/2342 – SAS summary
WO 219/2389 – SAS ops
WO 309/226 – NW Europe War Crimes
WO 309/474 – SAS War Crimes Cases
WO 309/830 – Poitiers case
WO 311/627 – SAS WCIT
WO 311/628 – SAS WCIT
WO 311/629 – SAS WCIT
AIR 37/714 – 2nd TAF Ops
AIR 25/40 – 2 Group Ops
AIR 25/41 – 2 Group Ops
AIR 25/42 – 2 Group Ops

AIR 27/1068 – 161 Squadron Ops

AIR 26/204 – 140 Wing Ops

AIR 27/956 – Ops Book 138 (SD) Squadron

HS 1/82 – interview, Major Maingard

HS 6/515 – debrief, Major Maingard

HS 9/1017/8 – SOE Files

HS9/976/9 – Major A. Maingard

HS 6/579 – report, Squadron Leader M. Southgate

TS 26/861 – Court Records

British Army Service Records – CASTELOW, Herbert
FGFO/85/1 3321164

French Archives:
Service Historique de la Défense

GR 16 P433726 – MOUHOT Jacques

GR 16 P363270 – LEOSTIC Pierre

GR 28 P 3 20 – 2 Rapport de fin de mission du capitaine Bergé

GR 28 P 3 20 – 2 Savanah Dossier Rapport BERGÉ

Other Published Sources

'Obituary, General Georges Bergé', M. R. D. Foot, 21/9/1997,
The Independent

'France honours the last SAS original', Ben Macintyre, *The
Times*, 23/06/2018

*United States Army in World War II. Three Battles: Arnaville,
Altuzzo and Schmidt*, by Charles B. Macdonald and Sidney

T. Mathews, Centre of Military History, United States Army, Washington DC, 1993

Battle Analysis: The Moselle River Crossing, Hasty and Deliberate River Crossings at Dornot and Arnaville, France, September 1944, Staff Group B, Section 22, Major William Thomas et al., CSI Battlebook 22-B (AD-A156 949)

'Obituary, Anthony Grenville-Bell', *The Times*, 28/03/2008

'50 ans plus tard les souvenirs resistant', *Republicain*, Vert-Le-Petit

A. J. Liebling, A Reporter at Large, 'Gafsa, The Eighth Army from Gabes', *The New Yorker*, 6/11/1943: https://www.newyorker.com/magazine/1943/11/06/gafsathe-eighth-army-from-gabes

Sergeant Duvivier, 'Paratrooper's Nine Lives', *Sutton Times & Cheam Mail*, date unavailable.

Non-published Sources

Philippe Autrive, 'La Ferté-Alais – the War Years: 1939 to 1945' (2017), https://www.lafertealais.com/world-second-war-39-45/

'Sabotage 62', IMK (Historical Museum of Crete), 2006: https://www.historical-museum.gr/eng/exhibitions/view/sabotage-62

'The Free French, June 1940 to July 1943, Jacques A. M. E. Mouhot': https://www-francaislibres-net.translate.goog/liste/fiche.php?index=86789&_x_tr_sch=http&_x_tr_sl=fr&_x_tr_tl=en&_x_tr_hl=en&_x_tr_pto=sc

Anon., 'IMK Studies & Texts, Testimonies Series, Mission en Crete': https://www.historical-museum.gr/store/category.php?id_category=6&mc_cid=ecace03a7c&mc_eid=%5B6848a13e85%5D&id_lang=1&p=2

Anon., 'WWII Escape & Evasion Information Exchange –
Escapers from Germany': http://www.conscript-heroes.com/
escapelines/EEIE-Articles/Art-16-Escapers-from-Germany.
htm

Kevin Walton, 'Obituaries, John Elliot Tonkin', Published
online by Cambridge University Press: 27 October 2009:
https://www.cambridge.org/core/services/aop-cambridge-
core/content/view/AB58C504739E354944F96DB99FAD63AE/
S0032247400027753a.pdf/obituaries.pdf

Anon., 'Obituary – Jacques L. Sibard: https://www.
historical-museum.gr/gr/news/view/h-ekim-apochaireta-to-
jack-sibard/2022

Selected Bibliography

Lorna Almonds-Windmill, *Gentleman Jim*, Barnsley: Pen & Sword, 2011

Lorna Almonds-Windmill, *A British Achilles*, Barnsley: Pen & Sword, 2011

Anon., *The SAS War Diary*, London: Extraordinary Editions, 2011

Daniel Allen Butler, *Field Marshal*, Casemate Publishers, 2017

J. V. Byrne, *The General Salutes A Soldier*, London: Robert Hale, 1986

Roy Close, *In Action With the SAS*, Barnsley: Pen & Sword, 2005

Johnny Cooper, *One of The Originals*, London: Pan Books, 1991

Virginia Cowles, *The Phantom Major*, Barnsley: Pen & Sword, 2010

Ex-Lance-Corporal X, QGM, *The SAS & LRDG Roll of Honour 1941–47*, SAS-LRDG-ROH, 2016

Raymond Forgeat, *Remember: Les Parachutistes de la France Libre*, Vincennes: Service Historique de l'Armée de Terre, 1990

Paul Gaujac, *Special Forces in The Invasion Of France*, Paris: Histoire et Collections, 1999

Lyman Hafen, *Far from Cactus Flat*, Arizona Strip Interpretive Association, 2006

Max Hastings, *Das Reich*, London: Michael Joseph, 1981

Stephen Hastings, *The Drums of Memory*, Barnsley: Pen & Sword, 1994

Malcolm James (Pleydell), *Born of The Desert*, Barnsley: Frontline Books, 2015

Nicholas Jellicoe, *George Jellicoe*, Barnsley: Pen & Sword, 2021

W. B. Kennedy Shaw, *Long Range Desert Group*, Barnsley: Frontline Books, 2015

Damien Lewis, *Churchill's Secret Warriors*, London: Quercus, 2014

Damien Lewis, *SAS Ghost Patrol*, London: Quercus, 2018

Damien Lewis, *SAS Band of Brothers*, London: Quercus, 2020

Damien Lewis, *SAS Great Escapes*, London: Quercus, 2020

Damien Lewis, *SAS Brothers in Arms*, London: Quercus, 2022

B. H. Liddell Hart, *The Rommel Papers*, New York: Harcourt Brace & Company, 1953

Corétra Ltée & Streak Design (ed.), *Lieutenant John H. Wiehe*, Precigraph Ltd, 2016

David Lloyd Owen, *The Desert My Dwelling Place*, London: Cassell & Company, 1957

David Lloyd Owen, *The Long Range Desert Group*, Barnsley: Leo Cooper, 2001

Jan Maingard, *Agent S.O.E. Ils l'appelaient SAMUEL*, Imprimerie et Papeterie Commercial, 2018

Ben Macintyre, *SAS Rogue Heroes*, London: Viking, 2016

Carol Mather, *When the Grass Stops Growing*, Barnsley: Leo Cooper, 1997

Paul McCue, *Behind Enemy Lines with the SAS*, Pen & Sword, 2007

Paul McCue, *SAS Operation Bulbasket*, Barnsley: Pen & Sword, 2009

J. Fraser McLuskey, *Parachute Padre*, Nottingham: Spa Books, 1985

Gavin Mortimer, *The SAS in Occupied France*, Barnsley: Pen & Sword, 2020

Gavin Mortimer, *David Stirling*, London: Constable, 2022

Gearoid O'Dowd, *He Who Dared and Died*, Barnsley: Pen & Sword, 2011

John O'Neill, *Legendary Warrior of The SAS*, Eastbourne: Menin House Publications, 2015

Sean Rayment, *Tales from The Special Forces Club*, London: Collins, 2014

Christian Richard, *1944 Le Special Air Service en Poitou*, La Crèche: Geste Editions, 2017

Jacques L. Sibard, *Mission en Crète*, Heraklion: IMK, 2006

Philip Vickers, *Das Reich*, Barnsley: Leo Cooper, 2000

A.P. Wavell, *Other Men's Flowers,* London: Jonathan Cape, 1968

Ian Wellsted, *With the SAS Across The Rhine*, Barnsley: Frontline Books, 2020

Index

Vaculik, Serge, 267, 271, 274–5, 294

Varey, Trooper, 271

Vassilopoulos, Ivy, 106

Verrières, France, 202–3, 225–6, 233, 238

Vert-le-Grand, France, 278

Vert-le-Petit, France, 276, 278–85, 295, 300–301

Vienne, France, 200

Wadi El Faregh, Libya, 42–3

Wadi Gamra, Egypt, 129, 132, 141

Wadi Zem-Zem, Tunisia, 163

Walker, Trooper, 271

Walton, Kevin, 209

war crimes, 251, 254

Weaver, Peter, 218–24, 228, 233, 253

Weber, Marcel, 217–18, 224, 228

Webster, James, 130, 138–9, 160

Westland Lysander 'Lizzies', 246

Wiehe, John H. 'Rex', 267, 271, 275

Willys jeeps, 174, 193

Young, Trooper, 271

AFPSAS

WHO DARES WINS

The AFPSAS (Association des familles des parachutistes S.A.S. de la France Libre), includes the Free French SAS from 3rd and 4th SAS (Special Air Service) regiments and their families.

The 'French SAS Squadron' traces its origins to 1940 when the 1ere Compagnie d'Infanterie de l'Air (1ere CIA) was formed by Capitaine Georges Bergé. Initially operating in North Africa, its men joined David Stirling upon the creation of the Special Air Service (SAS). They would return to the UK in 1943 and form the 3rd and the 4th SAS squadron. They would operate across Nazi-occupied territories and in particular in France. Along with the men of 1st and 2nd SAS, they would be the first forces to land on French soil on D-Day, parachuting during the night of 5th to 6th June 1944. The Regiment would continue to operate throughout the war, undertaking daring missions in occupied territories, harassing enemy troops by organising sabotage and ambushes as well as training the local resistance. The French SAS squadrons would complete their final missions helping to liberate Holland.

The AFPSAS promotes the social well-being of the veterans from those units, as well as supporting their families. It also aims at commemorating the history and esprit de corps of the SAS regiment and passing that on to younger generations. It works with the media, researchers, historians and writers focused on the history of the SAS regiment during World War II. It also supports specialised re-enacting teams and relevant museums.

The association operates out of France with a local liaison in the UK and also works in partnership with the Belgian and Dutch associations. It supports commemorative events across those countries. In November 2022, it co-sponsored the unveiling of a commemorative plaque dedicated to the 3rd and 4th SAS regiments, in London. In recent years, the AFPSAS has set up the first freely accessible, online memorial listing of the men of the 3rd and 4th SAS regiments. It can be viewed here: https://memorial.afpsas.fr

The AFPSAS is affiliated to the *Souvenir Français au Royaume-Uni* a.k.a. the *French War Graves Commission in the UK*, a registered Charity in England and Wales, charity number 1185088.

It can be contacted at the following address: getintouch@afpsas.fr

Who Dares Cares supports our Armed Forces, Emergency Services and Veterans including their families who are suffering from Post-Traumatic Stress Disorder (PTSD). They provide weekend retreat facilities where individuals and families can spend a weekend away from the daily grind and relax in fun activities, Walk, Talk and Brew Groups where they have teams of volunteers across the United Kingdom meeting with groups of people who maybe just want to clear their head and have the support of charity volunteers through participating in some gentle exercise or attending a PTSD awareness group or individual session to help provide a better understanding of what the signs and symptoms of PTSD are, how to manage symptoms and ways that families can better support in a way that is helpful to the individual. The charity recognises the importance of exercise as part of recovery and they work to encourage this and make this accessible for those who are struggling with PTSD and anxiety related issues.

The charity was founded in Hamilton, Scotland in 2016 by two former serving soldiers, Calum MacLeod (King's Own Scottish Borderers) and Colin Maclachlan (Royal Scots and Special Air Service). After Calum and Colin met, sharing their own stories, and becoming friends, bound by their own experiences, they both realised they could help so many other people, who were left 'alone' to deal with their experiences, thoughts and traumas.

They decided to build a platform that would provide help and support to individuals and their families, all in the way of Who Dares Cares.

There are a number of volunteers that support the charity, all with varying skills, from military backgrounds to nurses, who offer help and support to all of their followers in many different ways. The volunteers are just that, volunteers. They are dedicated to the charity and give up their own time and effort to support other people in so many different ways. Without them, Who Dares Cares wouldn't be able to provide the dedicated support that they can.

Anyone with a service record and a history of PTSD should apply for support, even if you're not sure you meet the criteria, each application is assessed on an individual basis. For more details please email the Who Dares Cares Support Team Mailbox on wdc@who-dares-cares.com and if you wish to learn more about this amazing charity and how you can support its vital work, please visit www.who-dares-cares.com.

> It is not about suffering from PTSD,
> it is about learning to live with PTSD!

Rebuilding lives after sight loss

Blind Veterans UK helps vision-impaired ex-Servicemen and women to rebuild their lives after sight loss. They provide rehabilitation, training, practical advice and emotional support to veterans regardless of how or when they lost their sight.

The charity was founded in London in 1915 by publisher and newspaper owner Sir Arthur Pearson. Sir Arthur, who was blind himself, recognised that the substantial numbers of veterans losing their sight during the First World War needed help. Originally called the Blinded Soldiers and Sailors Care Committee, the charity soon became known as St Dunstan's, which was the name of the first headquarters in Regent's Park, London.

Drawing on his own experience of sight loss, Sir Arthur's aim was to help veterans acquire new skills to adapt to their sight loss and live a fulfilling, independent life.

Blind Veterans UK has supported those blinded in subsequent wars and military engagements, including the Second World War and, more recently, the conflicts in the Falklands, Iraq and Afghanistan. They have two specially designed veterans' centres – in North Wales and on the South Coast of England – where beneficiaries can receive rehabilitation, respite, training and care.

In 1952 Her Majesty The Queen became Patron of St Dunstan's, after the death of their previous Patron, her father, King George VI. HM The Queen remained as Patron until December 2016 whereupon HRH The Countess of Wessex became Patron.

In 2018 HRH The Countess of Wessex unveiled a statue to

commemorate the achievements of blind veterans supported since the First World War. The statue, entitled Victory Over Blindness, depicts seven blinded First World War soldiers leading one another away from the battlefield with their hand on the shoulder of the man in front. It stands proudly outside Manchester Piccadilly station as the only permanent memorial to the injured of that conflict.

In 2022 Blind Veterans UK updated their Articles of Association to be able to provide their specialist vision-rehabilitation support to those affected by war-like activity, including terrorist activities. As a consequence, they are now able to support the people of Ukraine by offering their expertise to those who have sustained blindness through war-like activity.

Anyone with a service record and a vision impairment should apply for support, even if you're not sure you meet the criteria, each application is assessed on an individual basis. For more details please call the support team on 0800 389 7979 and if you wish to learn more about this amazing charity and how you can support its vital work, please visit www.blindveterans.org.uk